T0330128

The Law and Economics of Federalism

The Law and Economics of Federalism

Edited by

Jonathan Klick

University of Pennsylvania Law School, USA

Cheltenham, UK • Northampton, MA, USA

Published by
Edward Elgar Publishing Limited
The Lypiatts
15 Lansdown Road
Cheltenham
Glos GL50 2JA
UK

Edward Elgar Publishing, Inc.
William Pratt House
9 Dewey Court
Northampton
Massachusetts 01060
USA

A catalogue record for this book
is available from the British Library

Library of Congress Control Number: 2016949944

This book is available electronically in the **Elgar**online
Law subject collection
DOI 10.4337/9781786433602

MIX
Paper from
responsible sources
FSC
www.fsc.org   FSC® C013056

ISBN 978 1 84980 362 5 (cased)
ISBN 978 1 78643 360 2 (eBook)

Typeset by Servis Filmsetting Ltd, Stockport, Cheshire
Printed and bound in Great Britain by TJ International Ltd, Padstow

Contents

Contributors

Terry L. Anderson, Senior Fellow, Hoover Institution, Stanford, CA and Senior Fellow, Property and Environment Research Center, Bozeman, MT, USA

Marianne P. Bitler, Professor of Economics, University of California, Davis, USA

John A. Dove, Assistant Professor, The Manuel H. Johnson Center for Political Economy, Troy University, USA

Michael Faure, Professor, Maastricht University and Erasmus School of Law, the Netherlands

Robert K. Fleck, Professor, Department of Economics, Clemson University, USA

Brian Galle, Professor of Law, Georgetown University Law Center, USA

Jonah B. Gelbach, Professor of Law, University of Pennsylvania Law School, USA

F. Andrew Hanssen, Professor, Department of Economics, Clemson University, USA

Jonathan Klick, University of Pennsylvania Law School, USA

Russell S. Sobel, Professor of Economics & Entrepreneurship, School of Business, The Citadel, USA

Dominic P. Parker, Assistant Professor, Department of Agricultural and Applied Economics, University of Wisconsin-Madison, USA

Joshua D. Wright, University Professor, Antonin Scalia Law School at George Mason University; Senior of Counsel, Wilson Sonsini Goodrich & Rosati; former Commissioner, Federal Trade Commission

Madeline Zavodny, Professor, Agnes Scott College, USA

Introduction: law and economics of federalism

Jonathan Klick

The economic theory of federalism has been well discussed through the years. Wallace Oates (1972) largely started the systematic study of economic federalism, from both normative and positive perspectives, and the subsequent fiscal federalism literature is well developed.[1] The basic theoretical framework involves the recognition that there is preference heterogeneity across jurisdictions (which can affect the optimal level of public good provision) pushing in favor of smaller decision-making units, balanced by the possibility that cross-jurisdictional externalities exist as well as the potential gains from scale economies in production. The optimal system, then, is one that sets the marginal loss from increasing the jurisdictional level at which decisions regarding a public good are made equal to the gain achieved by internalizing jurisdictional externalities and exploiting economies of scale. The so-called decentralization or subsidiarity principle embodies this trade-off.

Subsequent economic discussions of federalism have included their political economy aspects (see, for example, Inman and Rubinfeld 1997 and Weingast 2009), including analyses from a constitutional economics perspective (Mueller 1996; Buchanan 2001). Legal scholars have used the economic model of federalism, but have also critiqued it for failing to recognize important practical limitations, such as a failure to distinguish between regulatory and fiscal federalism (see, for example, Super 2005). Beyond these criticisms, legal scholars have distinguished among cooperative and competitive federalism, as well as "uncooperative federalism" (Bulman-Pozen and Gerken 2009). All of these models and perspectives help to elucidate the ways that various levels of government interact, making the normative prescriptions somewhat more complicated than the decentralization principle would otherwise suggest.

While the literatures, in economics and law, on federalism are vibrant,

---

[1]   For overviews, see Oates (1999, 2005) and Inman and Rubinfeld (forthcoming).

insightful, and challenging, they have been well covered in collections like this previously.[2] Instead, in this collection, the focus is on using federalism as a vehicle for the empirical identification of policy effects. In some sense, this collection takes one of the oldest theoretical takes on federalism in the law and puts it in the service of the new empirically minded law and economics. In 1932, in the case *New State Ice Co. v. Liebmann*, Justice Louis Brandeis famously stated "[a] state may, if its citizens choose, serve as a laboratory; and try novel social and economic experiments without risk to the rest of the country."[3]

It is through state experimentation that we have learned much of what we know regarding the effects of many policies. A federalist structure, at least in principle, allows for quasi-experimental examinations and evaluations of the effects of various policies that would be more difficult in unitary systems. Because the lower level jurisdictions share much in common with each other (since all are affected by identical federal laws) they potentially serve as decent counterfactual comparisons for each other when one engages in a policy experiment. Further, the existence of instances where the federal government steps in (e.g., through the passage of a binding national law or the preemption of the law of the lower jurisdiction) plausibly creates additional policy variation that may be conditionally random, allowing for the credible identification of causal effects.

Such an approach has been used to examine laws in the US states for at least two decades. In the chapters that follow, there is a generalized discussion of much of this work in the environmental context (Fleck and Hanssen) and social welfare programs (Gelbach; Bitler and Zavodny). Additionally, largely new empirical work is provided on the effect of state regulations on entrepreneurism (Sobel and Dove), consumer protection law (Wright), and crime policies (Owens). This volume also provides an analysis of inter-jurisdictional arrangements on the development of Native American communities (Anderson and Parker), as well as the interplay among the levels of government when it comes to budgetary issues (Galle). Lastly, because this kind of empirical work is under-developed in the European Union, this volume provides institutional background for the way the effectively federalist system works in Europe with some discussion of issues that hopefully spur comparable empirical work in that context.

---

2   See, for example, Kobayashi and Ribstein (2007), Ahmad and Brosio (2006), Oates (1998), etc.
3   *New State Ice Co. v. Liebmann*, 285 U.S. 262 (1932).

REFERENCES

Ahmad, Ehtisham, and Giorgio Brosio (2006), *Handbook of Fiscal Federalism*, Edward Elgar Publishing.

Buchanan, James M. (2001), *The Collected Works of James M. Buchanan*, Volume 18: Federalism, Liberty, and the Law, Liberty Fund, Inc.

Bulman-Pozen, Jessica, and Heather K. Gerken (2009), "Uncooperative Federalism," *Yale Law Journal*, 118(7): 1256–310.

Inman, Robert P., and Daniel L. Rubinfeld (1997), "The Political Economy of Federalism," in *Perspectives on Public Choice: A Handbook*, D.C. Mueller, ed., Cambridge University Press.

Inman, Robert P., and Daniel L. Rubinfeld (forthcoming), "Economics of Federalism," in *Oxford Handbook of Law and Economics*, F. Parisi, ed., Oxford University Press.

Kobayashi, Bruce H., and Larry E. Ribstein (2007), *Economics of Federalism*, Edward Elgar Publishing.

Mueller, Dennis C. (1996), *Constitutional Democracy*, Oxford University Press.

Oates, Wallace E. (1972), *Fiscal Federalism*, London, Harcourt Brace Jovanovich.

Oates, Wallace E. (1998), *The Economics of Fiscal Federalism and Local Finance*, Edward Elgar Publishing.

Oates, Wallace E. (1999), "An Essay on Fiscal Federalism," *Journal of Economic Literature*, 37(3): 1120–49.

Oates, Wallace E. (2005), "Toward A Second-Generation Theory of Fiscal Federalism," *International Tax and Public Finance*, 12(4): 349–73.

Super, David A. (2005), "Rethinking Fiscal Federalism," *Harvard Law Review*, 118(8): 2544–652.

Weingast, Barry R. (2009), "Second Generation Fiscal Federalism: The Implications of Fiscal Incentives," *Journal of Urban Economics*, 65(3): 279–93.

1. Congressional control of state taxation: evidence and lessons for federalism theory

Brian Galle*

INTRODUCTION

Theories of the "political safeguards" of U.S. federalism have frequently been aired but seldom tested. The basic claim, beginning with Wechsler (1954), is that state influence is sufficient to preserve state autonomy from federal encroachments. For example, Kramer (2000) argues that the dependence of federal officials on state party support gives state officials bargaining leverage to fend off incursions (see also Choper 1980, La Pierre 1985, Rubin & Feeley 1994, Dana 1995). Critics counter that state autonomy as a whole is a public good, such that officials may have little incentive to exercise whatever influence they hold, and so only courts can adequately ensure that states in the long run will retain independence from federal control (Derthick 1986, Baker & Young 2002, McGinnis & Somin 2004).[1] Others accept Wechsler's and Kramer's claims only partially, arguing that one or more of the branches of federal government are more or less apt to respect state autonomy (Mendelson 2004, Nzelibe 2006, Metzger 2008, Sharkey 2008, Pursley 2010).

In a parallel debate, commentators also disagree over which federal institution should be responsible for ensuring a free flow of trade among the states. In the current U.S. arrangement, courts and Congress share power, with Congress holding final say. Courts fill in interstitially, striking

* The author gratefully acknowledges helpful comments from Wally Hellerstein, John Kincaid, Jon Klick, Rob Mikos, Austin Nichols, Larry Ribstein, Scott Taylor, Samantha Zyontz, and attendees of presentations at the American Law & Economics Association, the Conference on Empirical Legal Studies, and George Washington University Law School.
[1] For extended discussion of this argument and exploration of the instances in which autonomy would not represent a public good, see Galle & Seidenfeld (2008) and Galle (2008).

down sub-national taxes and regulations that discriminate against inter-state commerce. Since at least the 1950s, however, the Court has urged Congress to assume more responsibility for reviewing state taxation. In recent decades the Court has seemed to take steps to force Congress to do so. And prominent scholars have suggested retreat from or wholesale abandonment of federal judicial oversight of state taxes (Redish & Nugent 1987, Zelinsky 2002).

This chapter breaks from the existing literature by offering quantitative evidence of how Congress has actually used its authority to regulate state taxing power.[2] Utilizing a hand-collected dataset of every federal statute affecting state power to tax since the beginning of the republic—though only a handful predate the 20th century—I analyze what features, con-ditional on enactment, characterize congressional behavior in this area. I find that when Congress acts, it tends to reduce rather than expand

---

[2]   Several earlier authors examine the evidence on the safeguards hypothesis, but their efforts are purely qualitative, generally consisting of the historical back-ground of one or two statutes (Lee 1988, Dinan 1997, Hamilton 2001, Pickerill 2004, Jones 2004, Resnik 2008, Dinan 2009). Bowman & Krause (2003:302) lament this state of affairs. Frymer & Yoon (2002) also present qualitative descrip-tions of the sources of funding for modern political parties, which they argue bears on the Kramer hypothesis. Jenkins & Roscoe (2014) find evidence that local party activity affects national party success, a key assumption of the political safeguards theory, but they do not connect these findings to congressional behavior. Kam and Mikos (2007) present a quantitative study of voter attitudes towards federal-ism, but similarly do not observe legislative outcomes. There is a somewhat more extensive literature examining the determinants of *judicial* federalism decisions (e.g., Cross & Tiller 2000, Joondeph 2003, Solberg & Lindquist 2006, Collins 2007); this chapter can be thought of as a congressional complement to those studies.

Perhaps the closest to an antecedent quantitative study is Nicholson-Crotty (2008), who reports that Congress proposes and enacts fewer pieces of state-autonomy-affecting legislation during election years. However, Nicholson-Crotty does not examine whether legislation is simply shifted from one year to another, so that his findings appear to speak only to the timing, rather than the volume, of congressional action. His results can be equally well explained by two competing hypotheses. On the one hand, legislation may decrease because of heightened state influence during crucial periods. Alternatively, federalism-type legislation may decrease because of opportunity costs: federalism legislation is less important, and creates fewer rents, than others, and so is shifted aside when stakes are higher. Only the first of these would support the political-safeguards hypothesis.

I do not mean to suggest that quantitative analysis is necessarily superior to qualitative efforts. Indeed, the quantitative analysis here necessarily must omit important details that may be critical to the outcome of any particular piece of attempted legislation. The point is only that this contribution differs from the existing literature in its wider focus on the commonalities across statutes.

state autonomy, except in the case of state power to tax Indian tribes and tribal resources. I also find that public-choice factors appear to play a significant role in congressional decisions: narrow, concentrated interests are considerably more likely to win relief from state taxes. Surprisingly, this tendency holds true even when there are potentially competing concentrated interests, although competition somewhat blunts the efficacy of special interests.

These findings arguably weigh against wholesale judicial retreat in both of the areas I have mentioned. On the state autonomy front, I cannot observe the statutes that failed to pass, so I cannot draw strong conclusions about whether "political safeguards" may suffice to defeat legislation in some or even most instances. I can, though, confirm empirically the theoretical prediction that safeguards are unlikely to be fully effective in the face of strongly opposed congressional self-interest. Prior qualitative observations of federal lawmaking have noted many instances where federal authority has appeared to expand but has not generally inquired whether these expansions might serve to enhance state autonomy in the long run. My quantitative approach allows me to control, to some extent, for that possibility, and so I argue that my evidence represents a useful advance over the current state of the literature.

In this respect I may provide support for current judicial practices, which allow many forms of congressional regulation of states but prohibit certain so-called "unfunded mandates." Likewise, it is a familiar point in the theoretical literature that political economy factors may lead to excessive federal legislation if the federal government is not obliged to incur significant costs for its decisions. (La Pierre 1985). In that situation, enacting or threatening legislation allows the federal actor to extract rents, but the costs of the legislation are largely externalized. My results help to confirm this pattern: when Congress regulates state taxation, it tends to enact statutes that pass costs on to others (i.e., reduce state taxing authority) while generating rewards for itself (taking credit for enacting a tax cut).

On the free-trade front, my evidence again casts some doubt on the wisdom of placing full authority in the hands of an unrestrained Congress. Here my own hypotheses were that Congress is a dubious caretaker of state taxing power, for two reasons. For one, as I have just explained—although the literature has not fully recognized it—congressional regulation of state taxes has exactly the political-economy structure of an unfunded mandate. For another, Congress and the States arguably compete over the same tax base, meaning that any reduction in state authority potentially results in less political resistance to congressional revenue-raising.

These hypotheses are not mutually exclusive, and indeed I find support for both. Again, I find that opportunities to extract rents from concentrated interest groups correlate highly with enactment of federal legislation reducing state taxing power. As for the second hypothesis, I note that Indian tribes and Indian tribal lands are, as the Constitution states, "not taxed" by the federal government. Congress therefore does not compete with the States for the opportunity to tax them. I find, accordingly, that Congress is considerably more permissive in its treatment of state efforts to tax the tribes, although I cannot entirely rule out the possibility that tribes are simply much worse than anyone else at lobbying Congress.

Part I of the chapter provides a brief overview of the legal context for my investigation. Part II reviews the prior literature, and offers several hypotheses about the expected dynamic between states and the Congress that regulates them. Part III explains my methodology, and Part IV reports the results. Part V offers interpretation and caveats.

I.   LEGAL FRAMEWORK FOR FEDERAL CONTROL OF STATE TAXES AND TRADE

The U.S. Constitution grants overlapping taxing authority to states and the federal government. On the face of the Constitution the states' power is plenary, aside from bars on tariffs on imports and exports, and "dut[ies] of tonnage." The text also suggests that the federal government's taxing power is virtually unlimited, although until the enactment of the 16th Amendment in 1913 it imposed the burdensome procedural hurdle that all "direct" taxes had to be apportioned; "income" taxes now are exempt from that requirement. One other notable federal restriction is that the Constitution suggests that "Indians [are] not taxed" by the national government (U.S. Const. Art. I § 2).

At the same time, both courts and Congress have used federal authority to protect free trade among the states to modify state taxing power. Congress, of course, can "regulate Commerce ... among the several states, and with the Indian Tribes" (U.S. Const. Art. I § 8 cl.3). It has often used this power to alter the scope of state authority. For example, in ERISA, the Employee Retirement and Income Security Act of 1974, Congress invoked national uniformity to sweep aside all subnational regulation of employee benefit plans, including any efforts to tax such plans or their assets.

Even when Congress has stood still, the Supreme Court has defended free trade against perceived state threats. Beginning with Chief Justice Marshall's opinion striking down New York regulation of steam boats, in *Gibbons v. Ogden*, the Court has interpreted the constitutional grant of the power to regulate "Commerce" as also impliedly requiring a common economic market among states free of unnecessary state burdens. Most lawyers refer to this judicial enforcement of free-trade principles as the "dormant" commerce clause, following a coinage of one of the early 19th-Century cases (*Willson v. Black Bird Creek Marsh Co.*, 27 U.S. (2 Pet.) 245 (1829)). Congress, however, can authorize any judicially-suspect state action if it so chooses (see Metzger 2007 for more discussion).

Similarly, for much of the 19th and early 20th centuries federal courts presumed that the federal government was immune to taxation by the states. This immunity extended, at its high-water mark, even to the salaries of contractors working for the federal government. Even then, though, immunity was waivable by Congress. But this immunity doctrine waned beginning in 1936, and today extends only to entities that are functionally indistinguishable from the federal government itself.

Much as with federal instrumentalities, Indian tribes have long been held to be presumptively beyond the reach of taxation both for the states and also for the federal government. The status of transactions between tribes and outsiders, of outsiders conducting business on Indian land, and of individual native Americans, has been less clear and remains a source of some legal uncertainty. For example, the U.S. Treasury ruled in the 1930s that, while tribes themselves were not subject to the federal corporate income tax, individual members were responsible for paying their own federal income and social security taxes. Congress, however, may authorize states to tax transactions occurring in Indian territory, apparently including profits inuring directly to tribes, and modern doctrine permits states to collect many general taxes, such as cigarette excises, within Indian lands even in the absence of express authorization.[3]

I exploit the variations among and within these different legal regimes in an effort to identify trends in how Congress exercises its power to regulate state taxing authority, as I now will detail.

II. HYPOTHESES

The basic research question for this study is to examine how Congress has employed its authority to curtail states revenues: has it been a bully, a defender of national interests, an indifferent by-stander, or a sell-out? The existing literature offers several competing hypotheses about how Congress will behave. Roughly speaking, they run the gamut from

---

[3] For more discussion of this complex area, see Frickey (1990), Taylor (2007), and Jensen (2008).

predicting that Congress will seek to maximize national welfare to predicting that it will instead maximize the rent-seeking opportunities of
individual members of Congress. These hypotheses come from different
strands of the legal, economic, and political science literatures, and have
not been fully synthesized before, so that some discussion is warranted.

The most optimistic assessments come directly from judicial decisions applying the dormant commerce clause and the bulk of the legal
commentary on them. Courts and commentators alike observe that the
fundamental flaws the Constitution was designed to solve were that state
decisions affecting interstate trade gave rise to externalities, and that
Coasean interstate bargaining was fraught with coordination difficulties
(e.g., Tribe 1999). As a nationally representative body, Congress is supposed to internalize all nationwide costs and benefits.

According to the literature, federal courts, too, can play this internalization role, but the contemporary trend is to prefer Congress. The judicial
role was justified, most famously by Justice Jackson, as a necessary supplement to Congress in a large nation whose Constitution was designed to
make national legislation difficult. But modern decisions and commentary
emphasize instead the putatively superior democratic pedigree and fact-
finding abilities of Congress (Hellerstein 1941, Eule 1982, Swain 2003).
Some important voices, including Justice Thomas, have called for complete abandonment of the dormant commerce clause and a full takeover
by Congress (Redish & Nugent 1987, Zelinsky 2002; Eule 1982 opposes
the dormant commerce clause but would retain some role for judges).

There have been very few skeptics in the other direction. Shaviro (1992)
and Galle (2007a) observe that Congress is not necessarily a nationally-
representative body. Instead, of course, its members serve a regional con-
stituency, and it is only by bargaining, log-rolling, and other coordination
mechanisms that its outcomes approximate some national interest. Basic
free-rider theory suggests, then, that issues of general importance to the
states will not garner a devoted congressional following, while issues that
disproportionately affect one or a few regions will have strong supporters
who cannot expect to free ride on the efforts of others. Voters who are
concerned about division of power between tiers of government cannot
generally punish the national government as a whole when it overreaches
(Bednar 2007). Thus, the prediction would be that Congress will often
enact, or at least overlook, measures that allow some states to burden the
rest (Galle 2007a).

In a related vein, turning from the dormant commerce clause to the
broader field of federalism theory generally, many commentators point to
public-choice factors that would likely tend to lead members of Congress
to neglect national welfare-maximization in favor of self-interest. For

example, Zelinsky (1993) and McGinnis and Somin (2004) point out that to the extent that political autonomy for lower-tier governments improves long-term national welfare, that gain is a public good for the nation as a whole. We therefore should expect defenders of state autonomy to free ride on one another, so that state autonomy tends to lose out to the preferences of concentrated interest groups in political struggles.[4] Similarly, Mayhew (1974) predicts that federal restrictions may be imposed to appease special interests, and Macey (1986) predicts that members of Congress will assert exclusive federal power over some policy areas in order to monopolize rents from the regulated industries.

In other instances Congress may share power in order to pass along costs but retain credit. That is the standard explanation for the popularity of so-called "unfunded mandates," in which Congress enacts policies but requires state governments to carry them out (Zelinsky 1993, Garrett 1997). The costs of implementation, and potentially the political blame for policy failures, can be passed on to others (see Bednar 2007 for a formal model). Critics argue that unfunded mandates are likely welfare reducing because Congress does not internalize the costs of its decisions (LaPierre 1985). [5]

It might be argued that internalization is not an important consideration because members of Congress are relatively insensitive to cost. Of course, to the extent that Congress is motivated by non-budgetary factors, the importance of budget internalization diminishes (Dana 1995, Levinson 2005), but would still be significant on the margin. Levinson (2005:928–9) goes further, arguing that members of Congress are at best only weakly motivated by the size of the federal budget, since the effect of any one actor on the budget as a whole is largely an externality for individual members. If so, we would expect that budgetary factors will be more predictive for smaller legislative bodies, since in that case the externality is smaller and Coasean bargaining over externalities somewhat more straightforward.

---

[4] For more general assertions of the superiority of the executive in maximizing national welfare, see Olson (1982), McGinnis (2001) and Kagan (2001).

[5] In addition to curtailing "excess" federal legislation, however that concept might be defined, internalization serves another important federalism function by preserving state power to bargain with the federal government. As Hills (1998) explains, when Congress must pay states for their agreement, or must pay for the administrative apparatus to enforce its laws in the absence of state cooperation, states gain some hold-up power. Arguably, this heightened bargaining power increases state autonomy, although in instances in which individual hold-outs are an impediment to collective action, this power may be counter-productive. See Galle (2008) and Bulman-Pozen and Gerken (2009) for more extensive discussions of this latter point.

While these observations are now commonplace in the general federalism literature, they have not generally been applied to the question of the dormant commerce clause. Indeed, a leading proponent of exclusive congressional control over free trade has also been a significant critic of unfunded mandates (compare Zelinsky 1993 with Zelinsky 2002). Yet a congressional decision to prohibit certain state taxes would appear to have a similar political structure to other unfunded mandates: the state loses money, while Congress can take political credit with the affected interest group.

Of course, the claim that Congress does not internalize the costs of imposing mandates on states, or of otherwise reducing state authority, assumes that state officials have no way of influencing their federal counterparts (Adler 1997). In fact, though, there is a robust tradition in the legal literature arguing that state officials have powerful sway, such as through their ability to provide get-out-the-vote support during federal elections (Kramer 2000; for a skeptical treatment of these claims, see Schleicher 2016). Alternatively, in the modern regulatory state in which many programs are vertically integrated between the States and the federal government, states have hold-out power; they can refuse to provide the information and on-the-ground enforcement that federal programs depend on (Bulman-Pozen and Gerken 2009). Or, in the case of federal law that is enacted as a condition attached to a federal grant, states can simply refuse to accept the conditional funds.

The extent of state influence is likely to be contingent on institutional arrangements and other factors. For instance, hold-out power depends on whether states in fact have any real leverage: refusal to accept a conditional grant is a more meaningful threat if the federal government lacks constitutional authority to enact the grant's conditions outright (Galle 2004). To take another example, some scholars have argued that state-official lobbying is not a meaningful constraint on Congress' ability to curtail state prerogatives because of free riding among those officials (Derthick 1986, Baker & Young 2002, McGinnis & Somin 2004). Bellia (2006) presents a nice case study of this effect, finding that federal regulation of the power of state courts to hear civil suits was facilitated by the fact that the legislation offered concentrated benefits for interstate businesses while diminishing the power of most states uniformly. But in some cases state resistance to federal law may be more like a private good to the official, such as when there is local interest-group pressure in opposition (Levinson 2005, Galle 2008).

Putting together these various political-economy observations, we should expect that Congress will be especially apt to reduce state authority when several factors coincide. If members of Congress can extract rents from a concentrated interest group, if Congress faces little opportunity cost in enacting legislation, if the states have no hold-up opportunities, and if the state interests affected are shared widely and similarly by most states, we should expect the effectiveness of the "political safeguards" of state lobbying and other influence to be at its nadir. Many of these factors occur with great frequency in the federal regulation of state taxing authority.

Competition for revenues, a factor not mentioned elsewhere in the literature, also warrants some attention. Other commentators have often assumed that overlapping taxing authority shared by two sovereigns leads to crowding out: citizens are willing to tolerate only so much taxation, and so higher taxes by one government are said to put pressure on the other to reduce its own revenues (e.g., Baker 1995). Brennan and Buchanan (1984) go so far as to argue that a shared tax base is a common pool that overlapping sovereigns race to fish from. This competition theory is at least as old as Hamilton, who discussed it in the federalist papers, and Madison, who thought that vertical competition between the States and the federal government would restrain the size of both. And normatively, overlapping tax bases are arguably inefficient to the extent that they increase the total marginal rate facing economic actors, and therefore increase the deadweight loss of taxation, an effect that is likely an externality for each of the overlapping levels (Hanson & Stuart 1987; see Klick & Parisi 2005 for a formal model).

It is not clear that crowd-out in fact happens, or that it is normatively undesirable, but it is certainly a piece of conventional wisdom (for evidence, see Galle 2013). Overlap also has benefits, such as reduced compliance costs for citizens and the opportunity for economies of scale and scope for governments (Galle 2007b). Descriptively, recent evidence suggests citizens may not consider one level of tax when making political decisions about the other (McCaffrey & Barron 2006). Nonetheless, courts and politicians have long assumed that taxation at one level threatened the ability of the other sovereign to tax the same base. For example, crowd-out was the Supreme Court's asserted basis for constitutional limits on state taxing power in the mid-19th Century, was one of the Court's recent justifications for limits on federal conditional spending (*Nat'l Federation of Indep. Bus. v. Sebelius*, 567 U.S. __, 132 S.Ct. 2566, 2662 n.13 (2012)) and was the main rationale offered by Congress in 1963 for the federal income-tax deduction for state and local taxes paid.

In any event, to the extent that Congress is motivated by budgetary pressures and believes that crowd-out is a possibility, we should expect that Congress is not a fully trustworthy custodian of state taxing power. Just as Congress may use its preemption power to monopolize opportunities for political rents, so too might it use the commerce power to control the tax base.

As a result, I hypothesize that when Congress acts to alter state authority to tax, it will tend to reduce that power rather than expand it. I expect that to be particularly true in the instance where the tax at issue falls on a narrow interest, while the budget burden of repeal would fall equally on most or all state budgets. If my predictions are incorrect, though, that finding would strengthen considerably the argument of those who claim that the political safeguards of federalism are sturdy in all contexts.

III. METHODOLOGY

In order to test these hypotheses, I compiled a dataset consisting of every statute enacted by the U.S. Congress affecting state taxing power. I then coded each statute for a variety of factors relating to my hypotheses, and conducted regression analysis to test those theories.[6]

The dataset was drawn from a keyword search on HeinOnline's "U.S. Statutes at Large" database.[7] I found HeinOnline's search function to be somewhat unreliable, returning slightly different results at different times with identical searches. However, at the time of this writing HeinOnline is the only searchable database of year-by-year statutory text extending back to the 19th Century. I ran the search repeatedly and cross-checked the results against one another to be certain I had found every statute.

Next, I attempted to identify for each statute a prior authority affecting the same form of state tax, such as an earlier statute or Supreme Court decision. This was important to the study for two reasons. First, I am interested primarily in how Congress *changed* what the states could do, because the direction of change offers better evidence about how Congress behaves. For example, if Congress enacts a statute that leaves state taxing power heavily constricted, but the law in place before was even stricter, I think that represents a victory for states, and vice-versa. Thus coding only the end result, and not the change from baseline, could produce misleading results. Second, and relatedly, the extent of pre-existing restrictions at the time of enactment is potentially important for hypothesis-testing; we

---

[6]   A Statutory Appendix with a complete listing of statutes, prior authorities, and scores is available from the author upon request.

[7]   The search was "tax* state*" ~15 OR "tariff* state*" ~15 OR "levy state*" ~15 OR "impost* state*" ~15 OR "excise* state*" ~15 NOT treaty. The search returned 976 hits, of which 116 proved to be related to state taxing power.

have to control for the possibility that existing law might influence states' ability to affect federal legislation.

I then coded both the statutes and the corresponding prior authorities. I coded statutes for both their absolute and relative-to-baseline constraints on state power, while the prior authorities were coded only for absolute scores. Both categories were coded on a scale of one to seven. For the absolute score, a "one" represented a complete prohibition on a major source of state revenues, while a "seven" was no restrictions. For relative scores, a "four" was no change relative to baseline, while "one" was a severe narrowing and "seven" was major expansion of the States' authority. I employed three research assistants to assist with coding, and independently coded each statute and authority without looking at the assistants' scores; where opinions ended up differing I used the average of the scores, weighting my own twice as heavily.

Alternatively, I also report regression analyses in which I code no change as zero, new constraints as -1, and new expansions of state taxing authority as 1. While I believe that coding scores over a wider range allows me to exploit additional information available in the sample, I recognize that there may also be increased subjectivity in the coding of the degree rather than simply direction of change. My results are robust to the use of this alternative measure.

Before proceeding with additional coding, I dropped from the dataset 30 statutes that lacked a prior authority, leaving 85 observations, nearly all from the 20th and 21st Centuries. The reasoning for dropping observations with no prior authority was that by default state taxing power (other than power to tax Indian tribes) is unlimited; therefore, in the absence of any prior reduction in state authority, the only direction for Congress to go would be down. That, of course, would have prevented us from drawing meaningful inferences from any finding that Congress tended to reduce state power. So I instead confined my analysis to statutes in which Congress had an opportunity either to further constrain states or instead to undo the prior restraints. Editing the data in this way does raise some interpretation questions of its own, as I will discuss further in Part V.

Finally, I coded for additional aspects of my hypotheses I wished to test. I created a dummy variable for each statute reflecting its fit with basic public-choice factors: if the state tax affected had burdened a relatively concentrated interest group, but its budget effects were shared widely within states and across states, I coded that statute a "1" in the public choice category. I also added a dummy variable, called "rival," which was coded "1" when the congressional enactment in question would also place another concentrated interest group at a competitive disadvantage. For example, Public Law 86-272, which restricts state sales taxes on remote sales, was coded "1" in both categories, because it favored out-of-state distributors over local retailers.

In an effort to tease apart the public-choice and base-competition hypotheses, I also compared statutes regulating state efforts to tax Indian tribes (and, before 1934, individual Native Americans) with all others. Congress does not and has never taxed the tribes directly, and arguably the Constitution prohibits them from doing so. Until the 1930s it was assumed that members of tribes, too, were exempt from federal tax, but the Treasury ruled otherwise and that ruling has apparently been followed ever since. Thus, I expect that competition for the opportunity to tax the Indian tribes is considerably less intense than other forms of taxation. Accordingly, I created a dummy variable to indicate statutes affecting "Indians not taxed" by the federal government. Where there was legal uncertainty whether Congress could tax the affected source of revenue, I coded the enactment "0," on the view that this was the assumption most contrary to my hypothesis of differential treatment. Of the 85 observations, 20 of them were coded "1" for statutes affecting untaxed tribes.

I test Levinson's theory about the insensitivity of Congress to its own budget in several ways. My Indian variable sheds light indirectly on that question, since one possible explanation for more generous treatment of state laws affecting the tribes is that Congress is less concerned with its own revenues in that instance. A more direct measure I employ is to include the log of the number of members of the House of Representatives as an explanatory variable.[8] Again, if members of Congress treat the budget as a common pool, a smaller pool should result in greater cost internalization. And, finally, I include measures of slack or strain in the federal budget, such as annual debt or surplus as a percentage of GDP.

The statistical analysis took several forms. I performed a simple f-test to estimate the mean relative score within the restricted data set, and also performed that test separately for Indian and non-Indian statutes. Due to the small number of Indian statutes, I could not perform a chi-square test to compare the two. I did, however, include the Indian dummy variable in a series of regression analyses.

Because OLS is unbiased for ordered rankings, I estimate results

---

[8]   I do not report results for the number of Senators because of the small variation in that variable in the sample. I do find significant results for Senate membership when it is included in the regressions, but those results appear to be driven almost entirely by three extreme outlier observations from the 19th Century.

Table 1.1   *Descriptive statistics*

Variable	Obs	Mean	Std. Dev.	Min	Max
public choice	85	.4705882	.5020964	0	1
Indian	85	.2588235	.4405878	0	1
year	85	1960.882	33.70545	1864	2007
efficient?	85	.2705882	.4469003	0	1
coordination?	85	.2823529	.4528157	0	1
rival	85	.2941176	.4583492	0	1
absolute score	85	4.423529	1.257136	2	7
relative score	85	3.835294	1.213486	1	6
prior authority score	85	4.364706	1.502752	2	7
surplus per gdp	85	−2.391176	3.891649	−22.7	2.4
house members	85	427.1765	34.61701	184	437
percent dem house	85	.5566555	.0948279	.3011494	.7402299
senate seats	85	97.24706	6.502574	52	100
percent dem senate	85	.5439583	.1022101	.1923077	.7395833
house med dim. 1	85	.0224471	.1798338	−.255	.414
house med dim. 2	85	.0111529	.0885928	−.135	.23
h maj party med 1	85	−.0226824	.3523874	−.388	.526
h maj party med 2	85	.1227882	.1792056	−.369	.53
sen med dim. 1	85	−.0336941	.1290925	−.301	.318
sen med dim. 2	85	−.0389765	.1004343	−.303	.162
sen maj party med 1	85	−.0097765	.3301069	−.502	.459
sen maj party med 2	85	.0287882	.2503121	−.462	.33

utilizing both OLS and an ordered probit.[9] A probit model assumes a normal underlying distribution; however, the literature advises against use of heteroskedasticity-corrected ordered probit in models with fewer

---

[9]   I also utilized an ordered logit, which (once adjusted for the expected differences in coefficients between a probit and logit model) resulted in similar predicted marginal results as the ordered probit. As a result, I do not report the ordered logit findings.

than 100 observations (Keele & Park 2006). Therefore I limit use of the probit model to serving as a double-check on the accuracy of the OLS regressions.[10]

I estimate a series of regressions using relative change in restrictions as the dependent variable. To test several aspects of my hypothesis, described in more detail in the "Interpretation and Caveats" section, I constructed indicator variables for whether a given statute could plausibly be described as efficiency-enhancing under conventional microeconomic analysis, and for whether it resolved coordination problems among the states. I further control for year, absolute score of prior authority, ideological composition of the two houses of Congress,[11] and, where available, popular attitudes towards the federal government, federal taxation, and taxes in general.[12] I measure congressional ideology using historical DW-nominate scores calculated by Carroll et al. (2011).[13] I include measures for both the median position of the majority party as well as for Congress as a whole.

Thus, the OLS regressions estimate the equation:

$$R_i = \alpha + \beta_1 \, PublicChoice_i + \beta_2 \, Rival_i + \beta_3 \, PublicChoice_i * Rival_i + \beta_4 Efficient_i + \beta_5 \, Coordinate_i + \beta_6 \, Xi + C_i \qquad (1.1)$$

IV. RESULTS

My findings provide support for both the public choice and tax-base competition hypotheses. When Congress acts, it tends to reduce state

---

[10] Unlike the ordered probit, OLS assumes that the "width" of the bins counted is uniform. However, the "cut" point estimates in the ordered probit model are relatively evenly dispersed, except at the very top of the 1 to 7 range where there are few observations. This further supports the use of OLS.

[11] Because prior literature suggests that Democrats have a lower propensity to vote for "states' rights" legislation (Hero 1989, Weissert & Schram 1996), I also alternatively employed measures of the percentage of democrats in the House and Senate. Neither measure was significant and I do not report those results.

[12] These latter controls were available only from the 1970s on, and because they proved insignificant, I do not report them.

[13] DW-nominate provides estimates of two different forms of congressional ideology. The first dimension "can be interpreted in most periods as government intervention in the economy" (Carroll et al. 2011). The second reflects views on civil rights and race relations. For discussion of how DW-nominate is computed, see Carroll et al. (2008).

taxing power, and this effect is more pronounced where there is tax-base competition and where public choice theory predicts.

Even a casual inspection of the data suggests significant support for the base competition theory. The mean change in restrictions is in the more restrictive direction for non-Indian statutes, and is in the less-restrictive direction for Indian statutes, see Figures 1.1 and 1.2 below. An f-test indicates that the mean relative score for non-Indian statutes is 3.51, with a 95 percent confidence interval of 3.23 to 3.79—statistically significantly

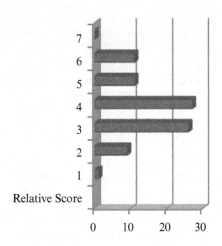

Figure 1.1 Relative scores for statutes affecting Indian tribes

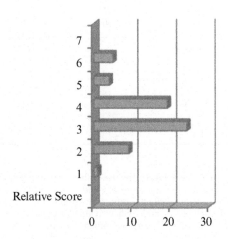

Figure 1.2 Relative scores for all non-Indian statutes

The law and economics of federalism

different from the null hypothesis of 4, no change. The mean relative score for Indian statutes is 4.70, with a 95 percent confidence interval from 4.39 to 5.00— again, significantly differing from 4, but in the opposite direction.

Turning to the regression analysis, I find strong support for the public-choice hypothesis in the form of a large negative coefficient for the public choice variable, as reported in Table 1.2 below. In other words, when

Table 1.2 Determinants of relative change in restrictiveness

	Range 1 to 7: OLS	Range 1 to 7: Ordered Probit	Range −1 to 1: OLS	Range −1 to 1: Ordered Probit
Public Choice	**−0.844***	**−1.385***	**−0.683***	**−2.200***
	(0.232)	(0.399)	(0.172)	(0.558)
Indian	**0.647***	**1.010***	**0.497***	**1.460***
	(0.209)	(0.344)	(0.170)	(0.435)
Rivals	−0.246	−0.343	−0.245	−0.626
	(0.329)	(0.422)	(0.194)	(0.495)
Surplus/GDP	−0.035	−0.073	0.001	−0.026
	(0.029)	(0.052)	(0.019)	(0.073)
Log house size	**2.250***	3.185*	**2.143***	**6.987**
	(0.797)	(1.764)	(0.565)	(2.837)
Rivalxpubchoice	0.612	0.823	**0.609**	**2.120***
	(0.558)	(0.593)	(0.305)	(0.788)
Efficiency	**0.733**	**1.112***	**0.481**	**1.348***
	(0.342)	(0.355)	(0.187)	(0.441)
Coordination	0.230	0.344	0.132	0.378
	(0.229)	(0.314)	(0.132)	(0.425)
Year Enacted	−0.009*	−0.011	**−0.008**	**−0.019**
	(0.005)	(0.008)	(0.004)	(0.009)
Prior Authority	0.009	0.006	0.071	0.220
	(0.077)	(0.094)	(0.047)	(0.136)
Net Marginal Effect of Pub. Choice, Rival=0	**−.844***		**−.683***	
	(.232)		(.173)	
Net Marginal Effect of Pub. Choice, Rival=1	−.232		−.074	
	(.508)		(.804)	
R-squared	0.61		.68	

Notes:
Standard errors in (parentheses). OLS estimates with robust standard errors. Controls include DW-nominate scores on dimensions one and two for Senate and House majority party and median. "Net marginal effects" reports the sum of the coefficients for public choice and rival x public choice variables when rival takes each indicated value, with standard errors calculated using the margins command in Stata14.
*: Statistically significant at the 10% level. **: Statistically significant at the 5% level.
***: Statistically significant at the 1% level. N: 85.

Congress alters state taxing power, if the state tax falls on a concentrated interest group (while providing undifferentiated revenue benefits to the whole population of the state), Congress is considerably more likely to limit that tax. This finding was statistically significant at the 1 percent level.

As predicted, concentrated interest groups in opposition tend to weaken the influence of interest-group lobbying. However, the impact of these public choice factors is considerably diminished in the presence of rival groups. In the presence of interaction terms, the true marginal effect of one of the factors in the interaction is the sum of the main effect (the coefficient of the variable standing alone) and the coefficient on the interaction term, conditional on the value of the other factor (Brambor et al. 2006). In my set-up, in other words, the true marginal effect of the public choice variable is the sum of $\beta_1 + \beta_3$ *Rival*$_i$. These values are reported for the OLS regressions in the bottom rows of Table 1.2.[14] When the *Rival* variable is zero, the net public choice effect is negative and significant. When rival interests are present, however, it is still negative but small and not statistically significant. This combination of outcomes supports the hypothesis that contrary concentrated private lobbying interests can block rent-seeking tax legislation.

For ordered choice variables, the net marginal effect can vary with the outcome, making summary in tabular form difficult. Figure 1.3, below, depicts the impact of the interaction of the rival and public choice variables for the ordered probit regression in which relative scores are coded from one to seven (although there are no observations of a score of seven in the sample). The point estimates are reporting the impact of the public choice variable on the probability of a given relative change in tax restrictions, conditional on the presence of rivals. Point estimates on the left border of the figure are for *Rival*=0, while the right border estimates are for *Rival*=1. We see that the relative scores on the right-hand side of the figure are clustered much more closely around zero, suggesting that the presence of rivals considerably diminishes the impact of interest group lobbying. For example, the top line shows the likelihood of a relative score of three, a small increase in tax restrictions, dropping considerably when rivals are present.

Additionally, when I control for other factors I continue to find that whether a statute affects Indian tribes has a highly significant positive effect on the relative score. As reported in Table 1.2, statutes affecting

---

[14]   I compute these values and their standard errors using the margins command in Stata14.

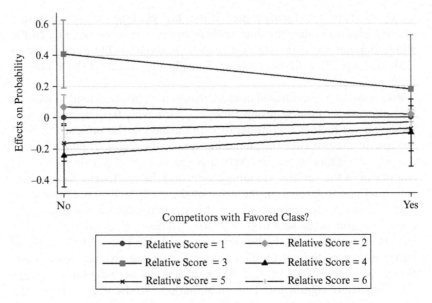

Figure 1.3   Marginal effects of public choice, conditional on rival

Indian tribes on average have considerably higher relative scores than others. Although the confidence intervals are fairly wide, I find a p-value of less than .01 in all of the models. Subject to some caveats, as discussed below, I interpret this finding as evidence in support of both the base-competition hypothesis as well as the notion that Congress is sensitive to budget pressure.

Other efforts to evaluate the base-competition hypothesis were less successful. I find that measures of Congress' need for funds, such as annual deficit, generally have the predicted negative sign (that is, I find that larger deficits result in greater state restrictions) but are not statistically significant. It may be that my measures are poor proxies for Congressional need for funds, or that I lack enough observations to use those measures meaningfully. Alternately, it may simply be that Congress' need for funds is not an important driver of its state-tax policy.

I do, however, find additional evidence bearing on the budget-pressure question. Congress is less restrictive of state authority as the size of the House increases.[15] Again, if Levinson (2005) is correct that members of Congress treat the budget as a commons, then we should expect to see

---

[15]   Since House size trends monotonically upwards, it is possible this result reflects some secular trend, rather than the effect of House size. I do, however,

fewer restrictions on competing state revenue sources when the legislative chamber expands and each member internalizes a smaller fraction of each budget-related decision. My results are consistent with that story. The fact that I find variation, though, suggests that Levinson somewhat overstates his case: the commons problem diminishes legislative sensitivity to budget pressure, but this effect varies with chamber size rather than being stuck at a uniform zero sensitivity. And, again, my base-competition result implies that Congress does appear to care about its revenue stream.

Additionally, I find the expected results for the political controls (not tabulated). The ideology of the dominant party affects to a statistically significant degree decisions to curtail state autonomy, especially ideological views on "states' rights" related race questions. The ideology of the minority party—represented in my data by the chamber median[16]—points in the opposite direction of the majority party, and the impact of this effect is more pronounced in the Senate.

Finally, I find some evidence that time matters. There is a fairly straight negative linear relation between relative score and year, at least for the period 1900 to present, although in the one to seven specifications this result is only marginally significant in the OLS model and not significant at all in the ordered probit.

V. INTERPRETATION AND CAVEATS

Overall, these findings suggest that political self-interest plays a role in Congress' regulation of the states' power to tax. When states seek to tax Indian tribes, who are not sources of revenue for Congress, Congress is considerably more forgiving. And unopposed interest groups fare rather better than others in winning congressional protection, implying that state lobbying can be overcome by interest-group pressure. Indeed, when Congress acts with regard to state tax power, the mean result is a moderate reduction in that power.

One potential concern with these findings is that they could be artifacts of the research design. For example, it might be argued that I find a negative trend in the relative score variable simply because Congress is acting

---

also control for simple time trends, which should soak up some portion of any unobservable changes in congressional practices.

[16] When the controlling party and chamber median positions are included together as explanatory variables, the coefficient of each represents the effects of that variable holding the other constant.

against a baseline of no or few restrictions, leaving more room in the downward direction.

In my view this is only a minor concern, for several reasons. For one, as noted I restricted the sample to statutes for which there was a pre-existing restriction—that is, where the absolute score of the prior authority was less than seven. By definition, then, every observation in the dataset offered Congress at least some opportunity to relax restrictions as well as to tighten them.[17] The reported results also include a control for the absolute score of the prior authority; adding this control reduces somewhat the impact of the Indian dummy but does not otherwise affect the outcome. Thus, the restrictiveness of the prior restraint is not a significant predictor of Congress' subsequent behavior. Further, most observed reductions in state authority were by a relatively small amount, which implies that even for statutes with fairly unrestrictive prior authorities there was at least equal room for an equivalent move in the other direction.

Of course, by limiting the dataset to instances where a prior authority, usually the Supreme Court, had already found it necessary to rein in states, I may have introduced selection bias. Of greatest concern is the possibility that the results support the alternative hypothesis that Congress is maximizing national welfare by prohibiting inefficient state taxation. Arguably, subjects of taxation already restricted by the Supreme Court are more likely to be inefficient than others. On the other hand, it could be argued that rules already policed by the Court would need no further oversight by Congress.[18] In any event, to account for these possibilities, I also coded each enactment for efficiency, a dummy variable.[19] I find

---

[17]   There were no observations in the sample with a prior authority absolute score of 1, either.

[18]   Yet another possible reason to expect correlation between Supreme Court decisions and later congressional action is that both are essentially driven by interest groups, who provide resources both for litigation leading to judicial resolution as well as the ensuing legislation (Collins 2007, Staudt et al. 2007). This alternative, though, actually supports my hypothesis that interest-group influence drives commerce-clause outcomes.

[19]   Since all tax reduction tends towards efficiency in the sense that it reduces deadweight loss, I coded a statute as efficient if its enactment could arguably cure some inefficiency other than the excess burden of taxation. In some cases I balanced pro-efficiency gains against inefficiency losses. Admittedly, some of these scores could be disputed. For example, the Internet Tax Freedom Act bars states from forcing internet service providers to collect sales and use taxes. Arguably this is efficient in the sense that ISPs may generate network externalities, and so subsidies for the industry may be warranted under classic public finance theory. But at the same time this rule results in large geographical distortions, since it permits retailers to escape tax if they have no physical presence in a taxing jurisdiction.

that efficiency, if anything, is correlated with fewer restrictions on state authority.[20] Including efficiency as an explanatory variable changes slightly the coefficients of the other variables but does not affect their sign. Additionally, I find no statistically significant difference in the absolute scores of observations within the restricted dataset and those in the dataset as a whole.

Another form of selection bias that I indisputably face is that I can observe only legislation that actually passed. It is possible that states routinely defeat much larger threats to their taxing power than those observed, or that defeated proposals otherwise differ systematically from those in my dataset. Thus, my results are best characterized as describing the common features of enacted legislation, rather than of the legislative process as a whole. Accordingly, I cannot say that political safeguards of federalism are never effective; for all we know, they may well be effective 99 percent of the time. States may also be effective lobbyists on behalf of their local interest groups. What I can say is that the safeguards are likely not 100 percent effective at protecting generalized state interests, and that the observed instances of failure match well with theoretical predictions of failure.[21]

Of course, there is already substantial qualitative evidence that Congress at times diminishes state autonomy, such as through preemption, cross-cutting conditions on federal grants, and outright commands to states (NCSL 2004). In many cases, though, what may appear to be a restriction

---

It also distorts the flow of capital between remote and "brick and mortar" businesses. And government could mitigate the geographical distortions while subsidizing the industry just as effectively by using direct cash payments. So I coded the ITFA as inefficient.

[20] It appears this correlation is driven mostly by federal immunity. I coded judicial protection of federal contractors and property from state taxation as an inefficient distortion of capital flows towards the tax-favored firms, so that when Congress waived these protections, the result was efficiency-enhancing.

[21] I say that it is only "likely" that states are not 100 percent effective in their lobbying efforts, notwithstanding my results here, because I cannot rule out the alternative that states themselves were the impetus for federal legislation reducing their own taxing power. That seems at best a minor possibility, though, since any story along those lines seems rather strained. It might be argued, for instance, that states whose neighboring, rival state drew large revenues from a particular source, such as oil, might lobby the federal government to cut off that source of comparative advantage. Or states that are subject to significant tax-exporting might seek to close off the exporting at its source (Rose-Ackerman 1981). But neither story fits particularly well with any of the statutes in the sample. It may be that some states have industries that could benefit from favorable tax treatment, but there is no obvious way to disentangle that possibility from the pure public choice story.

on state autonomy in fact maximizes state well-being overall, just as constraints on individual liberty (such as prohibitions on theft and assault) may increase net personal freedom. (*Charles C. Steward Mach. Co. v. Davis*, 301 U.S. 548, 587 (1937).) As is well known, federal action can be a mechanism for resolving coordination or other collective-action problems states might otherwise face (Oates 1999, Cooter 2002). Congress, for example, may be a low-transaction-cost venue for Coasean bargaining between those states that create and those that are affected by externalities (Kobayashi & Ribstein 2007). The existing literature studying federal impositions on states does not clearly distinguish between these two forms of federal enactment. Thus, the extant literature is unclear on whether federal authority actually reduces state autonomy.

This study advances significantly over the prior, qualitative, literature by controlling for the possibility that federal legislation may be state autonomy-enhancing. As noted, I find no correlation between the efficiency of a statute and the direction of change in state power. Additionally, I created another dummy variable, termed "coordination," to identify federal statutes that arguably could be said to resolve some sort of state-level coordination or other collective-action problem (such as a race to the bottom).[22] I found, however, that there was no correlation between whether a statute solved coordination problems and the direction of change in state authority: the relation between the two was essentially random, and including the coordination variable in the regression analyses did not meaningfully change the coefficient for any other variable. Of course, this does not prove that coordination is *not* motivating Congress, but the fact that my evidence shows strong support for a public-choice story and no support for a coordination story is suggestive.

My inability to observe failed legislation is less significant for the purely tax-related aspects of my hypotheses. As noted, the contention in the literature is that Congress will outperform courts in safeguarding national well-being against state-level externalities. In order for Congress to carry out that function, it must act (or at least threaten credibly to act). Thus, in testing claims about how Congress performs when it is able to overcome

---

[22]   For instance, I coded as "1" federal enactments that established one and only one state to be the exclusive income-taxing jurisdiction for employees of the railroad, bus, air, and shipping industries. These statutes are not necessarily efficient, in that they tend to distort the choice of state residence. The cumulative burdens of compliance and auditing costs, though, are largely an externality for each state (Shaviro 1992), suggesting that in the absence of coordination workers subject to tax in many states might be forced to comply with a confusing array of regimes.

legislative inertia, it makes sense to focus narrowly on Congress' actual output. Admittedly, I cannot rule out the possibility that even more forceful judicial efforts to prod Congress might result in passage of more benevolent laws than in the past. But the Supreme Court has already employed what look to be significant penalty defaults in an effort to force congressional action, without any effect measurable in this data or otherwise (see Galle 2007a for more discussion).

Moving beyond selection bias concerns, I must acknowledge that there are alternative interpretations for the influence of the Indian variable. Most significantly, it may be that the reason states have a freer hand to tax Indian tribes is because the tribes are politically weaker than other interest groups affected in the data set. Scholars of U.S.–tribal relations argue that states used tax law, and especially the power to seize the property of tax debtors, as a tool for pillaging tribal property (Taylor 2007). If this were the story, we might perhaps expect a trend towards parity in the modern era as outright oppression faded. I do not, however, observe a significant difference in the time trends between statutes affecting the tribes and others.[23] Another factor that supports my explanation over this alternative is that, for the alternative to be true, it would have to be the case that Indian tribes are even less effective than the general public at lobbying. But I find to the contrary that the mean relative score for Indian statutes does not differ significantly from the mean for non-Indian, non-public choice statutes; Congress treats tribes roughly the same as the public at large.

Another aspect of the data worth some comment is the frequency with which Congress appears to enact legislation that does not change existing law. Given the difficulty of enacting legislation, that is somewhat puzzling. Staudt et al. (2007) offer several explanations, such as the possibility that legislation expands a judicial decision to new contexts (which I do not observe in my data) or clarifies a confusing precedent. I would further hypothesize that clear notice to the public is valuable in its own right, especially in eras that lack easy access to judicial decisions or computerized searches. I continue to observe in my data simple codification in modern statutes, however, which inclines me towards other explanations. Codification locks in outcomes against possible changes in judicial personnel, and may also, as Staudt et al. (2007) hint at, allow for rent-extraction from constituencies which are relatively unsophisticated about current law. Thus, the extensive codification efforts seen in the data here provide some additional evidence of rent-seeking behavior by Congress.

---

[23] Interactions of the year term with the Indian variable also yielded no significant results.

One final riddle is how to interpret the linear, albeit in some specifications insignificant, negative relationship between year and relative score. Percentages of national government expenditures spent at the state level, as well as attitudes towards federal taxes (Kincaid & Cole 2007, Kincaid & Cole 2000), exhibit a similar overall negative trend, while measures of overall policy centralization (Bowman & Krause 2003) show no correlation with our result. Another possible explanation could be a learning story, in which special interests have over time developed expertise in influencing Congress, or members of Congress have become more aware of the potential for rent-extraction through tax legislation (Posner 2005). I found no significant results with any interaction terms between the year, public choice, and rival variables. Still, this might simply represent the limitations of the data.

VI.   CONCLUSION

While my evidence here certainly does not end any debates over federalism, it is suggestive. Claims that states never need to fear inefficient federal expansions seem likely to be overstated. I find that, at least in the case where special interest influence is strong, and Congress can export the costs of regulation to the States, congressional action in fact does tend to diminish state prerogatives. Further, I find no evidence that this diminution might be serving to preserve state autonomy in the long run by facilitating coordination among states.

I therefore provide at least modest support for a continuing judicial role in federalism decisions. To be sure, the possibility of occasional bad deeds by Congress is not the only factor in play. Unfunded mandates might still be justified as efficient allocation of the social costs of regulation (Dana 1995, Adler 1997, Roin 1999), or shrugged off as simply another opportunity for states to hold up the federal government within a cooperative regime (Caminker 1995, Siegel 2006, Bulman-Pozen & Gerken 2009). And courts may simply be so bad at federalism decisions that even a Congress that can at times be captured by special interests looks good by comparison. In some areas, however, such as the dormant commerce clause, commentary to date has assumed uncritically that Congress is both the superior fact-finder and also a trustworthy maximizer of national welfare. At a minimum, my findings here warrant consideration of how to balance the strengths and weaknesses of the three branches in regulating free trade, a project I take up elsewhere.

In addition, my results shed some light on the motivations of Congress. Levinson (2005) argues that members of Congress are at best only weakly motivated by the size of the federal budget, since the effect of any one actor on the budget as a whole is largely an externality for individual members. I find, in contrast, that opportunities for reducing budget pressure do seem to play a role at least in statutes affecting state tax policy. Internal institutional factors, such as party leadership and budget rules, may outweigh the collective action problems members would otherwise face, a possibility that merits further investigation.

Lastly, it is worth emphasizing the institutional dimension of these findings. I study here only Congress and, indirectly, the President as veto player. I have argued elsewhere that administrative agencies are relatively more likely to take care with state autonomy, at least in the case where judicial review demands that they do so (Galle & Seidenfeld 2008). My results therefore suggest the possible appeal of a federalism doctrine that shifts more authority to agencies, although more empirical work into the performance of the executive is needed to confirm whether in fact agencies function better than Congress.

REFERENCES

Adler, Robert. 1997. "Unfunded Mandates and Fiscal Federalism: A Critique," 50 *Vanderbilt Law Review* 1137.

Baker, Lynn A. 1995. "Conditional Federal Spending after Lopez," 95 *Columbia Law Review* 1911.

Baker, Lynn A. & Ernest A. Young. 2002. "Federalism and the Double Standard of Judicial Review," 51 *Duke Law Journal* 75.

Bednar, Jenna. 2007. "Credit Assignment and Federal Encroachment," 15 *Supreme Court Economic Review* 285.

Bellia, Anthony J., Jr. 2006. "Congressional Power and State Court Jurisdiction," 94 *Georgetown Law Journal* 949.

Bowman, Ann O'M. & George A. Krause. 2003. "Power Shift: Measuring Policy Centralization in U.S. Intergovernmental Relations, 1947–1998," 31 *American Politics Research* 301.

Brambor, Thomas, William Roberts Clark, & Matt Golder. 2006. "Understanding Interaction Models: Improving Empirical Analysis," 14 *Political Analysis* 63.

Brennan, Geoffrey & Buchanan, James. 1984. "Towards a Tax Constitution for Leviathan," in *The Theory of Public Choice II*. Ann Arbor: University of Michigan Press.

Bulman-Pozen, Jessica & Heather K., Gerken. 2009. "Uncooperative Federalism," 118 *Yale Law Journal* 1256.

Caminker, Evan. 1995. "State Sovereignty and Subordinacy: May Congress Commandeer State Officials to Implement Federal Law?" 95 *Columbia Law Review* 1001.

Carroll, Royce et al. 2011. "DW-Nominate Scores with Bootstrapped Standard Errors." http://www.voteview.com/dwnomin.htm.

Carroll, Royce et al. 2008. "Measuring Bias and Uncertainty in DW-Nominate

Ideal Point Estimates Using the Parametric Bootstrap." Working Paper. http://papers.ssrn.com/sol3/papers.cfm?abstract_id=1281667.

Choper, Jesse H. 1980. *Judicial Review and the National Political Process: A Functional Reconsideration of the Role of the Supreme Court.* Chicago: Chicago University Press.

Collins, Paul M., Jr. 2007. "Towards an Integrated Model of the U.S. Supreme Court's Federalism Decision Making," 37 *Publius: The Journal of Federalism* 505.

Cooter, Robert. 2002. *The Strategic Constitution.* Princeton: Princeton University Press.

Dana, David. 1995. "The Case for Unfunded Environmental Mandates," 69 *Southern California Law Review* 1.

Derthick, Martha. 1986. "Preserving Federalism: Congress, the States, and the Supreme Court," *The Brookings Review* Winter/Spring: 32.

Dinan, John. 2009. "The State of American Federalism 2007–2008," 38 *Publius* 381.

Dinan, John. 1997. "State Government Influence in the National Political Process: Lessons from the 104th Congress," 27 *Publius* 129.

Eule, Julian N. 1982. "Laying the Dormant Commerce Clause to Rest," 91 *Yale Law Journal* 425.

Frickey, Philip P. 1990. "Congressional Intent, Practical Reasoning, and the Dynamic Nature of Federal Indian Law," 78 *California Law Review* 1137.

Galle, Brian. 2013. "The Effects of National Revenues on Sub-National Revenues: Evidence from the United States," 37 *International Review of Law & Economics* 147.

Galle, Brian. 2008. "Federal Grants, State Decisions," 88 *Boston University Law Review* 875.

Galle, Brian. 2007a. "Designing Interstate Institutions: The Example of the Streamlined Sales and Use Tax Agreement," 40 *U.C. Davis Law Review* 1381.

Galle, Brian. 2007b. "A Republic of the Mind: Cognitive Biases, Fiscal Federalism, and Section 164 of the Tax Code," 82 *Indiana Law Journal* 673.

Galle, Brian. 2004. "Getting Spending: How to Replace Clear Statement Rules with Clear Thinking about Conditional Grants of Federal Funds," 37 *Connecticut Law Review* 155.

Galle, Brian & Mark Seidenfeld. 2008. "Administrative Law's Federalism: Preemption, Delegation, and Agencies at the Edge of Federal Power," 57 *Duke Law Journal* 1933.

Garrett, Elizabeth. 1997. "Enhancing the Political Safeguards of Federalism: The Unfunded Mandates Reform Act of 1995," 45 *University of Kansas Law Review* 1113.

Hamilton, Marci A. 2001. "The Elusive Safeguards of Federalism," 574 *Annals of the American Academy of Political and Social Science* 93.

Hanson, I. & Stuart, C. 1987. "The Sub-Optimality of Local Taxation under Two-Tier Fiscal Federalism," 3 *European Journal of Political Economy* 407.

Hellerstein, Jerome. 1941. "State Taxation in a National Economy," 54 *Harvard Law Review* 949.

Hero, Rodney. 1989. "The U.S. Congress and American Federalism: Are 'Subnational Governments' Protected?" 42 *Western Political Quarterly* 93.

Hills, Roderick M., Jr. 1998. "The Political Economy of Cooperative Federalism: Why State Autonomy Makes Sense and 'Dual Sovereignty' Doesn't," 96 *Michigan Law Review* 813.

Jensen, Erik M. 2008. "Indian Gaming on Newly Acquired Lands," 47 *Washburn Law Journal* 675.

Jones, Renee M. 2004."Dynamic Federalism: Competition, Cooperation and Securities Enforcement," 11 *Connecticut Insurance Law Journal* 1.

Joondeph, Brad. 2003. "Exploring the 'Myth of Parity' in State Taxation: State Court Decisions Interpreting Public Law," 13 *Washington University Journal of Law and Policy* 86–272.

Kagan, Elena. 2001. "Presidential Administration," 114 *Harvard Law Review* 2245.

Kam, Cindy D. & Robert A. Mikos. 2007. "Do Citizens Care about Federalism? An Experimental Study," 4 *Journal of Empirical Legal Studies* 589.

Keele, Luke & David K. Park. 2006. "Difficult Choices: An Evaluation of Heterogeneous Choice Models," unpublished working paper.

Kincaid, John & Richard L. Cole. 2007. "Public Opinion on Issues of Federalism in 2007: A Bush Plus?" 38 *Publius: The Journal of Federalism* 469.

Kincaid, John & Richard L. Cole. 2000. "Public Opinion and American Federalism: Perspectives on Taxes, Spending, and Trust—An ACIR Update," 30 *Publius: The Journal of Federalism* 189.

Klick, Jonathan & Francesco Parisi. 2005. "Intra-Jurisdictional Tax Competition," 16 *Constitutional Political Economy* 387.

Kobayashi, Bruce H. & Larry E. Ribstein. 2007. "Introduction," in *Economics of Federalism*. Northampton: Edward Elgar Press.

Kramer, Larry. 2000. "Putting the Politics Back into the Political Safeguards of Federalism," 100 *Columbia Law Review* 215.

La Pierre, D. Bruce. 1985. "Political Accountability in the National Political Process – The Alternative to Judicial Review of Federal Issues," 80 *Northwestern University Law Review* 577.

Lee, Carol. 1988. "The Political Safeguards of Federalism?: Congressional Responses to Supreme Court Decisions on State and Local Liability," 20 *Urban Lawyer* 301.

Levinson, Daryl J. 2005. "Empire-Building Government in Constitutional Law," 118 *Harvard Law Review* 915.

Macey, Jonathan R. 1986."Promoting Public-Regarding Legislation through Statutory Interpretation: An Interest-Group Model," 86 *Columbia Law Review* 223.

Mayhew, David. 1974. *Congress: The Electoral Connection*. New Haven: Yale University Press.

McCaffrey, Edward J. & Jonathan Barron. 2006. "Thinking about Tax," 12 *Psychology, Public Policy, and Law* 106.

McGinnis, John O. 2001. "Presidential Review as Constitutional Restoration," 51 *Duke Law Journal* 901.

McGinnis, John O. & Ilya Somin. 2004. "Federalism vs. States' Rights: A Defense of Judicial Review in a Federal System," 99 *Northwestern University Law Review* 89

Mendelson, Nina A. 2004. "Chevron and Preemption," 102 *Michigan Law Review* 737.

Metzger, Gillian. 2008. "Administrative Law as the New Federalism," 57 *Duke Law Journal* 2023.

Metzger, Gillian. 2007. "Congress, Article IV, and Interstate Relations," 120 *Harvard Law Review* 1468.

National Conference of State Legislatures. 2004. *Mandate Monitor*. Washington, DC: NCSL.

Nicholson-Crotty, Sean. 2008. "National Election Cycles and the Intermittent Political Safeguards of Federalism," 38 *Publius: The Journal of Federalism* 295.

Nzelibe, Jide. 2006. "The Fable of the Nationalist President and the Parochial Congress," 53 *UCLA Law Review* 1217.

Oates, Wallace. 1999. "An Essay on Fiscal Federalism," 37 *Journal of Economic Literature* 1120.

Olson, Mancur. 1982. *The Rise and Decline of Nations*. New Haven: Yale University Press.

Pickerill, J. Mitchell. 2004. *The Impact of Judicial Review in a Separated System*. Raleigh: Duke University Press.

Posner, Paul. 2005. "The Politics of Preemption," 38 *PS: Political Science and Politics* 371.

Pursley, Garrick B. 2010. "Preemption in Congress," 71 *Ohio State Law Journal* 511.

Redish, Martin H. & Nugent, Shane V. 1987. "The Dormant Commerce Clause and the Constitutional Balance of Federalism," 1987 *Duke Law Journal* 569.

Resnik, Judith. 2008. "Lessons in Federalism from the 1960s Class Action Rule and the 2005 Class Action Fairness Act: 'The Political Safeguards' of Aggregate Translocal Actions," 156 *University of Pennsylvania Law Review* 1929.

Roin, Julie A. 1999. "Reconceptualizing Unfunded Mandates and Other Regulations," 93 *Northwestern University Law Review* 351.

Rose-Ackerman, Susan. 1981. "Does Federalism Matter? Political Choice in a Federal Republic," 89 *Journal of Political Economy* 152.

Rubin, Edward L. & Feeley, Malcolm. 1994. "Federalism: Some Notes on a National Neurosis," 41 *UCLA Law Review* 903.

Sharkey, Katherine M. 2008. "Products Liability Preemption: An Institutional Approach," 76 *George Washington University Law Review* 449.

Shaviro, Daniel. 1992. "An Economic and Political Look at Federalism in Taxation," 90 *Michigan Law Review* 895.

Siegel, Neil S. 2006. "Commandeering and its Alternatives: A Federalism Perspective," 59 *Vanderbilt Law Review* 1629.

Solberg, Rorie S. & Stefanie A. Lindquist. 2006. "Activism, Ideology, and Federalism: Judicial Behavior in Constitutional Challenges before the Rehnquist Court, 1986–2000," 3 *Journal of Empirical Legal Studies* 237.

Staudt, Nancy, Rene Lindstadt, & Jason O'Connor. 2007. "Judicial Decisions as Legislation: Congressional Oversight of Supreme Court Tax Cases, 1954–2005," 82 *New York University Law Review* 1340.

Swain, John A. 2003. "States Sales and Use Tax Jurisdiction: An Economic Nexus Standard for the Twenty-First Century," 38 *Georgia Law Review* 343.

Taylor, Scott A. 2007. "A Judicial Framework for Applying Supreme Court Jurisprudence to the State Income Taxation of Indian Traders," 2007 *Michigan State Law Review* 841.

Tribe, Laurence. 1999. *American Constitutional Law: Volume One*, 3rd edn. New York: Foundation Press.

Wechsler, Herbert. 1954. "The Political Safeguards of Federalism: The Role of States in the Composition and Selection of the National Government," 54 *Columbia Law Review* 543.

Weissert, Carol S. & Sanford F. Schram. 1996. "The State of American Federalism, 1995–1996," 26 *Publius: The Journal of Federalism* 1.

Zelinsky, Edward. 2002. "Restoring Politics to the Commerce Clause: The Case for Abandoning the Dormant Commerce Clause Prohibition on Discriminatory Taxation," 29 *Ohio Northern Law Review* 29.

Zelinsky, Edward. 1993. "Unfunded Mandates, Hidden Taxation, and the Tenth Amendment: On Public Choice, Public Interest, and Public Services," 46 *Vanderbilt Law Review* 1355.

2. Harmonisation of private law in Europe

Michael Faure*

1. INTRODUCTION

Although the institutional structure and history of the United States (US) and the European Union (EU) are quite different, the impressive body of law and economics literature that has been used to analyse federalism issues within the American context has to an increasing extent, also been used to look at the division of competences between the Member States and the central level in Europe. In this chapter I will sketch some evolutions in Europe and address how these have been viewed by law and economics scholarship. The chapter will not review the entire law and economics literature with respect to federalism in Europe, but rather focus on a particularly interesting, although limited, domain of private law. The reason is that many academics interested in private law in Europe have for many years now advocated that Europe should have a civil code.[1] This seemed to be at first merely an academic interest with a strong symbolic value.[2] This idea seems to be taken over at the European political level as well. Whereas the European integration process and hence the focus of European legislative action originally focused on harmonisation of economic regulation, thus removing barriers to interstate trade, increasingly Europe also started legislating on rules of private law, such as product liability,[3] environmental liability[4] or unfair terms in consumer contracts.[5]

* I am grateful to Marianne Breijer (Rotterdam Institute for Law and Economics) for useful comments on an earlier draft of this chapter.
[1] See for example Hartkamp and others (2011).
[2] Like Napoleon succeeded in uniting France with a Code Civil of 21 March 1804 it is hoped that a European Civil Code will also promote the political unification in Europe.
[3] Directive of 25 July 1985, *OJ* L 210/29 of 7 August 1985.
[4] Directive 2004/35 of 21 April 2004, *OJ* L 143 of 30 April 2004.
[5] Directive 93/13 of 15 April 1993, *OJ* L 095 of 21 April 1993.

The idea that rules of private law should also be harmonised at central (European) level therefore received increasing support at the political level.

Moreover, increasingly a variety of private initiatives were taken, usually academic projects, aiming to achieve a European harmonisation in the area of private law. One example constitutes the European Group on Tort Law which drafted Principles of European Tort Law (2005) (Jansen 2001; Spier and Haazen 1999). This is an academic exercise addressing the common roots of tort law in various laws of Member States, more comparable to the American restatement. However, one particular initiative goes much further. It is a major project concerning a European Civil Code, supervised by Prof. Christian von Bar from Osnabrück. His ideas led to the drafting of a so-called Draft Common Frame of References (DCFR) (Von Bar, Clive and Schulte-Nölke 2008). This is according to some nothing less than a draft of a European Civil Code and has also been financially supported by the European Commission (Commission) (Von Bar, Clive and Schulte-Nölke 2008). It gave rise to many critical reflections, especially as far as the ambitions of this document are concerned (see e.g. Eidenmüller et al. 2008a, 2008b). A particular strong reaction followed by the well-known comparative lawyer Pierre Legrand who pointed at the impossibility of legal transplants (more particularly between the common law and the civil law (Legrand 1997) and who published an article with the meaningful title 'Antivonbar' (Legrand 2008).

This brief sketch shows that there is in Europe an increasing interest now in harmonisation of private law, not only in academic circles, but increasingly also at decision-making level. This is interesting from a comparative perspective given that Europe still lacks, even after the Treaty of Lisbon, a completely integrated federal structure whereas in the US domains belonging to private law (e.g. contract, tort and property) traditionally would belong to state law and only under particular strict conditions to federal law. Not surprisingly the increasing Europeanisation of private law has therefore been the subject of a lot of criticism from law and economics scholarship. This literature uses traditional arguments advanced in (mainly North-American) law and economics scholarship against centralisation of decision-making and harmonisation of legal rules.

This chapter will review some of this law and economics literature. The chapter has therefore to be read within this particular limited context of rules dealing with private law. After all, for other domains (like economic regulations) arguments in favour of centralisation may be much stronger.

After this introduction first the institutional background for decision-making at EU-level will briefly be sketched (2) and a few examples of European Directives in domains of private law will be provided (3).

Next, traditional economic arguments with respect to centralisation will be briefly reviewed and applied to the cases of private law harmonised in Europe. The focus will be on transboundary externalities (4) and the race-to-the-bottom argument (5). Specific arguments often advanced in European legal scholarship in favour of harmonisation will be reviewed as well. One refers to the necessity of harmonisation in order to harmonise marketing conditions (6); another to the fact that harmonisation would generally lower transaction costs (7). Sometimes it is argued that harmonisation would not be needed for economic reasons, but simply to provide a minimum level of protection to European citizens (8). The chapter concludes with a few policy considerations, including a brief public choice perspective (9) and with a few concluding remarks (10).

Given the fact that harmonisation of private law in Europe has been the subject of an extensive law and economics scholarship it will not be possible to review this literature in this chapter in detail. The main arguments will therefore be presented; the reader is referred to the list of references for further reading.

2.   INSTITUTIONAL BACKGROUND

A leading author on environmental policy wrote 'The European Union ... does not enjoy the prerogatives of a state; it may act only where it has been expressly so authorized by the (Maastricht) Treaty (that created the EU)' (Krämer 2002). The Member States of the EU hence in principle retain full sovereign status. EU Member States are independent nations with distinct cultures and languages and until recently substantial barriers to mobility of capital, labour and residency within the EU existed that do not exist in the US (Faure and Johnston 2009, 210). A consequence of the European Member States remaining sovereign nations is that under the so-called "principle of attribution" European institutions' powers extend only as far as has been expressly confirmed by the Treaty. Despite this principle the power of the European bureaucracy (that is, the Commission) has steadily increased and led to a steady shift of regulatory competences to the European level. For example in a domain like environmental law today 66 per cent of environmental law in a Member State such as the Netherlands is based on European directives and regulations (Douma et al. 2007).

Given the principle of attribution the European institutions needed a formal legal basis to take legislative action. For a long time the Commission found this authority in Article 100 of the (then) European

Economic Community (EEC) Treaty.[6] This Article 100 allowed for European measures to harmonise national legislation in order to remove or prevent barriers for the internal market. Precisely because an express legal basis for legislative action in the domain of private law was lacking in the Treaty this old Article 100 was often found as a basis for harmonising actions in the domain of private law.[7]

As far as the division of labour between Member States and the EU is concerned the Maastricht Treaty has introduced the so-called subsidiarity principle according to which powers should be granted to the EU institutions only when it has been established that they cannot be satisfactorily exercised by the Member States. This subsidiarity principle applies with the exception of the so-called exclusive competences of the EU institutions. The subsidiarity principle hence guides, after the entering into force of the Treaty on the Functioning of the European Union (better known as the Lisbon Treaty) the division of competences between the central and decentralised level and generally puts the burden of proof of the necessity of centralised action on the EU institutions.[8]

A result of this brief sketch of the institutional background concerning European federalism is that, as far as private law is concerned, the legal basis for EU action is usually to be found in improving the functioning of the internal market.[9] Nevertheless, as was mentioned in the introduction, some (academic) projects like the DCFR go much further to the extent that they would like to establish a truly European Civil Code.

3. EXAMPLES

A few examples of European action in the field of private law, already mentioned in the introduction, will be presented in order to show the domains of private law on which the EU has been active or has proposed action. It concerns a relatively old (1985) Directive on Product Liability and a more recent one (2004) on Environmental Liability. The contents of the directives will be briefly sketched in order to give some flavour of how

---

[6] Meanwhile this Article 100 has been renumbered many times.
[7] As a consequence the European Commission only has competence to regulate to the extent that cross-border transactions are stimulated (see Weatherill 2005, 74).
[8] See further on this principle Berman (1994) and Edwards (1986) as well as Marquardt (1994).
[9] This follows clearly from a decision of the Court of Justice in the well-known *Tobacco Advertising* judgment (Case C-376/98, ECRJ, 2000, 8419). For a comment see Hervey (2001).

EU private law works. Moreover, the arguments presented at EU level for EU legislative action in this field will be reviewed as well; these will then be critically reviewed in the following sections (4–7) using the economic perspective on federalism.

3.1 Product Liability

Probably one of the first EU actions in the domain of private law was the Directive 85/374 of 25 July 1985 on the approximation of the laws, regulations and administrative provisions of the Member States concerning liability for defective products. The directive introduces a strict liability for damage caused by defective products (Art. 1). The following articles develop what is meant by the different notions which are used in Article 1. A product is considered to be defective under the directive when it does not provide the safety which a person is entitled to expect. Non-liability clauses are invalid, but certain exclusion grounds for the producer apply.

Reading the considerations preceding the directive the goal of this directive is formulated as follows:

> Whereas approximation of the laws of the Member States concerning the liability of the producer for damage caused by the defectiveness of his product is necessary because the existing divergences may distort competition and affect the movement of goods within the common market.

The reasoning is in other words that differing levels of product liability might affect the free movement of goods within the common market. The legal basis of the directive was therefore the (old) Article 100 of the EEC Treaty which allowed harmonisation through directives in all cases where the functioning and establishment of the common market were directly concerned. In addition to the possible distortion of competition a second goal of the directive is mentioned, that of consumer protection. The argument is advanced that the existing divergences in the product liability rules of the Member States might 'entail' a different degree of protection of consumer protection. The notion of 'protection of the consumer' is mentioned as often as 12 times in the considerations preceding the directive. The goal of the Product Liability Directive is therefore not just to harmonise existing laws, but to harmonise them at a higher level of consumer protection (Faure 2000, 468–70).

3.2 Environmental Liability

On 21 April 2004 the Directive 2004/35 on Environmental Liability with regard to the prevention and remedying of environmental damage was promulgated. The directive introduces strict liability for environmental damage caused by specific activities listed in an Annex to the directive; for other activities a fault regime applies. Environmental damage is defined as damage to protected species and natural habitats, water damage and land damage. When environmental damage has occurred the operator is obliged to take remedial action and he shall bear the costs of this pursuant to the directive. The Environmental Liability Directive has no retroactive effect.

As far as the reasons for EU action in this field are concerned the considerations preceding the directive mention the implementation of the polluter-pays principle and contributing to EU environmental policy. A document preceding the directive, the so-called White Paper on Environmental Liability of February 2000[10] provides more information on the reasons for European action. The White Paper inter alia states that harmonisation should be accepted under the subsidiarity principle as the Member States cannot adequately deal with transboundary environmental pollution. A directive is therefore necessary 'to avoid inadequate solutions to transfrontier damage'. However, the Commission also argues that a regime dealing exclusively with cross-border harm 'would leave a serious gap where liability for bio-diversity damage is concerned'. This could have as a consequence that purely national and cross-border cases will be treated differently, which could possibly violate the principle of equal treatment. The Commission again argues that an EU wide regime 'may contribute to creating a level playing field in the internal market'.[11]

After now having reviewed two directives in the field of private law I will in the next four sections examine these arguments for harmonisation of private law using the law and economics perspective on federalism.

4.   TRANSBOUNDARY EXTERNALITIES

4.1   General

The transboundary character of the problem to be regulated is presented in economic theory as an argument in favour of centralisation from two different angles. One aspect is that in case of transboundary externalities

---

[10]   Communication of the European Communities, White Paper on Environmental Liability, COM(2000) 66 final, Brussels, 9 February 2000.

[11]   For a further analysis of the arguments presented by the Commission see Faure and De Smedt (2001).

States will have no incentive to impose stringent regulations upon their own citizens if the consequences of harmful actions are only felt outside their own territory. Transboundary externalities may thus create inefficiencies in the absence of central regulation (Revesz 2000, 67). A second argument is that if the problem to be regulated crosses the borders of competence of the regulatory authority the decision-making power should be shifted to a higher regulatory level, preferably to an authority which has jurisdiction over a territory large enough to deal with the problem adequately (Esty 1996). 'Economic theory provides a straightforward but unrealistic answer to regional problems: draw "optimal" jurisdictional boundaries' (Rose-Ackerman 1995, 38).

Although this argument may favour centralisation, e.g. with respect to transboundary torts, European law and economics scholars have argued that in the area of private law European law cannot be considered an effective remedy to the interstate externality problem: in some cases European law goes further than is necessary to cure transboundary externalities; in other cases less comprehensive legal instruments than total harmonisation could be used to remedy the problems. In other cases the transboundary externality could be cured by an extraterritorial application of national law (Van den Bergh 1998, 143–6).

This can be illustrated by the cases of private law discussed before.

4.2   Application

As far as product liability is concerned at first blush the transboundary externality argument plays an important role. In the US context it was argued that since products are sold throughout the federal nation product liability may be a good candidate for centralised law (Ackerman 1996, 451; Schwartz 1996, 924). However, within the European context Van den Bergh has argued that in EU Member States different communities may have different preferences concerning both the level of product safety and product liability law (Van den Bergh 1998, 133). Moreover, within the European context the transboundary externality argument is not particularly strong for the simple reason that exporters remain liable in foreign (European) countries. A Dutch manufacturer cannot, for example, externalise harm to Belgian consumers for the simple reason that he will remain liable in the (Belgian) export market. The Belgian victim can also sue the Dutch manufacturer in the place where the harm occurred (e.g. Belgium) as a result of a (now transformed into an EU regulation) European convention with respect to the jurisdiction and execution of judgments (Faure 2000, 476–8).

As far as environmental liability is concerned the transboundary externality argument is valid to the extent that the environmental liability regime applies to transboundary externalities (Bergkamp 2000, 107). However, the Environmental Liability Directive essentially applies to damage to natural habitats, water damage and land damage, which is surely not only transboundary. The option of a 'transboundary only' regime was, however, rejected by the Commission since it would lead to inequalities in the treatment of victims in Member States depending on whether they were the victims of transboundary or local pollution. In that case, the Commission no longer argues within the scope of the subsidiarity principle, but simply pleads for uniformity (see Bergkamp 2000, 107).

5. RACE TO THE BOTTOM

5.1 General

Centralisation has also been advanced as a remedy to the prisoner's dilemmas that could arise in case of a race to the bottom: the assumption is that local governments would use lenient regulation as a competitive tool to attract industry (see e.g. Rose-Ackerman 1992, 166–70). The validity of this race to the bottom argument is strongly debated among law and economics scholars who tend to stress the benefits of competition between States and point out the dangers of centralisation (see especially Revesz 1992, 1996). Others point at the potentially destructive effects of this inter-state competition and hence attach more belief to the race to the bottom rationale (see e.g. Esty 1996; Esty and Geradin 1998).

The race to the bottom argument has as such not been explicitly discussed in the European legal debate. It does, however, pop up in the argument that conditions of competition should be harmonised. European law and economics scholars, however, argue that the race to the bottom rationale only provides an argument for centralisation on the condition that there is (empirical) evidence that States can and do indeed attract industry with lenient rules (see Van den Bergh 2000, 445). The question therefore arises whether industry will relocate as a result of lenient rules of private law or whether these rules will play an important role in location decisions of firms.

5.2 Application

Again, the race to the bottom argument could in theory play a role in case of product liability. It would assume that governments compete with lenient product liability rules to attract industry (compare Rose-Ackerman

1992, 166–70). There are, however, several weaknesses in this argument. First, increased costs of product liability can be passed on to purchasers of the product (Van den Bergh 1998, 137–9). Second, engaging in a race to the bottom will not be effective in attracting manufacturing industries that largely depend upon an export market. After all manufacturers will remain liable in export markets (Ackerman 1996, 458; Faure 2000, 479). Third, it is more likely that European States would wish to protect accident victims instead of corporate interests. There is hence rather a danger of a 'race to the top', leading to an overprotective product liability law.

The same can be argued as far as environmental liability is concerned. North-American research has already showed that effects of environmental regulations on location decisions of industry are 'either small, statistically insignificant or not robust to tests of model specification' (Jaffe, Peterson, Portney and Stavins 1995). Although more recent evidence somewhat relaxes these earlier findings (Faure and Johnston 2009, 246–50) it certainly does remain valid in the area of environmental liability. It is, certainly as far as the old EU Member States are concerned, doubtful whether they would engage in a game in which they would strive for low level environmental liability in order to attract industry. Also, elements other than environmental liability may be far more important in the location decision of businesses. Moreover, also as far as environmental liability is concerned, it is more likely that States would wish to protect victims of environmental pollution instead of corporate interests, thus engaging in a race for the top (Ogus 1999, 48; Vogel 1995, 13). This story may only have changed after EU enlargement to Central and Eastern Europe, as a result of which now many Member States with substantially lower environmental standards have been included in the EU. Although the argument in favour of centralisation (to counter a race to the bottom) has thus increased one can expect, paradoxically, the contrary. The reason is that many Western-European companies moved to the East, also benefitting from lower (environmental and labour) standards there. Such firms would, if anything, have an incentive to favour environmental regulatory decentralisation, so that they can take advantage of lax environmental standards in new Member States with slower development (Faure and Johnston 2009, 267–71). Although enlargement may thus have interesting consequences for the EU federalistic model, that cannot be an argument to justify the Environmental Liability Directive, which was adopted in 2004, prior to the enlargement to Central and Eastern Europe.

6. HARMONISATION OF MARKETING CONDITIONS

6.1 General

The race-to-the-bottom argument, that competition among jurisdictions for economic activity will be 'destructive', corresponds – to some extent – with the European legal argument that the creation of harmonised conditions of competition is necessary to avoid trade distortions. This argument was traditionally used to harmonise legislation of the Member States in a variety of areas. Simply stated, the argument is that complying with legislation imposes costs on industry. If legislation is different, these costs would therefore differ as well and the conditions of competition within the common market would not be equal. The argument apparently assumes that total equality of conditions of competition is necessary for the functioning of the common market. 'Levelling the playing field' for European industry is the central message.

There are, however, some problems with this traditional European argument which in fact claims that any difference in legislation between the Member States might endanger the conditions of competition and therefore justifies harmonisation of legal rules. The latter argument seems particularly weak (Spier and Haazen 1999, 478). From an economic point of view, the mere fact that conditions of competition differ, does not necessarily create a race-to-the-bottom risk. There can be differences in marketing conditions for a variety of reasons, and if the conditions of competition were indeed totally equal, as the argument assumes, there would also be no trade.

Also, Europe has developed an elaborate set of rules that guarantees, inter alia, a free flow of products and services and thus contributes to market integration without the necessity of harmonising all rules and standards.[12] In this context, the case law of the European Court of Justice with respect to the free movement of goods versus environmental protection springs to mind. This shows that the goal of market integration can be achieved through (other) less comprehensive instruments than total harmonisation (Esty and Geradin 1997, 296–9; Ogus 2004, 177–9), which can remove barriers to trade just as effectively. Hence, one should make a distinction between the political ideal of creating one common market in

---

[12] See generally on the potential conflict between free trade and environmental protection Esty (1999).

Europe on the one hand and the (economic) race-to-the-bottom argument on the other hand.[13]

6.2   Application

The problems with the 'harmonisation of marketing conditions' argument becomes clear when addressing specific directives in more detail. If the directives were to aim at a 'harmonisation of marketing conditions' they should create a full harmonisation of liability law in the EU Member States. That was for example the formal goal as stated in the preamble to the Product Liability Directive: harmonisation was necessary to 'avoid distortions of competition'. However, when addressing the Product Liability Directive in detail it becomes clear that the directive could in fact never reach a harmonisation at all (see Van Wassenaer Van Catwijck 1986). For example, according to Article 13 of the directive all the different, already existing, product liability laws remain in effect. This means that differences that already existed will remain unchanged. In addition, at many points the directive itself refers to national legislation, for example, with respect to the rights of contribution or recourse (Art. 5 and Art. 8(1)); with respect to non-pecuniary losses (Art. 9); and the suspension or interruption of the limitation period (Art. 10(2)). Moreover, in three cases the directive expressly allowed the Member States to derogate from the provisions of the directive – mainly whether liability for primary agricultural products would be included, liability for development risks and the introduction of a financial limit on liability. It is therefore clear that this directive can never reach a harmonisation of marketing conditions (Faure 2000, 485–6).

A similar conclusion can be reached as far as the Environmental Liability Directive of 21 April 2004 is concerned. For example, the question whether compliance with regulation and more particularly with a licence excludes liability in tort is not regulated. In fact Article 8(4)(a) allows the Member States to provide for such a 'compliance with regulation' defence. Also, one of the most important issues in environmental liability, being causation and the regulation of causal uncertainty, is not regulated. Article 9 of the directive provides that it is 'without prejudice to any provisions of national regulations concerning cost allocation in cases of multi-party causation especially concerning the apportionment of liability between the producer and the user of a product'. Also, the directive

---

[13]   See also Revesz (1997, 1331), who equally argues that these are separate points which should be distinguished.

introduces a strict liability rule, but does not oblige Member States to force potential polluters to obtain financial security (like compulsory insurance) to cover for the potential insolvency. Article 14(1) merely provides that 'Member States shall take measures to encourage the development of financial security instruments and markets by the appropriate economic and financial operators'. However, the Member States are not forced to require financial guarantees from operators. Finally, Article 16 of this Environmental Liability Directive also provides that the directive 'shall not prevent Member States from maintaining or adopting more stringent provisions in relation to the prevention and remedying of environmental damage'. These examples show that the directives are apparently not able to lead to a harmonisation of legal rules. The 'harmonisation of marketing conditions' argument was rather used to provide an appropriate legal basis on which to ground the legislative power of the EU.

It has been equally shown that harmonisation of rules of private law is not necessary to facilitate transboundary trade. Differences in regulatory standards can of course impose costs upon enterprises (see Vogenauer and Weatherill 2006), but companies are not deterred from cross-border sales even when this means that they have to adapt to local legal rules (see Wagner 2002, 1004–14). The idea that full harmonisation of contract law would be necessary to increase competition within the internal market was even strongly rejected by business organisations (Ott and Schäfer 2003, 236). Empirical evidence indeed shows that a lack of cross-border trade is not related to the differences in private law, but to other causes (Thommes, Faure and Heine 2014 and Van den Bergh 2007a, 202–3). Law and economics scholarship also criticises the fact that the Commission completely neglects the fact that traditional economic arguments (transboundary externalities and the race to the bottom) do not apply to the area of contract law or to the area of consumer law (see Van den Bergh 2002).

7. REDUCTION OF TRANSACTION COSTS

7.1 General

An argument strongly linked with the market integration argument is that the current differences between private legal rules in the EU Member States lead to substantial administrative costs (see e.g. Lando 1993). The assumption simply holds that uniform rules are easier to apply than differentiated legal rules, as a result of which substantial savings on costs are available. At first sight, this argument is seductive: uniform rules reduce information costs because study of the different legal systems in the Member States is no longer necessary.

There are, however, several problems with the simplicity of this argument. One problem is that the argument suggests that the costs of harmonisation would be nil or at least very low. Many scholars have pointed at the fact that introducing a new legal concept (imposed by a directive) within a particular legal culture in fact imposes high costs, according to some, even prohibitive costs (Legrand 1997). As a result of the many differences between legal cultures and traditions in Europe the costs of those legal transplants may indeed be extremely high (see Majone 2008; Legrand 2008). Van Dam also pointed at the diversity in national legal cultures and the correspondingly high costs of harmonisation in Europe (Van Dam 2007).

A second, related problem is that not only are the administrative costs of harmonisation neglected, but so are the benefits of differentiation. Law and economics scholars point at the fact that varying legal rules should not be considered as problematic as long as they reflect varying preferences of citizens (Van den Bergh 2000, 435 and Ogus 1999, 405). Uniformity hence always creates a cost related to the loss of differentiation.

7.2   Application

In general law and economics scholars have pointed to the fact that for the domain of private law the potential of transaction cost reduction is not large, given the huge differences between legal cultures in this respect today in Europe. From an economic perspective it has been argued that only when legal rules in fact serve the same goal, whereby only the legal techniques used differ and not the underlying values and preferences, harmonisation may be beneficial (Van den Bergh 2007b). From an economic perspective it can be held that the argument of harmonisation based on the potential of reduction of administrative costs (through a simplification by uniform legal rules) is valid only when the marginal costs of this harmonisation are indeed lower than the marginal benefits of such a unification (Van den Bergh 1998, 146–8).

Looking at some cases of (attempted) harmonisation in the area of private law there is in fact a lot of evidence which shows the high costs of harmonisation, for example, in the case of the European directive concerning product liability, discussed above. There were many interpretation problems concerning the concepts used in the directive, as a result of which the savings on transaction costs were minimal (see Van den Bergh 1998, 146–7). Moreover, as was explained above, the directive itself provided plenty of scope for Member States to apply their own rules, and, as a consequence, the directive merely added an additional layer of complexity to already existing differences while creating no reduction in transaction costs (Faure 2000). The story is the same for the Environmental Liability Directive where it was also shown that on the crucial issues (causation, compliance with licence defence and compulsory insurance) no decision could be taken as a result of which these issues were either not regulated or left to the Member States. Again, this points in the direction of the high costs of harmonisation. In one particular case, being a draft of a directive on the liability of service providers, the differences between Member States and the resulting costs of harmonisation were apparently so high that the project was entirely abandoned.

8. PROVIDING A MINIMUM LEVEL OF PROTECTION

8.1 General

Some may of course argue that harmonisation of private law in Europe should not merely be based on economic arguments, but that a minimum level of protection should be provided. It is an argument which clearly plays a role in the field of private law in Europe, as the particular examples show. For example, in the preamble of the product liability directive it is repeatedly argued that the directive should also aim at the protection of consumers; a similar argument is made in the Environmental Liability Directive, stating that the directive should further the polluter-pays principle as well as the principle of sustainable development. There are, not only from an economic, but also from a policy perspective, various problems with this argument. The economic problem is obviously that it reflects a type of legal paternalism that clearly shows little respect for national differences in preferences and in legal culture (Van Dam 2007, 53–76). The economic perspective suggests on the other hand that local authorities are more likely to have better information for creating rules that better correspond with the preferences of the citizens in particular Member States (see Van den Bergh 2007a, 192). From a policy perspective one can also wonder whether it is, more particularly in the area of private law, necessary to provide a minimum level of protection e.g. to consumers, victims of accidents or other 'weaker parties' whereas at the regulatory level this type of minimum protection is largely failing in Europe. Social security is indeed, to an important extent, not yet harmonised; for example, compensation after industrial accidents or occupational diseases can still be very different in the Member States. This is of course also related to the fact that, for example, minimum wages in say, the Netherlands, are substantially higher than in say, Portugal, let alone in comparison with Member States from Central or Eastern Europe. From that perspective, given existing differences, it would be rather odd to argue in favour of providing a minimum level of protection in the area of private law, whereas this largely fails in much more important areas touching upon, for example, health care or minimum wages.

8.2　Application

The argument that European private law should provide a minimum level of protection is hardly rooted in European legal scholarship. The debate concerning the amounts awarded for non-pecuniary losses can illustrate this point. There are today still considerable differences between the amounts awarded in that respect (Van Dam 2006, 322). Differences exist as far as the question is concerned whether some victims (and their relatives) are entitled to non-pecuniary losses, but also as far as the amounts awarded are concerned (see Rogers 2001). Some private lawyers have therefore argued that it is unacceptable that within Europe a victim who, for example, suffers the loss of an arm would receive less in say, Portugal than in say, Germany. They argue that there is no reason to treat those victims differently and that the call for harmonisation of the amounts awarded for non-pecuniary losses is justified (see Magnus and Fedtke 2001; Magnus 2002; Magnus 1995).

Several reactions can be formulated against this argument: first, the differences in amounts awarded for non-pecuniary losses are not pointless, but may reflect differing preferences of citizens in the various Member States (Faure 2011, 993). Second, according to the Coase theorem the increased protection can always be passed on to consumers via the price mechanism. Hence, if it is argued that the Portuguese should pay higher amounts for non-pecuniary losses, this would lead to an increase in prices for which Portuguese consumers may not be willing to pay. Third, lower amounts of non-pecuniary losses can of course be related to general welfare and income levels (see also Hartlief 2002).

The proponents of harmonisation also argue that there is now a higher amount of travel in Europe today (tourism) as a result of which it could not be understood why, say, a German professor would receive less for his pain and suffering if he were to have an accident in Portugal rather than in Germany (see Magnus and Fedtke 2001). Again, it can be argued that travelling is hardly an argument to force the Portuguese to come up to the German level, just to please the German tourists. The latter could, moreover, being aware that they will not enjoy the same level of protection abroad as in Germany, seek additional protection in the form of a voluntary first party insurance (Faure 2011, 994).

This debate illustrates that some European private lawyers strongly believe in the values and benefits of harmonisation, rather as a mission and political statement, than that this is based on rational arguments. Such a call can undoubtedly lead to paternalistic measures disrespecting varying preferences between citizens in Europe.

9.   POLICY ISSUES

9.1   General

The result of applying economic criteria to the question of whether tort law should be harmonised is that there would only be arguments in favour of centralised European rule making: (1) if inefficiencies were created by national tort law so that damage could be externalised to other countries; or (2) if it could be established that States would attract industry by their lenient tort law standards. The latter is, however, unlikely since States would, on the contrary, be more likely to enact legislation to protect victims of accidents within their own jurisdiction with high standards. However, there may be transaction cost savings if European intervention were able to create legal certainty and achieve full harmonisation. Other arguments, such as the need to create a level playing field or the harmonisation of marketing conditions cannot, at least from an economic perspective, justify centralisation.

Looking more specifically at the Product Liability Directive and comparing this to the criteria for centralisation we can conclude as follows:

1. The Product Liability Directive is not able to correct for the risk of interstate externalities caused by product damage, if such a risk already exists.
2. There is no empirical evidence of a risk that States could attract manufacturers with lenient product liability legislation (the directive would only apply to manufacturers). On the contrary, there might be a risk of a race to the top, protecting national victims of product-related accidents.
3. The Product Liability Directive, given its high reliance on national law, can never lead to a 'levelling of the playing field' or a 'harmonisation of marketing conditions'.
4. The Product Liability Directive, which in fact, adds an additional layer of complexity to the labyrinth of conflicting standards of liability, does

not lead to uniformity or a lowering of transaction costs (Ackerman 1996, 454).

A similar conclusion could probably also be reached as far as another piece of European tort law is concerned, namely, the Environmental Liability Directive.

9.2 Public Choice Considerations

A question which obviously cannot be avoided when inefficiencies are found is whether this can be explained on the basis of public choice theory. Indeed, one notices that many of the harmonisation efforts in the domain of private law do not fit into the economic theory of centralisation and would hence, at least from an economic perspective, not be considered as promoting social welfare. If a certain legislative action cannot be said to promote public interest, public choice scholars would ask whether the legislation favours special interest groups.[14] Of course, one can generally hold that the lack of transparency at the European level is a highly useful cover for lobbying activities. In fact, the desire to create a European liability regime sometimes simply serves the interests of industry and is the result of lobbying.

Some have argued that the comparative lawyers themselves can be considered as a lobby group. Harmonisation efforts will undoubtedly serve their interests since harmonisation requires knowledge of the various legal systems that need to be harmonised. A call for harmonisation does undoubtedly create a demand for comparative lawyers and may hence serve their interests.[15]

Finally, in the context of public choice analysis, one should obviously also mention the interests of the European bureaucracy itself. Until 1985 Europe had done relatively little as far as the harmonisation of private law was concerned (because differing legal cultures hampered it). Maybe a European Product Liability Directive, although it did not fulfil the economic criteria for centralisation, might have served the interests of the Brussels bureaucracy to show that Europe could bring about a piece of legislation in an area which is considered important by many lawyers and is, moreover, very sensitive to public opinion. Hence, the fact that the

---

[14] For a discussion of harmonisation efforts in Europe from a public choice perspective, see Van den Bergh (1998, 148–51) and Van den Bergh (2000, 448–51), and see Revesz (2000).

[15] See Ogus (1999, 405), and Ogus (2001, 28–32), as well as Van den Bergh (2000, 449).

Commission wanted e.g. a European Product Liability Directive may to some extent also simply have been due to the prestige that this directive, as one of the first in the area of private law, would give the European Commission.

9.3 Example: Environmental Liability

We concluded that relatively few economic arguments can be found to justify centralisation in the area of environmental liability. Only trans-boundary pollution justified it and even then the question arose whether the same result could not be reached through different, less extensive legal instruments than total harmonisation.

Nevertheless, there seemed to be strong forces striving for a European environmental liability regime, at least for damage to biodiversity. This resulted, as mentioned above, in the Environmental Liability Directive.[16] To some extent this can still be explained on public interest grounds, since non-economic, ecological arguments, could also be advanced in favour of a minimum quality of restoration for polluted soils. However, public choice scholars have taught that there is always a risk that regulation in fact serves the interests of particular pressure groups.[17]

Indeed, another non-economic reason why the European Union would like to harmonise liability legislation can be found in public choice theory. With respect to environmental standard-setting, intensive rent-seeking behaviour by interest groups can be identified. European industries may be confronted at state level by 'green' non-governmental organisations (NGOs), whereas these countervailing powers might have less force in Brussels. Moreover, the lack of transparency in the decision-making process will stimulate European industries to engage in serious lobbying.

The lobbying does not necessarily have to result in lower environmental standards. In particular cases, special interest groups representing industry might, understandably, lobby in favour of harmonisation at a higher level of environmental protection (Esty and Geradin 1997, 303). Interest groups in areas that are already heavily regulated may have incentives to extend their strict (national) regulations to the European level, forcing foreign competitors to follow the same strict regulation with which they already comply. The result is that industry will lobby to erect artificial barriers to

---

[16] See Directive 2004/35/EC of 21 April 2004 on environmental liability with regard to prevention and remedying of environmental damage. For a comment see the contributions in Betlem and Brans (2006).

[17] For a public choice analysis of (de)centralisation of environmental law see Ferejohn (2000).

entry. In addition, green NGOs will be pleased with this lobbying and will obviously support the demand to transfer strict national standards into a European standard.[18] Thus, industry in heavily regulated (and probably polluted) areas can (supported by green NGOs) force their very stringent standards upon their (southern) competitors, although these Member States probably would not need these stringent standards if the policy goal were only one of reaching a uniform level of environmental quality.

Thus it becomes clear that the 'harmonisation of conditions of competition' argument is used to serve the interests of industries in heavily regulated areas by erecting barriers to entry. Environmental law can thus be used to limit market entry and environmental law is abused to serve private interest goals.

This leads to the conclusion that the 'harmonisation of conditions of competition' argument, as presented in European rhetoric, can be problematic, from both the economic and ecological points of view, and in fact serves the interests of industrial groups in heavily regulated areas.[19] It can actually be in their interests that 'conditions of competition' are harmonised.

It is not clear yet whether the harmonisation efforts with respect to environmental liability should be considered as an attempt by interest groups to create barriers to entry. One could still run the risk that industry in Member States with stringent soil sanitation would strive for centralisation, thus creating a barrier to entry for competitors from countries where these strict standards do not yet apply. It is too early to assess whether the desire to create a European environmental liability regime in fact serves the interest of industry. One should, however, be aware of the fact that this risk, that centralisation may be abused to create barriers to entry, may appear in any attempt towards centralisation.

10.   CONCLUDING REMARKS

I started this chapter by mentioning a striking tendency in Europe to move towards a harmonisation of private law. This tendency is especially

---

[18]   These "alliances" between environmentalists and domestic producers are also discussed in Vogel (1995, 52–5).

[19]   This is not to say that there is no risk of regulatory capture resulting in inefficient standards at the level of the Member States, compare (in the US context) Rose-Ackerman (1992, 166 and 173). However, in Europe, it is especially the untransparent Brussels bureaucracy which is feared from a public choice perspective.

strong among academics, best reflected in the idea to come to a 'European Civil Code'. First steps towards such a project have been set by drafting a Common Frame of Reference, which in fact is nothing less than such a draft European Civil Code. Although this is still (at least at this stage) merely an academic project, criticised by many, the EU institutions themselves have also attempted to harmonise private law in various fields.

Interestingly, law and economics scholarship has been quite critical of the tendency to harmonise private law in Europe and especially concerning the way in which it has been undertaken by the EU institutions. The arguments pro and contra centralisation based on the economics of federalism, central to this volume, are apparently well known, both to European law and economics scholars and to (some) European lawyers as well and have been applied to harmonisation attempts in Europe in the domain of private law. Although these arguments hence play an important role, at least at academic level, scholarship is equally critical of the fact that the Commission seems to (at least in some cases) only stress the benefits of harmonisation, disregarding potential costs and arguments in favour of differentiation, as has been stressed by economic literature.

In that respect the application of economic theory to some of the examples discussed (product liability and environmental liability) shows that, according to this literature, the Commission often goes too far in harmonising private law, beyond what would be useful based on economic grounds (transboundary externalities, race to the bottom or reduction of transaction costs). Sometimes the internal market is still used as an argument to harmonise legal rules of all sorts, as also in the domain of private law, whereas law and economics scholarship showed that it is quite possible to create an internal market, also with differentiated rules of private law. The argument that 'marketing conditions should be harmonised' was thus often used by the Commission in a stereotypical way because (at least in the past) this was needed to provide a legal basis for European action in particular domains.

It is not always clear why European institutions go further in harmonisation than what would be necessary according to economic criteria for centralisation. Undoubtedly, the power of the European bureaucracy (e.g. the Commission) may be an important reason. After all, creating directives in particular fields of private law may add to the prestige and power (and hence budget) of the Commission.

It is important to stress that from an economic perspective probably the most important reason in favour of centralisation of tort law is the potential for reducing transaction costs. To some extent one can certainly argue that various tort rules in the Member States reflect similar preferences and only differ as a result of differing legal techniques. If it were possible to align rules of tort law that reflect similar preferences, this could certainly be considered a gain. That is precisely the approach chosen in a variety of (mostly privately initiated) academic projects on harmonisation of tort law. In most of these projects the academics involved analyse the existing differences between the various aspects of tort law in the Member States and try to find a common denominator. This approach seems to be more promising than that chosen by the Commission. That top-down approach of imposing directives on Member States has so far not been very successful. The approach chosen by the academic groups focuses on the search for a *ius commune* and can therefore be called 'bottom up'. If these groups succeed in showing that some differences are merely of a technical nature and can thus be considered as pointless incompatibilities which do not touch upon or relate to differing preferences, then this harmonisation approach of searching for a common denominator may well prove to be more successful than the approach chosen by the Commission so far.

Finally it should be stressed that in this chapter I have merely focused on one aspect of European federalism, being private law and hence, paraphrasing the words of Calabresi and Melamed (1972) I only provided 'one view of the cathedral'. Indeed, as far as private law is concerned European law and economics scholars have traditionally been rather critical of attempts towards full harmonisation. It goes without saying, however, that in many other domains the harmonisation attempts and generally the regulations issued by EU institutions have had enormous benefits as far as creating the European internal market is concerned. It is more particularly in the domain of private law, the central focus of this contribution, that, given the many differences that still exist between Member States in this domain today, questions arise on the desirable scope of a European intervention.

REFERENCES

Ackerman, R.M., 'Tort Law and Federalism: Whatever Happened to Devolution?', *Yale Law and Policy Review, Symposium Issue*, 1996, 429–63.
Bar, C. Von, Clive, E. and Schulte-Nölke, H. (eds), Principles, Definitions and Model Rules of European Private Law, Draft Common Frame of Reference (DCFR), Munich, Sellier, 2008.
Bergkamp, L., 'The White Paper on Environmental Liability', *European Environmental Law Review*, 2000, 105–14.
Berman, G., 'Taking Subsidiarity Seriously: Federalism in the European Community and the United States', *Columbia Law Review*, 1994, vol. 94, 331–456.
Betlem, G. and Brans, E. (eds), *Environmental Liability in the EU. The 2004 Directive Compared with US and Member State Law*, London, 2006.

Calabresi, G. and Melamed, D., 'Property Rules, Liability Rules and Inalienability: One View of the Cathedral', *Harvard Law Review*, 1972, vol. 85, 1089–128.

Douma, W.Th. et al., 'Europese invloed op regelgeving meetbaar (European Influence on Legislation can be Measured)', *Nederlands Juristenblad*, 2007, 1828.

Edwards, D.J., 'Fearing Federalism's Failure. Subsidiarity in the European Union', *The American Journal of Comparative Law*, 1986, vol. 44, 537–83.

Eidenmüller, H. et al., 'Der gemeinsame Referenzrahmen für das Europäische Privatrecht. Wirtungsfragen und Kodifikationsprobleme', *Juristenzeitung*, 2008a, 529–50.

Eidenmüller, H. et al., 'The Common Frame of Reference for European Private Law: Policy Choices and Codification Problems', *Oxford Journal of Legal Studies*, 2008b, vol. 28(4), 659–708.

Esty, D., 'Revitalising Environmental Federalism', *Michigan Law Review*, 1996, vol. 95, 625.

Esty, D., 'Economic Integration and the Environment', in Vig, N. and Axelrod, R. (eds), *The Global Environment: Institutions, Law and Policy*, Washington, CQ Press, 1999, 190–209.

Esty, D. and Geradin, D., 'Market Access, Competitiveness, and Harmonisation: Environmental Protection in Regional Trade Agreements', *Harvard Environmental Law Review*, 1997, vol. 21, 265–336.

Esty, D. and Geradin, D., 'Environmental Protection and International Competitiveness, A Conceptual Framework', *Journal of World Trade Law*, 1998, vol. 32(3), 5–46.

European Group on Tort Law, *Principles of European Tort Law. Text and Commentary*, Vienna, Springer, 2005.

Faure, M.G., 'Product Liability and Product Safety in Europe: Harmonisation or Differentiation', *Kyklos*, 2000, vol. 53, 467–508.

Faure, M.G., 'The Harmonization of Consumer Contractual Rights: An Economic Perspective', in Apathy, P., Bollenberger, B., Bydlinski, P., Iro, G., Karner, E. and Karollus, M. (eds), *Festschrift für Helmut Koziol zum 70. Geburtstag*, Vienna, Jan Sramek Verlag, 2010, 1385–99.

Faure, M.G., 'Economic Analysis of Tort Law and the European Civil Code', in Hartkamp, A., Hesselink, M., Hondius, E., Mak, Ch. & Du Perron, E. (eds), *Towards a European Civil Code*, 4th edn, Nijmegen: Ars Aequi Libri 2011, 977–1000.

Faure, M. and De Smedt, K., 'Should Europe Harmonise Environmental Liability Legislation?', *Environmental Liability*, 2001, 217–37.

Faure, M.G. and Johnston, J.S., 'The Law and Economics of Environmental Federalism: Europe and the United States Compared', *Virginia Environmental Law Journal*, 2009, vol. 27(3), 205–74.

Ferejohn, J., 'The Political Economy Pollution Control in a Federal System', in Revesz, R., Sands, Ph., and Stewart, R. (eds), *Environmental Law, the Economy and Sustainable Development*, Cambridge, Cambridge University Press, 2000, 96–103.

Hartkamp, A.S., Hesselink, M.W., Hondius, E.H., Mak, Ch. and Du Perron, C.E. (eds), *Towards a European Civil Code*, 4th rev. and expanded edn, Alphen a/d Rijn, Kluwer Law International, 2011.

Hartlief, T., 'Comments on Magnus, U. Towards European Civil Liability', in Faure, M., Schneider, H. and Smits, J. (eds), *Towards a European Ius Commune in Legal Education and Research*, Antwerp, Intersentia, 2002, 225–30.

Hervey, T., 'Community and National Competence in Health after Tobacco Advertising', *Common Market Law Review*, 2001, vol. 38, 1421–46.

Jaffe, A., Peterson, S., Portney, P. and Stavins, R., 'Environmental Regulation and the Competitiveness of US Manufacturing: What Does the Evidence Tell us?', *Journal of Economic Literature*, 1995, vol. 33, 132–63.

Jansen, N., 'Auf dem Weg zu einem Europäischen Haftungsrecht', *Zeitschrift für Europäisches Privatrecht*, 2001, 30–65.

Krämer, L., 'Thirty Years of EC Environmental Law: Perspectives and Prospectives', *Yearbook of European Environmental Law*, vol. 2, Oxford, Oxford University Press, 2002, 155–82.

Lando, O., 'Die Regeln des Europäischen Vertragsrecht', in Müller-Graff, P.C. (ed.), *Gemeinsames Privatrecht in der Europäischen Gemeinschaft*, Baden-Baden, Nomos, 1993, 473 and ff.

Legrand, P., 'The Impossibility of "Legal Transplants"', *Maastricht Journal of European and Comparative Law*, 1997, 111–24.

Legrand, P., 'Antivonbar', *Journal of Comparative Law*, 2008, vol. 1(1), 13–39.

Magnus, U., 'European Perspective of Tort Liability', *European Review of Private Law*, 1995, 427–44.

Magnus, U., 'Towards European Civil Liability', in Faure, M., Schneider, H. and Smits, J. (eds), *Towards a European Ius Commune in Legal Education and Research*, Antwerp, Intersentia, 2002, 205–24.

Magnus, U. and Fedtke, J., 'German Report on Non-Pecuniary Loss', in Rogers, H.W.V. (ed.), *Damages for Non-Pecuniary Loss in a Comparative Perspective*, 2001, 109–28.

Majone, G., 'Unity in Diversity: European Integration and the Enlargement Process', *European Law Review*, 2008, vol. 33, 457–81.

Marquardt, P.D., 'Subsidiarity and Sovereignty in the European Union', *Fordham International Law Journal*, 1994, vol. 18, 616–40.

Ogus, A.I., 'Competition between National Legal Systems: A Contribution of Economic Analysis to Comparative Law', *The International and Comparative Law Quarterly*, 1999, 405–18.

Ogus, A.I., 'The Contribution of Economic Analysis of Law to Legal Transplant', in Smits, J. (ed.), *The Contribution of Mixed Legal Systems to European Law*, Antwerp, Intersentia, 2001, 27–37.

Ogus, A.I., *Regulation: Legal Form and Economic Theory*, Oxford, Clarendon Press, 2004.

Ott, C.L. and Schäfer, H.B., 'Die Vereinheitlichung des Europäischen Vertragsrechts. Ökonomische Notwendigkeit oder akademisches Interesse?', in Ott, C.L. and Schäfer, H.B. (eds), *Vereinheitlichung und Diversität des Zivilrechts in transnationalen Wirtschaftsraum*, Tübingen, Mohr Siebeck, 2003, 203–36.

Revesz, R., 'Rehabilitating Interstate Competition: Rethinking the Race-for-the-Bottom Rationale for Federal Environmental Regulation', *New York University Law Review*, 1992, vol. 67, 1210–54.

Revesz, R., 'Federalism and Interstate Environmental Externalities', *University of Pennsylvania Law Review*, 1996, vol. 144, 2341–416.

Revesz, R., 'Federalism and Environmental Regulation: Lessons for the European Union and the International Community', *Virginia Law Review*, 1997, vol. 83, 1331–46.

Revesz, R., 'Federalism and Environmental Regulation: An Overview', in Revesz, R., Sands, Ph. and Stewart, R. (eds), *Environmental Law: The Economy and Sustainable Development*, Cambridge, Cambridge University Press, 2000, 37–79.

Rogers, H.W.V. (ed.), *Damages for Non-Pecuniary Loss in a Comparative Perspective*, Vienna, Springer, 2001.

Rose-Ackerman, S., *Rethinking the Progressive Agenda. The Reform of the American Regulatory State*, Toronto, Macmillan, 1992.

Rose-Ackerman, S., Controlling Environmental Policy: The Limits of Public Law in Germany and the United States, New Haven, Yale University Press, 1995.

Schwartz, G.T., 'Considering the Proper Federal Role in American Tort Law', *Arizona Law Review*, 1996, vol. 38, 917–51.

Smits, J., 'The Future of European Contract Law: On Diversity and the Temptation of Elegance', in Faure, M., Smits, J. and Schneider, H. (eds), *Towards a European Ius Commune in Legal Education and Research*, Antwerp, Intersentia, 2002a, 239–56.

Smits, J., 'On Successful Legal Transplants in a Future Ius Commune Europaeum', in Harding, A. and Örücü, E. (eds), *Comparative Law in the 21st Century*, The Hague, Kluwer Law International, 2002b, 137–54.

Smits, J., 'Toward a Multi-Layered Contract Law for Europe', in Grundman, S. and Stuyck, J. (eds), *An Academic Green Paper on European Contract Law*, The Hague, Kluwer Law International, 2002c, 387–98.

Spier, J. and Haazen, O., 'The European Group on Tort Law ("Tilburg Group") and the European Principles of Tort Law', *Zeitschrift für Europäisches Privatrecht*, 1999, 469–93.

Thommes, K., Faure, M.G. & Heine, K., "The Internal Market and the Consumer: What Consumers Actually Choose", *The Columbia Journal of European Law*, 2014, vol. 21(1), 47–70.

Van Dam, C., *European Tort Law*, Oxford, Oxford University Press, 2006.

Van Dam, C., 'European Tort Law and the Many Cultures of Europe', in Wilhelmsson, Th. (ed.), *Private Law and the Cultures of Europe*, The Hague, Kluwer Law International, 2007, 53–76.

Van den Bergh, R., 'Subsidiarity as an Economic Demarcation Principle and the Emergence of European Private Law', *Maastricht Journal of European and Comparative Law*, 1998, 129–52.

Van den Bergh, R., 'Towards an Institutional Legal Framework for Regulatory Competition in Europe', *Kyklos*, 2000, vol. 53, 435–66.

Van den Bergh, R., 'Forced Harmonisation of Contract Law in Europe: Not to Be Continued', in Grundmann, S. and Stuyck, J. (eds), *An Academic Green Paper on European Contract Law*, The Hague, Kluwer Law International, 2002, 249–68.

Van den Bergh, R., 'The Uneasy Case for Harmonising Consumer Law', in Heine, K. and Kerber, W. (eds), *Zentralität und Dezentralität von Regulierung in Europa. Schriften zur Ordnungsfragen der Wirtschaft*, Band 83, Stuttgart, Lucius & Lucius, 2007a, 184–206.

Van den Bergh, R., 'Der gemeinsame Referenzrahmen: Abschied von der Harmonisierung des Vertragsrechts?', in Eger, Th. and Schäfer, H.B. (eds), *Ökonomische Analyse der Europäischen Zivilrechtsentwicklung, Beiträge zum X. Travemünder Symposium zur ökonomischen Analyse des Rechts*, Tübingen, Mohr Siebeck, 2007b, 111–26.

Van Wassenaer Van Catwijck, A.J.O., 'Products Liability in Europe', *American Journal of Comparative Law*, 1986, vol. 34(4), 789–801.

Vogel, D., *Trading Up: Consumer and Environmental Regulation in the Global Economy*, Cambridge, MA, Harvard University Press, 1995.

Vogenauer, S. and Weatherill, S., 'The European Community's Competence to Pursue the Harmonisation of Contract Law – An Empirical Contribution to the Debate', in Vogenauer, S. and Weatherill, S. (eds), *The Harmonisation of European Contract Law*, Oxford, Hart, 2006, 105ff.

Weatherill, S., *EU Consumer Law and Policy*, Cheltenham, Edward Elgar, 2005.

3. Lessons in fiscal federalism from American Indian nations

Terry L. Anderson and Dominic P. Parker*

Fiscal federalism focuses on the tradeoffs inherent in comparing which governmental functions "are best centralized and which are best placed in the sphere of decentralized levels of government" (Oates 1999, 1120).[1] On the side of decentralization are lower agency costs between citizens (principals) and public officials (agents). It is easier for citizens to monitor what local public officials are doing and to create decentralized institutions that match local customs, culture and norms.[2] On the side of centralization are scale economies in the provision of "market-supporting public goods" (Besley and Ghatak 2006, 286) and networks of contract enforcement that are uniform across geographic space and socioeconomic groups (Dixit 2003). Theoretically, these two tradeoffs determine the optimal locus or size of government.

The market-supporting public good of interest here is the provision of a law and order system that facilitates market transactions. Scale economies exist in its provision because of the large fixed costs associated with organizing police forces, operating courts, writing legal codes, and compiling legal precedent.

* For helpful comments, we thank Richard Todd, Paul Glewwe, Ben Simon and participants at the Minneapolis Federal Reserve's Law and Economics of Indian Country Economic Development Conference (August 2012) and the Society of Government Economists Annual Conference (November 2012).

[1] What is "best" for tribes is, of course, difficult to define and measure just as it is difficult to define and measure what is "best" for populations within municipalities, counties, or states. In the public finance literature the typical approach has been to study the optimal division of responsibilities in a federal system assuming the goal is to maximize the public's welfare within a particular jurisdiction (see McKinnon and Nechbya 1997). Applying this reasoning to reservations, we can imagine a division of responsibilities that maximizes the welfare of a representative tribal resident.

[2] As North (1981) and Alesina and Spolare (2003) point out, local control allows rules, laws, and property rights befitting local culture to evolve without interference from outsiders.

Fiscal federalism provides an excellent lens through which to view the provision of law and order on American Indian reservations, which could be administered by federal, state, or tribal governments. Relative to tribal governments, federal and state legal systems encompass larger regions and populations and thus can exploit scale economies in establishing reputations and building precedent upon which market transactions rely.[3] For this reason, reservation economies may function better under federal or state legal systems, which provide relatively uniform contract enforcement that is built on large precedent and is therefore fairly predictable. On the other hand, decentralized tribal control better enables tribes to rely on rules and laws that match indigenous norms of legitimacy (Cornell and Kalt 2000). For Indian-to-Indian interactions, whether criminal or civil, adherence to such norms can be beneficial, but for Indian-to-non-Indian interactions, adherence to local norms can raise transaction costs and suppress economic exchange.

Fiscal federalism also provides a lens through which to view reservation property rights to land and natural resources. On one hand, individual tribes have time- and place-specific knowledge of local resource values and an incentive to capture those values. These incentive and information advantages imply that land and resource use will be optimized only if property rights are held by tribes or their members and defined as tribes choose. Such arrangements might include communal property of the type described by Ostrom (1990).[4] On the other hand, property institutions that comport with surrounding jurisdictions can better facilitate resource management and access to capital markets involving non-tribal members.

Ideally, the tensions between local and central control could be resolved through the endogenous and bottom-up process of letting an efficient division of governmental responsibilities emerge. On Indian reservations, a truly bottom-up process would likely take into account the tradeoffs described above. The process would allow each tribe to freely choose the exact dimensions of law over which to assert local control, and the exact dimensions over which to yield to state or federal governments. For some tribes, the optimal arrangement might be local definition and enforcement of criminal, family, and commercial contracts as well as reservation

---

[3] According to 2006–2010 U.S. Census Reports, only six reservations have American Indian populations exceeding 10,000. After the Navajo Reservation, which has a population of 169,321, the population of the next largest reservation – the Pine Ridge – is 16,906.

[4] For a discussion of how local tribal property management can improve resource use, in this case forests, see Berry (2009).

property rights. For other tribes, the optimal arrangement might include non-local enforcement of commercial contracts, for example.

Unfortunately, the history of legal and property institutions on Indian reservations has been anything but bottom up. Rather, those institutions have been mainly determined by the federal government, driven from top down. For example, tribal jurisdiction over contracts and crimes was stripped from some tribes during the 1950s and 1960s and given to the states surrounding reservations without tribal consent. Federal policy has since made it difficult for tribes to get their jurisdiction back. There are sometimes also barriers to tribes wanting to waive their local jurisdiction over certain subject matter to larger spheres of government or on a case-by-case basis.[5] Since the reservation era, the federal government has exerted control over property rights to reservation land and natural resources against the wishes of tribes. Again, it has been difficult for tribes to reassert local control. The top down changes in tribal, state, and federal control on reservations have created experiments from which social scientists can learn about fiscal federalism, but the experiments have often brought detrimental consequences for American Indians.

In what follows, we will argue that the muddy division of federal, state, and tribal control that exists on today's reservations is far from optimal for American Indians and their reservation economies. Single tribal units are typically responsible for their legal infrastructure, and this local jurisdiction over contracts has deterred some economic development. The problem is that tribal legal systems may lack the precedent needed to encourage trade with non-Indians. The mis-match runs in the other direction with respect to federal control over land and natural resources. Here the available evidence implies that non-local control has stunted reservation development. We conclude that tribes should be free to choose a different system of federalism than they are currently under and suggest how barriers to a freer choice might be removed.

CRIME AND CONTRACTS

The main doctrine governing tribal sovereignty comes from *Cherokee Nation v. Georgia* (30 U.S. 1 [1831]). In that case, the U.S. Supreme Court

---

[5] In some instances tribes have essentially been offered all-or-nothing opportunities to go under state jurisdiction and these all-or-nothing choices are suboptimal for tribes given the texture of case-specific tradeoffs between local and centralized control.

ruled that a tribe is "a distinct political society separated from others, capable of managing its own affairs and governing itself," but also that reservations are "domestic dependent nations," making the relationship between tribes and the federal government like that of "a ward to his guardian." Under this doctrine, tribal authority to create and enforce laws governing reservations is exclusive unless the federal government exercises its "guardian" power by extending federal or state jurisdiction to reservations.

The Imposition of Federal and State Jurisdiction

Tribal sovereignty over crimes and contracts eroded with the passing of two major acts of the U.S. Congress. The first was the Indian Major Crimes Act of 1885, in response to the trial of a Lakota Indian who killed another Lakota man on a reservation in South Dakota. In that case, the Lakota tribal court, using traditional methods of dispute resolution, required the perpetrator to compensate the family of the victim with goods and property but allowed him to go free. Non-Indian observers, arguing that tribal decisions such as this encouraged lawlessness on reservations, successfully lobbied Congress to pass the Indian Major Crimes Act. The Act gave the federal government jurisdiction to prosecute serious criminal offenses (e.g., murder and rape) committed on reservations regardless of the race of the perpetrator or victim (Harring 1994).

The other major act was P.L. 280, passed in 1953 during the termination era. Between 1945 and 1961 the federal government's explicit goal was to place reservation Indians under the same laws as other U.S. citizens as rapidly as possible (Getches et al. 1998). P.L. 280 can be viewed as a first step towards achieving this goal.

It required that jurisdiction over all criminal offenses (major and minor) and over civil disputes on some reservations be turned over to the state surrounding those reservations. P.L. 280 initially mandated that the transfer apply to most reservations located in Alaska, California, Minnesota, Nebraska, Oregon, and Wisconsin.[6] These states are known as the "mandatory" P.L. 280 states because Congress, not the state legislatures, initiated and required the jurisdictional shift. All states were eventually given the option to assume P.L. 280 jurisdiction through legislative action, and some exercised the option.

Table 3.1 below lists the states that ultimately assumed jurisdiction.

---

[6] Some reservations within Minnesota, Oregon, and Wisconsin were excluded from P.L. 280 and therefore retained tribal jurisdiction.

Table 3.1 States with Public Law 280 and related jurisdiction

State	Mandatory P.L. 280	Optional P.L. 280 Criminal	Civil	Notes
Alaska	Yes	No	No	Tribal jurisdiction over some criminal offenses committed on the Annette Island Reservation was retained by the Metlakatla Indian Community.
Arizona	No	No	Partial: the state assumed jurisdiction over water & air pollution (1967)	
California	Yes	No	No	
Florida	No	Full (1961)	Full (1961)	
Idaho	No	Partial: the state assumed jurisdiction over seven subject areas and full jurisdiction with tribal consent (1963).		The seven subject areas are: school attendance; juvenile delinquency; abused children; mental illness; public assistance; domestic relations; and operation of vehicles on state and county roads. The Nez Perce is the only tribe to consent, allowing state jurisdiction over additional criminal offenses.
Iowa	No	No	Full: over the Sac & Fox Reservation (1967)	A federal statute passed in 1948 conferred criminal jurisdiction to the state over the Sac & Fox Reservation.
Kansas	No	No	No	A federal statute passed in 1940 conferred criminal jurisdiction to the state over all reservations within the state.

Table 3.1 (continued)

State	Mandatory P.L. 280	Optional P.L. 280 Criminal	Civil	Notes
Minnesota	Yes	No	No	Red Lake Reservation was exempted. P.L. 280 jurisdiction over Bois Forte Reservation (formerly Nett Lake) was retroceded in 1972.
Montana	No	Full: over Flathead Reservation	Full: with tribal and county consent, but no tribe has consented (1963).	Most of the criminal jurisdiction assumed by the state over Flathead Reservation was retroceded in 1993.
Nebraska	Yes	No	No	The state retroceded criminal jurisdiction over Omaha Reservation in 1970, and over the Winnebago Reservation in 1986.
Nevada	No	Full: with tribal consent	Full: with tribal consent (1955)	P.L. 280 jurisdiction was conferred over a number of small reservations. Retrocession has now occurred over most reservations in this group.
New York	No	No	No	Federal statutes passed in 1948 and 1950 conferred criminal and civil jurisdiction to the state over all reservations.
North Dakota	No	No	Full: with individual or tribal consent, but no tribe has consented (1963).	A federal statute passed in 1948 conferred criminal jurisdiction to the state over Devil's Lake Reservation. Individual acceptance has been held invalid under the Supremacy Clause of the U.S. Constitution.
Oregon	Yes	No	No	Warm Springs Reservation was exempted from the list of mandatory reservations. The state retroceded criminal jurisdiction over the Umatilla Reservation in the 1980s.

State		
South Dakota	No	The state attempted to assume jurisdiction over criminal offenses and civil causes of action arising on highways, subject to federal government reimbursement of enforcement costs (1961).	The state supreme court held this assumption to be invalid.
Utah	No	Subject to tribal consent (1971).	No tribe has consented.
Washington	No	In 1957, the state assumed full P.L. 280 jurisdiction over nine reservations that had consented. In 1963, the state assumed jurisdiction without tribal consent over non-Indians and limited jurisdiction over Indians on the remaining reservations.	Criminal jurisdiction over Quinalt and Port Madison Reservations assumed through the 1957 legislation was retroceded in 1969 and 1972 respectively. The jurisdiction assumed over these reservations through the 1963 legislation remained intact. In 1986 the state retroceded jurisdiction over Indians for crimes committed on the Colville Reservations.
Wisconsin	Yes		The Menominee Reservation was exempted from the list of mandatory reservations and the reservation was terminated by federal statute in 1961. The Menominee Reservation was reinstated in 1973, and retrocession of P.L. 280 jurisdiction was granted shortly thereafter.

Source: Anderson and Parker (2008).

Table 3.2   Judicial jurisdiction on American Indian reservations

	Criminal Jurisdiction	
	Non-P.L. 280 Jurisdiction	P.L. 280 Jurisdiction
Tribal	Over American Indians; subject to a few limitations	Over American Indians; subject to a few limitations
Federal	Over major crimes committed by Indians; over interracial crimes	Same as off-reservation
State	Only over crimes committed by non-Indians against other non-Indians	Over Indians and non-Indians; subject to a few limitations
	Civil Jurisdiction	
Tribal	Over American Indians and non-Indians	Over American Indians
Federal	Same as off-reservation	Same as off-reservation
State	None, except some suits between non-Indians on fee-simple lands	Over suits involving non-Indians generally; subject to a few limitations

Source: Melton and Gardner (2000).

Today, more than half of the 327 federally recognized reservations are in states that assumed most or all of the jurisdiction available under P.L. 280. P.L. 280 added a layer of complexity to reservation jurisdictional authority which is summarized in Table 3.2 above.[7] It summarizes the main differences in criminal and civil jurisdiction between P.L. 280 and non-P.L. 280 reservations.

Congressional records indicate that P.L. 280 was advanced as an opportunity to improve criminal law enforcement on reservations. The 1953 Senate report on the law stated:

> As a practical matter, the enforcement of law and order among the Indians in Indian Country has been left largely to the Indian groups themselves. In many

---

[7]   With respect to the assumption of civil jurisdiction, it is important to note that P.L. 280 did not give states authority to impose taxes on reservations nor did it give states the authority to regulate reservation land use (Goldberg-Ambrose 1997). Regardless of whether or not a reservation is subject to P.L. 280 legislation, tribes retained their authority to impose taxes on tribal members, and to regulate land use within reservations. A tribe's flexibility to regulate land use, however, may be restricted by U.S. federal trust constraints on land as described in the following section.

States, tribes are not adequately organized to perform that function; consequently, there has been created a hiatus in law enforcement authority that could best be remedied by conferring criminal jurisdiction on the States indicating a willingness to accept such responsibility. (U.S. Senate 1953, 5)

The Senate report gives only a terse reference to civil jurisdiction, which was also extended to the mandatory states through P.L. 280. Goldberg-Ambrose (1997, 50) argues that the extension of civil jurisdiction was "an afterthought in a measure aimed primarily at bringing law and order to reservations, added because it comported with the pro-assimilationist drift of federal policy and because it was convenient and cheap." More generally, Goldberg-Ambrose (1997) argues that the main legislative purposes of P.L. 280 were to bring law and order to reservations and to save the federal government money (by unloading the jurisdictional obligations of major crimes onto states). Based on these factors and the pro-assimilation drift of federal policy during the 1950s, why were more reservations not placed under P.L. 280?

One reason more reservations were not placed under P.L. 280 is that they were in states with constitutions that had disclaimers of jurisdiction over Indian Country. These states were Arizona, Idaho, Montana, Nevada, New Mexico, North Dakota, Oklahoma, South Dakota, Utah, Washington, and Wyoming.[8] Given the option of assuming P.L. 280 jurisdiction, many states declined, apparently because it would have been costly to amend their constitutions. As shown in Table 3.1, the only disclaimer state that acquired major P.L. 280 jurisdiction was Washington. It did so without amending its constitution making the legal validity of its assumption uncertain.

For the purposes of this chapter, we view P.L. 280 as an experiment in centralized versus local control over criminal cases and contract enforcement. It is not a pure natural experiment because Congress did not roll dice to determine P.L. 280 status. This is evident because the assignment of mandatory P.L. 280 was based on history, geography, and claims of criminal activity rather than random draws. Importantly, however, we later show that the selection process ultimately did not target a biased sample of tribes as measured by average economic conditions in reservations prior to

---

[8] These disclaimers were required by the federal government as prerequisites to gaining statehood for any state not part of the Union as of 1881 (Wilkins 2002). The disclaimers were apparently in response to a U.S. Supreme Court ruling that states could adjudicate crimes committed on reservations by non-Indians against non-Indians. The forced disclaimers were meant to ensure federal jurisdiction over such crimes (Wilkins 2002).

1953. We return to our assessment of the economic effects of state versus tribal jurisdiction after first discussing the impact of P.L. 280 on tribal satisfaction with criminal law enforcement.

The Costs of State Jurisdiction

The passage of P.L. 280 was controversial, and much of the legal and sociology literature argues that the loss of sovereignty disadvantaged tribes. Goldberg-Ambrose (1997, ix–x), for example, refers to the federal legislation as a "calamitous event" and argues that tribes put under state jurisdiction had to "struggle even harder to sustain their governing structures, economies, and cultures." One of the major objections was that P.L. 280 was imposed upon Indian tribes without their consent in direct violation of the doctrine of tribal sovereignty. The other criticism of the law is that states are not well suited to handle criminal incidents involving Indians given that tribal norms differ significantly as to what constitutes a crime.[9]

Although state jurisdiction binds tribes to a larger and more extensive system of law and order, it does so at the cost of assigning rules and compliance procedures that are unlikely to match tribal cultures. According to Goldberg-Ambrose (1997), Indian elders, in particular, have expressed concerns of not being able to cope with the different language and culture of state courts. Indians have also expressed concerns about facing racial discrimination in state criminal courts and being subject to culturally insensitive law enforcement systems.

Goldberg and Singleton (2008) interviewed approximately 350 reservation residents, law enforcement officials, and criminal justice personnel from a non-random sample of 17 "confidential reservation sites – 12 subject to state/county jurisdiction under P.L. 280, four operating under the more typical federal/tribal criminal jurisdiction regime, and one, a 'straddler' with some territory in a state covered by P.L.280 and the remainder in a different state" (vi). They concluded that: "reservation residents in P.L. 280 jurisdictions typically rate the availability and quality of law enforcement and criminal justice lower than reservation residents in non-P.L. 280 jurisdictions" (vi). In addition, some tribal members reported a reluctance to report crimes to non-tribal police because of fear, distrust, and disagreement with rules and values of non-reservation police and courts.

---

[9] This helps explain why there is some controversy and objections to state jurisdiction over contracts and commercial activity, which also may lie outside tribal norms.

Their conclusion emphasizes the importance of local control with respect to policing and criminal law enforcement. Benefits arise because indigenous norms and preferences differ substantially from those of non-Indian criminal law methods, which is one of the key arguments for local control in a federalist system.

The Benefits of State Jurisdiction

The benefits from state jurisdiction emanate from having a legal system that binds tribes with a larger and more extensive system of contract enforcement, described by Besley and Ghatak (2006) as a key market-supporting public good. They argue that a well-functioning legal system makes it feasible for the poor to participate in markets and hence benefit from gains from trade. This reasoning is analogous to Dixit (2003), who argues that large and uniform systems of contract enforcement encourage trading across disparate parties and enable gains from trade to be captured. External jurisdiction also provides a credible commitment to a stable rule of law and there is evidence that this credible commitment encourages economic activity in various settings. In the case of former British colonies, for example, there is evidence that the former colonies still bound to British Privy Council appellate courts have achieved higher levels of investment and faster economic growth when compared to former British colonies that have established purely independent local court systems (Voight et al. 2007).

External, non-local jurisdiction is also plausibly beneficial on Indian reservations where the average tribal legal system is considered to be much less complete, more difficult to access, and less constrained by judicial precedent (Cooter and Fikentscher 2008, Haddock and Miller 2006).[10] These conditions, real or perceived, create an uncertain contracting environment, particularly for non-Indians contemplating doing business on reservations.

Using cross-sectional growth regressions, our earlier research (2008) provides a measure of the benefits of state rather than tribal jurisdiction

---

[10] Cooter and Fikentscher note that written commercial laws are absent on some reservations and legal codes are often not available in public places when they exist. Where there is precedent, "tribal judges seldom document their decisions in writings that outsiders can access" (p. 31). Similarly, Haddock and Miller (2006, 211) note that "vastly fewer cases have been litigated under tribal law" giving investors less precedent to rely upon, and "tribal precedents often have been poorly recorded, making the relatively sparse body of tribal precedent difficult for investors to discover."

over contracts by comparing per capita income growth from 1969 to 1999 for Native Americans on reservations under state versus civil tribal jurisdiction. Our analysis focused on the 71 reservations for which American Indian populations exceeded 1,000 in 1999, and we include an indicator variable for those reservations for which contracts were under the jurisdiction of state courts.[11]

Using a simple regression model that only includes 1969 per capita income as a control variable, we showed that growth was 35 percentage points higher on the 22 reservations under state jurisdiction. Controlling for land tenure, resource endowments, human capital, and economic conditions in surrounding counties, growth was still 31 percentage points higher under state jurisdiction. The relationship between P.L. 280 and growth was strongest between 1969 and 1979, and slightly less so between 1989 and 1999. We also found higher rates of income growth on reservations under state jurisdiction that were not explained by differences in the amount of casino gaming and in measures of acculturation.[12]

Lacking income data prior to the passage of P.L. 280, our 2008 research could not rigorously demonstrate a causal effect of state jurisdiction on growth, primarily because we could not rule out pre-existing differences in incomes and growth before the passage of P.L. 280. We could only argue that there was no evidence to suggest that the selection of P.L. 280 tribes was biased towards a subset of reservations that would have experienced faster growth in the absence of P.L. 280. Moveover, because census data on reservation income were only available starting in 1969, Dimitrova-Grajzl et al. (2014a, 130) criticized our study, noting that it focused "solely on the time period beginning two decades after P.L. 280's enactment." Dimitrova-Grajzl et al. also echoed a criticism of Goldberg (2010) who revisited the history of P.L. 280 in order to critique our empirical analysis. Goldberg (2010, 1048) suggests that Congress may have targeted tribes based on their ". . . inclination to participate in the market economy and strive for economic success as measured by per capita income."[13]

---

[11]   Our focus was not on criminal jurisdiction.

[12]   We measured acculturation by the percentage of reservation populations that were non-Indian and by the percentage of reservation residents speaking a native language.

[13]   This account differs from Goldberg's earlier writings. Golderg-Ambrose (1997, 50) dismisses the idea that Congress "knew or cared about the Indians' readiness for state jurisdiction." Furthermore, she notes "it is difficult to reconcile this theme of advanced acculturation with the prevailing notion that state criminal jurisdiction was necessary because Indians were disorderly and incapable of self-government." The possibility that Congress targeted economically successful and acculturated Native Americans for state jurisdiction is not addressed in Goldberg

Therefore, the "... possibility of this kind of selection bias makes it extremely difficult to attribute any causal force to state, as opposed to tribal, civil jurisdiction" (Goldberg 2010, 1050).

To address these and related concerns, we have assembled a longer panel data set of reservation per capita incomes spanning certain years from 1917 to 2010.[14] The 1917 data actually report the average per capita incomes of Indians on reservations during 1915–18. The 1917, 1938, and 1945 data come from reports of the Bureau of Indian Affairs (BIA). The 1938 and 1945 data are from the U.S. National Archives and the 1917 data are available online. The year 1945 is the closest year prior to 1953 for which we were able to find comprehensive income data.[15] The 1969, 1979, 1989, 1999 data come from decadal U.S. Census reports, which were used in our earlier study. To this we add 2010 data from American Community Surveys.[16] The 1917–2010 per capita income panel, the longest studied in the Native American development literature, spans a longer time period than most cross-country studies of institutions and growth.

Figure 3.1 below compares the mean per capita incomes (in 2010 dollars) for reservations put under state jurisdiction (with respect to contracts) for the years with available data. Panel A makes the comparisons for the 49 reservations for which data are available for each of the eight time periods. Panel B makes the comparisons for the larger set of reservations for which data are available for at least seven of the eight time periods. For both samples, there was no statistical difference in the mean incomes prior to P.L. 280. These results indicate that, unless there was systematic change during 1946–52, the average tribe put under P.L. 280 was not economically

---

and Singleton's (2008) analysis of the adverse impacts of state criminal jurisdiction on reservations. We infer that she now believes the issue of acculturation to be a potentially important source of selection bias with respect to income growth on reservations, but not with respect to the satisfaction of tribal members with state criminal enforcement.

[14] Some of the analysis that follows is also presented in Parker (2014).

[15] The 1950 U.S. Census reports summary information about incomes earned on Indian reservations but those data are aggregated up to a small number of large reservation areas and this makes the 1950 data not suitable for statistical analysis. Similarly, the 1960 U.S. Census also reports aggregated data for American Indians on reservations.

[16] The 2010 data come from the American Community Survey (ACS) which differs from the earlier decennial reservation census reports in certain ways. For geographic areas with populations less than 20,000, the ACS reports five-year estimates (i.e., 2006–10 averages). Because of this, the only data available for most reservations are the five-year estimates which are what we use in our analysis.

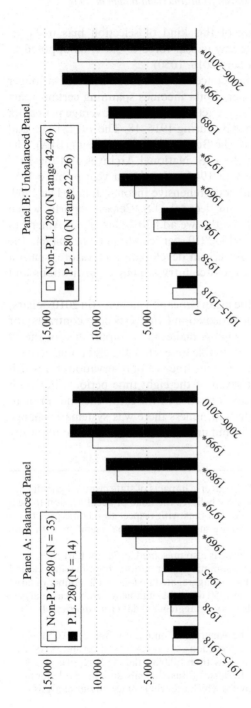

Note: For 1915–18, we are reporting the mean incomes over 1915, 1916, 1917 and 1918 based on income data from BIA reports available online at http://digicoll.library.wisc.edu/cgi-bin/History/History-idx?type=header&id=History.AnnRep90&isize=M. The 1938 and 1945 means are calculated from data contained in Bureau of Indian Affairs reports located at the U.S. National Archives in Washington, D.C. Because the 1945 reservation income estimates do not report reservation populations, we calculate per capita income by dividing 1945 aggregate income by the populations on reservation in 1943, which is the closest year to 1945 for which we have comprehensive Indian population data. The 1969, 1979, 1989, and 1999 means are based on data from decadal U.S. census reports. The 2006–10 means are based on data from the U.S. Census Bureau, American Community Surveys conducted during the 2006–10 period. * denotes rejection of the null hypothesis of no difference in means at p < 0.10 whether assuming equal or unequal variance. The "balanced" panel consists of reservations for which income data are available for each of the eight time periods. The "unbalanced" panel consists of reservations for which income data are available for seven of eight time periods. The definitions of P.L. 280 and non-P.L. 280 tribes come from Anderson and Parker (2008).

Figure 3.1   Mean per capita incomes for American Indians on reservations (in 2010 $)

advantaged in terms of per capita income prior to the law. Moreover, if P.L. 280 targeted acculturated tribes, the comparison of means suggests that acculturation was not an obvious economic advantage between 1915 and 1945.

By 1969, after P.L. 280 had been implemented, there were large, statistically significant differences in mean incomes that remained for nearly every decade thereafter. Something happened between 1945 and 1969 that improved relative incomes on P.L. 280 reservations, and the obvious candidate is a change in the administration of law and order brought about by P.L. 280.

To assess differences in per-capita income trends before and after P.L. 280, we first estimate the following regression model.

$$y_{it} = \alpha + \beta_1 t_{prePL280} + \beta_2 stjur \cdot t_{prePL280} + \beta_3 t_{postPL280} + \beta_4 stjur \cdot t_{postPL280} + \varepsilon_{it} \quad (3.1)$$

where y_{it} is the inflation-adjusted income per capita of American Indians on reservation i in time t. The parameter, β_1, is the linear time trend in income for all reservations prior to P.L. 280 (i.e., 1917–45) and β_2 is the difference in the 1917–45 time trend for reservations that were later put under state jurisdiction as a result of P.L. 280. Similarly, β_3 is the linear 1969–2010 t3.rend for all reservations, and β_4 is the difference for reservations put under P.L. 280.

Table 3.3 below shows regression results of (3.1) and Figure 3.2 displays the estimated linear trends. There is no statistically significant difference in income trends from 1917 through 1945. After P.L. 280, however, income growth diverges across the two sets of reservations as demonstrated by the positive sign and statistical significance of the coefficients on the interaction between state jurisdiction and the 1969–2010 trend. Visually, Figure 3.2 shows that the divergence in income trajectories begins after 1945, but not before.

The following panel regression model allows for more flexible time trends and controls for time-varying covariates:

$$y_{it} = \alpha_i + \theta_t + \beta st.jur_{it} + \delta state.pci_{st} + \eta oilwells.percap_{it} + \lambda slots.percap_{it} + \varepsilon_{it}. \quad (3.2)$$

Here y = per capita income, i = reservation, s = state, and t = time period. Each model controls for time shocks affecting all reservations (θ_t), and allows each reservation to have its own income intercept (α_i). The use of reservation-specific fixed effects controls for time-invariant differences across reservations (e.g., geographic location, reservation size, and land quality) that may cause persistent cross-sectional differences in income.

Table 3.3   Regression estimates of linear time trends

	BALANCED PANEL	UNBALANCED PANEL
1917–1945 Time trend	476.67***	924.28***
	(0.000)	(0.000)
1917–1945 Time trend × state jurisdiction	−21.058	−213.36
	(0.855)	(0.250)
1969–2010 Time trend	1186.42***	1309.74***
	(0.000)	(0.000)
1969–2010 Time trend × state jurisdiction	212.49**	286.79***
	(0.025)	(0.001)
Constant (1917 intercept)	1971.02***	1301.13***
	(0.000)	(0.000)
Observations	392	553
Adjusted R^2	0.741	0.650

Note: * $p < 0.10$, ** $p < 0.05$, and *** $p < 0.01$. P-values are reported in parentheses and are based on standard errors that are clustered at the reservation level. The "balanced" panel consists of reservations for which income data are available for each of the eight time periods. The "unbalanced" panel consists of reservations for which income data are available for seven of eight time periods. The definitions of P.L. 280 and non-P.L. 280 tribes come from Anderson and Parker (2008).

In addition, we introduce time varying covariates to control for economic shocks that might affect income growth. The first covariate we include is the per capita income of the state surrounding the reservation.[17] The second covariate is the number of oil and gas wells drilled on reservations divided by the reservation's Native American population in each of the relevant years.[18] The third covariate measures casino gaming activity on reservations with the number of slot machines per American Indian in

---

[17] Ideally we would prefer to include the per capita incomes of counties adjacent to reservations as we did in Anderson and Parker (2008) but the census first reports per capita income at the county level in 1959. The data on per capita income at the state level are from the Bureau of Economic Analysis and are available for 1929–2010.

[18] More specifically, this variable aggregates the number of oil and gas wells drilled on reservations in the five-year period preceding each year for which we have income data. We use this procedure because oil and gas drilling may have lagged effects on income due to the flow of oil and gas that subsequently occurs. For 1999, for example, the variable indicates the number of wells drilled during 1995–99 divided by a reservation's 1999 American Indian population.

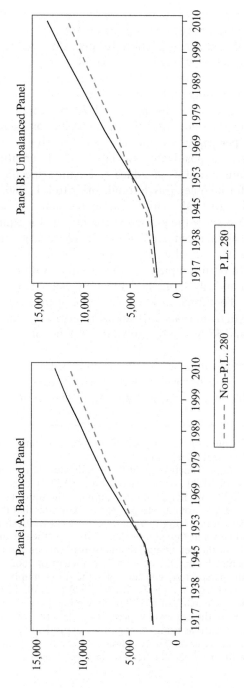

Note: The results plotted here come from the regression results reported in Table 3.3. The vertical bar in 1953 represents the passage of P.L. 280. The "balanced" panel consists of reservations for which income data are available for each of the eight time periods. The "unbalanced" panel consists of reservations for which income data are available for seven of eight time periods. The definitions of P.L. 280 and non-P.L. 280 tribes come from Anderson and Parker (2008).

Figure 3.2   Per capita incomes based on estimated linear time trends (in 2010 $)

1999, and 2010. The casino variable is zero prior to 1999 because reservations in these samples did not have casinos prior to 1999.[19]

Table 3.4 presents the panel regression results. Column 1, which employs the balanced panel of 392 reservations ($i = 49$, $t = 8$), shows that state jurisdiction is associated with a $1,243 increase in per capita income over the full time period. Adding the covariates in column 2, which forces us to drop 1917 data because of missing state-level per capita income data for that time period, does not affect the state jurisdiction coefficient, but, as expected, state per capita income, oil wells per capita, and slot machines per capita are all positively associated with reservation per capita income.[20] Columns 3 and 4 introduce reservation-specific linear time trends to control for income growth trends prior to P.L. 280, which increases the size and statistical significance of the state jurisdiction coefficients. Columns 5–8 show the estimated coefficients for equivalent specifications using the unbalanced panel, which enables a larger number of observations. The results in columns 5–8 are qualitatively similar to those in columns 1–4. In both samples, the coefficients on state jurisdiction are positive, economically large, and precisely estimated with the exception of column 7. To appreciate the magnitude of the coefficients, we note that mean growth from 1946–2010 across reservations was $8,393 in the balanced panel and $8,657 in the unbalanced panel, in 2010 inflation adjusted dollars.[21]

To address the possibility that the acculturation of tribes, rather than P.L. 280 itself, caused the difference in income growth over 1946–2010, we have collected data on blood quantum ratios that existed across

---

[19]   Prior to the Indian Regulatory Gaming Act of 1988, casino gaming on reservations was virtually non-existent (Cookson 2010).

[20]   For example, the column 2 coefficient of 0.273 indicates that an increase of state per capita income of $1.00 is associated with a $0.273 increase in per capita incomes of American Indians living on reservations in the state. To put the 4248.7 coefficient on the oil wells variable into perspective, consider that the mean number of wells drilled per capita changed from 0.065 in 1999 to 0.186 in 2010 for the eleven oil endowed tribes in this sample. The 4248.7 coefficient therefore implies an increase of $514 in the per capita income of residents on reservations with oil and gas endowments. To put the column 2 coefficient of 1662.6 on the slot machines variable into perspective, consider that the mean number of slot machines per capita increased from 0.23 to 0.37 from 1999 to 2010. The 1662.6 coefficient therefore implies an increase of $232.8 in per capita income.

[21]   To put the estimates in the context of percentage growth, we have also estimated the Table 3.4 specifications using the log of the dependent variable (not shown here but available on request). Those regression results show that state jurisdiction is associated with 26–67 percent increases in per capita income depending on the specification.

Table 3.4 *Panel regressions of per capita income on American Indian reservations*

	BALANCED PANEL				UNBALANCED PANEL			
	(1)	(2)	(3)	(4)	(5)	(6)	(7)	(8)
P.L. 280 Reservation (= 1 if yes, otherwise = 0)	243.3** (0.020)	1234.4*** (0.007)	1867.9** (0.022)	2771.0*** (0.001)	2065.9*** (0.000)	1302.7*** (0.001)	1232.5 (0.177)	2007.1** (0.015)
State per capita income		0.273*** (0.000)		0.348*** (0.000)		0.280*** (0.000)		0.355*** (0.000)
Oil wells drilled per capita		4248.7*** (0.011)		2696.9*** (0.003)		4104.9*** (0.001)		2670.5*** (0.004)
Slot machines per capita		1662.6** (0.017)		1701.5** (0.022)		1642.5*** (0.000)		1360.1 (0.113)
Year fixed effects	Yes	Yes	Yes	Yes	Yes	Yes	Yes	Yes
Reservation fixed effects	Yes	Yes	Yes	Yes	Yes	Yes	Yes	Yes
Reservation time trends	No	No	Yes	Yes	No	No	Yes	Yes
Observations	392	343	392	343	553	487	553	487
Adjusted (within) R^2	0.85	0.82	0.91	0.89	0.73	0.78	0.81	0.84

Note: * $p < 0.10$, ** $p < 0.05$, and *** $p < 0.01$. P-values are reported in parentheses and are based on standard errors that are clustered at the reservation level. The number of observations is lower in the specifications that control for state-level per capita income because we lack 1917 data on state per capita incomes. The state-level per capita income data come from the U.S. Bureau of Economic Analysis. The slot machines variable takes on a value of zero for all reservations prior to the 1989 Census. The data on slot machines for 1989 and 1999 were compiled by Anderson and Parker (2008) and also used in Cookson (2010). The data on slot machines in 2010 were compiled by the authors from www.500nations.com/Indian_Casinos.asp. This site provides the number of slots/gaming machines for all American Indian casinos in the U.S. Each casino can be tied to a reservation by looking at which tribe owns the casino and where the casino is located. We downloaded gaming machine data from the site in 2013, so our measure may include casinos built after 2010. The data on the number of oil and gas wells drilled come from our merge of ArcGis Shapfiles of U.S. Indian reservations boundaries with iHS data on the longitude and latitude of oils and gas wells drilled in the Western Region of the U.S. For this variable, we aggregate the number of oil and gas wells drilled over the four-year period prior to the year in which income data are reported. For example, our 1999 measure aggregates the number of wells drilled over 1995–99 and divides this number by the 1999 American Indian population of the reservation.

Table 3.5   Mean blood quantum on reservations prior to P.L. 280

	P.L. 280 Reservations (N)	Non-P.L. 280 Reservations (N)	t-stat for difference
Percent of "full blooded" American Indians			
Panel A			
Balanced Panel	38.98 (14)	62.97 (35)	2.71
Unbalanced Panel	41.29 (25)	62.58 (45)	3.05
Panel B			
Trimmed Balanced Panel	38.98 (14)	39.22 (17)	0.03
Trimmed Unbalanced Panel	41.29 (25)	41.47 (25)	0.03

Note: The data on blood quantum are for 1938, the closest year prior to P.L. 280 for which we have comprehensive reservation-level data. The variable measures the percentage of the American Indian population on a reservation with 100 percent American Indian blood. The blood quantum data come from BIA reports that are housed at the U.S. National Archives in Washington, D.C. The t-statistics above assume equal variance. Allowing for unequal variance, the t-statistics are 2.68 and 3.04 respectively for the Balanced and Unbalanced samples and 0.03 and for both of the trimmed samples.

reservations prior to the passage of P.L. 280. Table 3.5 above compares the mean percent of "full-blooded" American Indians in 1938, which is the closest pre-P.L. 280 year for which we have data. Panel A shows that a smaller percentage of Native Americans on reservations that were later put under P.L. 280 were full blooded.

Although having a greater percentage of American Indian residents with white blood would not necessarily advantage reservation income growth after 1946, it is possible that the relationships between P.L. 280 and income growth in Table 3.4 are confounded by this systematic difference in blood quantum.[22] To address this possibility, we create trimmed subsamples of reservations for which there is no mean difference in blood quantum across P.L. 280 and non-P.L. 280 reservations (see Panel B of Table 3.5). The samples were balanced by first ranking the non-P.L. 280 reservations in descending order based on percent full blood, and second sequentially dropping the highest ranked non-P.L. 280 reservations until the difference in means across P.L. 280 and non-P.L. 280 reservations was minimized for both the balanced and unbalanced trimmed samples. This process led to the dropping of 18 and 20

---

[22]   Kuhn and Sweetman (2002), for example, find evidence that having more white blood is related to higher wages among indigenous labor in Canada.

of the least acculturated reservations for the balanced and unbalanced samples, respectively.[23]

Table 3.6 below presents the results of the regression estimates that employ the trimmed samples. The eight columns of regression specifications are identical to those shown in Table 3.4. The relationship between P.L. 280 and per capita income remains positive, economically large, and statistically precise (again with the exception in column 7). Moreover, comparing the point estimates on the P.L. 280 coefficients across Table 3.4 and Table 3.6 shows they are effectively indistinguishable. This implies that the P.L. 280 coefficients in Table 3.4 are unlikely attributable to differences in acculturation as measured by blood quantum.

Overall we conclude from the Table 3.3, Table 3.4, and Table 3.6 regressions that:

1. state jurisdiction is positively related to income growth on reservations from 1946 to 2010, and
2. the relationship between jurisdiction and growth is not merely driven by differential state income growth, oil and gas development, tribal gaming, or pre-P.L. 280 trends in reservation income growth, and
3. the relationship is robust to using subsamples of P.L. 280 and non-P.L. 280 reservations with statistically indistinguishable mean levels of acculturation as measured by blood quantum prior to P.L. 280.

To summarize, the evidence suggests that either P.L. 280 increased per capita incomes on reservations, or some other set of events or policies that are correlated with P.L. 280 did so. Of course, even if one accepts that P.L. 280 caused the increased incomes, this does not mean the benefits exceeded the costs described above.[24] But our findings do suggest that tribes can further promote economic activity by attaching

---

[23] Seven of the 18 balanced panel reservations that are omitted by this criterion are located in Arizona. Other reservations that are omitted by this criterion are located in New Mexico, Utah, Colorado, Oregon, Idaho and South Dakota. A full list is available from the authors upon request.

[24] The conclusions we draw from Tables 3.4 and 3.6 differ from Dimitrova-Grajzl et al. (2014a), who use a sample of U.S. counties containing American Indian reservations to show that the adoption of P.L. 280 is correlated with relatively lower median family incomes over 1949–79. Because their income data include white and Native American families, and families living on and off reservations, we do not consider the findings to be comparable.

Table 3.6 Panel regressions of per capita income using subsamples trimmed by blood quantum

	TRIMMED BALANCED PANEL				TRIMMED UNBALANCED PANEL			
	(1)	(2)	(3)	(4)	(5)	(6)	(7)	(8)
P.L. 280 Reservation (= 1 if yes, otherwise = 0)	1374.4** (0.025)	1648.4*** (0.002)	1730.7** (0.040)	2694.1*** (0.002)	2397.9*** (0.000)	1679.8*** (0.000)	1102.1 (0.290)	1733.6** (0.047)
State per capita income		0.251*** (0.000)		0.356*** (0.000)		0.263*** (0.000)		0.410*** (0.000)
Oil wells drilled per Am. Indian		-1.3e+04 (0.639)		-2.0e+04 (0.328)		-1.0e+04 (0.680)		-2.5e+04 (0.175)
Slot machines per Am. Indian		1825.6** (0.014)		1564.1** (0.046)		1610.3*** (0.000)		1255.1 (0.158)
Year fixed effects	Yes	Yes	Yes	Yes	Yes	Yes	Yes	Yes
Reservation fixed effects	Yes	Yes	Yes	Yes	Yes	Yes	Yes	Yes
Reservation time trends	No	No	Yes	Yes	No	No	Yes	Yes
Observations	248	217	248	217	390	342	390	342
Adjusted (within) R^2	0.85	0.82	0.90	0.88	0.71	0.77	0.78	0.83

Note: * $p < 0.10$, ** $p < 0.05$, and *** $p < 0.01$. P-values are reported in parentheses and are based on standard errors that are clustered at the reservation level. Each sample is trimmed in order to equalize the mean percentage of full-blooded American Indians on P.L. 280 and non-P.L. 280 reservations prior to the law (see Table 3.5). The specifications here match those shown in Table 3.4.

to a larger system of contract enforcement as fiscal federalism principles suggest.[25]

The Choice of Jurisdictional Scale

The way in which P.L. 280 was implemented and has operated has impaired evolution toward a more optimal legal system for Indian reservations. P.L. 280 could have given tribes a way to accrue the benefits of state jurisdiction without incurring the costs had it allowed tribes to choose state jurisdiction over civil disputes, such as enforcement over debt contracts with non-Indians. But, as noted above, tribes in the mandatory P.L. 280 states were subjected to blanket state jurisdiction over crimes and civil disputes without their consent. Some optional P.L. 280 states did assume partial jurisdiction over certain subject matter but until the 1968 amendments to P.L. 280, these assumptions of jurisdiction did not require tribal consent.

The 1968 amendments of P.L. 280 gave tribes more choices, but fell short of giving tribes the authority to pick and choose the types of disputes over which states would have jurisdiction. The amendments required any state that had not yet assumed jurisdiction to first acquire tribal consent, which seems a marked improvement for tribes. In practice, some states did not want to assume jurisdiction over reservations or only offered to do so if tribes accepted blanket state jurisdiction over crimes and civil offenses. Since 1968 no tribe has consented to P.L. 280 jurisdiction.

The 1968 amendments also set up a process whereby a state (but not a tribe), could initiate the return or retrocession of state jurisdiction that was assumed prior to 1968. Had the tribes been given authority to initiate full or partial retrocession, their decisions to keep or dispose of state jurisdiction would provide valuable information about the relative costs and benefits of tribal control on different reservations. As it stands, we can only observe that a small number of tribes have undergone the process of retrocession, primarily over criminal jurisdiction.[26] According to five

---

[25] Evidence that demonstrates plausible channels from state jurisdiction over contracts to faster income growth on reservations is accumulating. Parker (2012), Dimitrova-Grajzl et al. (2015), and Brown et al. (2015), for example, find higher rates of credit use on reservations governed by P.L. 280, and Cookson (2014) finds evidence of greater capital investment in the counties of reservations that are under state jurisdiction. Although only suggestive, these studies are consistent with our reasoning that state jurisdiction, on average, makes non-Indian investors and creditors more willing to contract with tribal members.

[26] Goldberg and Singleton (2008, 8–11) lists 29 tribes as undergoing partial or full retrocession. Of these 16 are sparsely populated tribes in Nevada. Of the remaining 13 cases, nine cases were partial retrocessions.

case studies of retrocession provided by Goldberg and Singleton (2008), the retrocessions seem to have been motivated by one of two factors; tribal dissatisfaction with state and county law enforcement, or tribal desire to make criminal justice more consistent with overall assertions of sovereignty.

We can only speculate about the reasons for the lack of retrocession on the more than 150 other reservations still under P.L. 280 jurisdiction. It may mean that the majority of tribes believe that state jurisdiction provides net benefits, or it could be that states may be unwilling to withdraw their jurisdiction over these reservations.

There are also contracting challenges that P.L. 280 does not address. When a tribe is a party to a contract, rather than an individual tribal member, it faces difficulties in credibly agreeing to allow disputes to be adjudicated by an outside court regardless of P.L. 280 status. First, waivers of sovereignty must be explicit, as courts have held that commercial activities of tribes do not in themselves constitute implied waivers (McLish 1988). Second, as McLish (1988, 179) notes, there is "debate as to whether tribes can expressly waive their own immunity without congressional authorization." This means that federal courts might rule that a tribe had no authority to waive its immunity in a contract and thus disallow suits against the tribe for breach of contract in an outside court. More generally, federal courts have a record of ruling that tribal immunity from suit is always retained except when the tribe's ability to waive immunity is patently apparent (see Haddock and Miller 2006). According to both McLish (1988) and Haddock and Miller (2006), less stringent waiver requirements would help tribal businesses compete more effectively in the non-Indian business world.

To summarize, a better federalist arrangement would allow tribes to choose when to yield their jurisdiction and when to retain it. Without the freedom to choose many tribes are stuck with one of two second-best institutional arrangements. Either they establish a strong tribal law enforcement and court system that matches tribal norms and culture, but raises the cost of doing business with non-Indians or they accept state jurisdiction which facilitates contracting with non-Indians, but does not match tribal customs and norms, particularly with respect to criminal law enforcement.

LAND AND NATURAL RESOURCES

As noted in the introduction, land tenure on Indian reservations is another example of how fiscal federalism could work, but has not worked, on Indian reservations. The transfer of land out of Indian control – tribal and individual – is well documented (see Carlson 1981), but it has not been linked to fiscal federalism. To understand the link, it is useful to consider Chief Justice Marshall's opinion in *Cherokee Nation v. Georgia* (30 U.S. 1, 1831), wherein he described the relationship between tribes and the U.S. as "that of a ward to his guardian." Under this interpretation, the federal government monopolized treaty negotiations with tribes in order to reduce conflicts over land and forced tribes into a subservient position by declaring them wards. It is through this guardian role that the federal government has asserted trusteeship over reservation land and resources and limited each tribe's ability to evolve its own system of land tenure.

Federal Trusteeship

With the passage of the Allotment Act of 1887, the U.S. federal government made its first major attempt at bureaucratic control over how reservation land would be allocated. Prior to the act, informal property rights to reservation land varied significantly across reservations, and Carlson (1992, 73) provides evidence that locally evolved tenure systems were working well for some tribes.

> Once a tribe was confined to a reservation, it needed to find a land tenure system suitable to the new environment. On the closed reservations, the system that evolved was one of use rights. Typically, the [U.S. Bureau of Indian Affairs] agent and members of a tribe recognized an individual's title to animals and, where farming was practiced, a family's claim to the land it worked. ... What is remarkable is how similar this system of land tenure was to that which existed among agricultural tribes before being confined to reservations.

Under the Allotment Act, however, Congress intervened and began to shape property rights. The Allotment Act authorized the President to allot reservation land to individual Indians with the potential for them to obtain private ownership, including the right to alienate, after 25 years or if the allottee was declared "competent" (the word in the Act) by the Secretary of the Interior. For arable agricultural land the Indian head of a household would be allotted 160 acres and for grazing land 320 acres. Indians would become U.S. citizens upon receiving their allotments. On reservations for which total acreage exceeded that necessary to make the allotments, surplus land could be ceded to the federal government for sale with the proceeds deposited in a trust fund managed by the Department of Interior through the BIA.[27] A 1903 U.S. Supreme Court ruling, however,

---

[27]   Trust fund management was ultimately the focus of a major class action law

Table 3.7   Reservation acres in 1887 and 1933

	Acres
1. Reservation Land, 1887	136,394,895
2. Reservation Land, 1933	69,588,411
a. Tribal trust, 1933	29,481,685
b. Individual trust, 1933	17,829,414
c. Allotments no longer in trust	22,277,342
3. Surplus land surrendered, 1933	66,806,454

Source: Flanagan et al. (2010).

allowed surplus land to be opened to non-Indian settlement without tribal consent.

Through a combination of land sales once allotments owners were declared competent and title was alienable and sale or homesteading of surplus land, millions of reservation acres were transferred from reservation jurisdiction to state jurisdiction.[28] The Indian Reorganization Act (IRA) of 1934 halted such transfers, declaring those acres not already alienated to be held in trust by the BIA, either as individual trust land or as tribal lands. Table 3.7 reports that the number of reservation acres was cut from 136,394,895 in 1887 to 69,588,411 in 1934. This implies that 66,806,454 acres of surplus lands were ceded from Indian Country and sold to or homesteaded by white settlers or retained by the federal government. Of the land that was retained within Indian reservation boundaries, another 22,277,342 acres was out of trust status, and most of these non-trust acres were owned by non-Indians in 1934.

Under IRA, lands not already privately owned were locked into trust status, some for individual Indians who received allotments that were never released from trust – individual trust – and for tribes – tribal trust. Trust status means that the legal title to the land is held by the U.S. government, but the beneficial title – the right to use or benefit from the land – is held by either individuals or tribes. Trusteeship does keep land

---

suit, *Cobell v. Salazar*, filed against the federal government. For a brief discussion see Anderson (2012).

[28]   In general, allotment is criticized because it transferred land from Indian to non-Indian ownership (although some land cleared for fee simple ownership remains Indian owned), but, in the context of fiscal federalism, the issue is one of jurisdiction. Land transferred to fee-simple ownership is removed from tribal jurisdiction, and land held in trust, known as Indian Country, is technically under tribal jurisdiction, but subject to the trust authority of the federal government.

in Indian ownership, but the extra layer of bureaucracy that comes with it reduces productivity. As Carlson (1981, 174) concludes, "no student of property-rights literature or, indeed, economic theory will be surprised that the complicated and heavily supervised property rights that emerged from allotment led to inefficiencies, corruption, and losses for both Indians and society."

The combination of the Allotment Act, the IRA, and related land policies created a mosaic of land tenure – fee simple, individual trust, and tribal trust – on most western reservations. Fee-simple lands can be alienated and sold to Indians and non-Indians, and liens can be placed against the land title to collateralize loans. Trust lands, both tribal and individual, cannot be alienated and therefore generally cannot be used as collateral against loans.[29]

The burden of trusteeship is further complicated by the fact that individual trust lands have often been inherited several times leaving multiple landowners who must unanimously agree on land-use decisions. The website for the Indian Land Tenure Foundation explains how extreme fractionalization can arise:

> ... imagine that an Indian allottee dies and passes on the ownership of the allotment to her spouse and three children. Divided interest in the land is now split between four people. Now imagine those children becoming adults and raising families of their own, each consisting of three children. When the second generation dies, and if all the grandchildren survive, then ownership is divided between all of the grandchildren. The ownership of the original allotment is now split between nine different people or possibly more depending on whether the spouses of the second generation are still alive. As each generation passes on, the number of owners of a piece of land grows exponentially. Today, it is not uncommon to have more than 100 owners involved with an allotment parcel.

With so many owners, each individual owner has weak economic incentives to coordinate investments in the land that could increase the value of the property. Moreover, the cost of getting unanimous agreement from all owners rises exponentially.

Table 3.8 summarizes the mosaic of land tenure types. Of 82 reservations in 1999, an average of 58.3 percent of Indian Country was in tribal trust, 29.3 percent in fee simple, and 13.9 percent in individual trust.[30]

---

[29]   There are some exceptions through programs that allow foreclosure on trust lands so that they can be converted to fee simple with the consent of the secretary of the U.S. Department of Interior and allow the long-term leasing of trust land.

[30]   The source is Anderson and Parker (2008) and the authors' data.

Table 3.8 Land tenure categories on U.S. reservations

Characteristics	Land Tenure Status		
	Fee-Simple Land	Trust Land	
		Tribally Owned	Individually Owned
Legal title	Individual owner or tribal govt. owner	U.S. government	U.S. government
Beneficial title	Same as legal	Tribe	Individual
Alienation	Can be sold to non-tribal members	Cannot be sold to non-tribal members except under unusual circumstances	Cannot be sold to non-tribal members except under unusual circumstances
Collateral options	Can be used as lien and mortgaged in standard way	Loans secured by a leasehold interest are permissible	Can be used as a lien and mortgaged with approval of U.S. govt. Foreclosed land is converted to fee simple if it cannot be transferred within the tribe
Other issues	Land use may be subject to tribal law	Tribes may develop programs through which it executes a land lease as a lessor. The lessee can then offer up a leasehold interest as collateral, subject to U.S. govt. approval.	Beneficial title is conveyed to all descendants, often resulting in a large number of fractional owners

Source: Listokin et al. (2006, 98–99).

Economic Consequences of Federal Control

Because the BIA must approve or disapprove contracts for land use held in trust, the added cost of negotiating contracts can suppress development and investment. Trosper (1978) was one of the first economists to formally identify the importance of reservation land tenure to agricultural productivity after the allotment era. He observed that ranches operated by Indians on the Northern Cheyenne Reservation in Montana generated less output per acre than ranches operated by non-Indians adjacent to the reservation.

He identified possible sources of the productivity difference: (1) Indians lacked technical and managerial knowledge of ranching; (2) Indians had ranching goals other than profit maximization; and (3) land tenure on reservations constrained Indians from operating their ranches at an efficient scale and from using the optimal mix of land, labor, and capital.

Trosper argues that the lower output chosen by Indian ranchers on the Northern Cheyenne is actually profit maximizing. According to his estimates, Indian ranchers are as productive as non-Indians operating nearby ranches when accounting for the different input ratios. Given that Indian ranch managers are as technically competent as non-Indians, Trosper concludes that the effects of land tenure should be examined further.[31]

Anderson and Lueck (1992) take up this challenge by estimating the impact of land tenure on the productivity of agricultural land using a cross-section of large reservations. They benchmark the productivity of tribal and individual trust lands against those of fee-simple lands on reservations. When controlling for factors such as the percentage of trust lands managed by Indian operators and whether the tribe was indigenous to the reservation area, Anderson and Lueck estimate the per-acre value of agriculture to be 85–90 percent lower on tribal trust land and 30–40 percent lower on individual trust land. They attribute the larger negative effect of tribal trust land to collective action problems related to communally managed land. In addition to having to overcome BIA trust constraints, agricultural land held by the tribe is subject to common-pool resource management incentives that can lead to exploitation and neglect.

The U.S. Congress has authorized some noteworthy land reforms, but, for the most part, their impacts have not been rigorously studied by economists. One such reform is the Indian Long-Term Leasing Act of 1955, which increased the length of allowable leases of trust land for some tribes. Akee (2009) finds evidence that the increase in allowable lease tenure caused a significant increase in land values and in commercial and residential development on tribally owned trust land on California's Aqua Caliente reservation. This result suggests that the inability of tribes to commit to long-term leases elsewhere has hindered their ability to gain from commercial interest in their land.

BIA trusteeship goes beyond land management alone to include other natural resources such as coal, oil and gas, and timber. Just as it has thwarted more productive use of land, trusteeship has limited the ability

---

[31] Trosper also dismisses the claim that Indians on the Northern Cheyenne do not seek to maximize profits. His data suggest that Indian ranchers used inputs efficiently.

of tribes to manage and profit from other resources. Though federal paternalism has been described as a responsibility "to protect Indians and their resources from Indians" (American Indian Policy Review Commission on Reservation and Resource Development, quoted in Morishima 1997, 8), there is ample evidence that the BIA has failed to be a good guardian, not the least of which was the 2009 settlement of the long running class-action lawsuit in *Cobell v. Salazar*. The plaintiffs claimed the U.S. government mismanaged Indian trust assets, including money deposited in trust accounts, and therefore owed the beneficiaries billions of dollars. Eventually the government settled for $3.4 billion, likely a small fraction of what was actually lost.

To give tribal governments more control of their assets, Congress passed the Self Determination Act of 1976 (Public Law 93-638) and later the Self-Governance Demonstration Project Act in 1988. Under this legislation, the Confederated Salish and Kootenai Tribes (CSKT) on the Flathead Reservation became one of ten tribes to have more management autonomy. Finally in 1995, the confederated tribes' forestry department compacted with the BIA to take control of forest management decisions on the Flathead Reservation.

Berry (2009) documents the success of the experiment in fiscal federalism on the Flathead Reservation by comparing tribal forest management with U.S. Forest Service management on the neighboring Lolo National Forest. Not only did she find that the CSKT earned more than $2 for every $1 spent compared to the U.S. Forest Service just breaking even, Berry documents that timber quality, wildlife habitat, and water quality were all better under tribal management. In her words, "Since the CSKT rely on timber revenues to support tribal operations, they have a vested interest in continuing vitality of their natural resources ... The tribes stand to benefit of responsible forest stewardship – or bear the burden of mismanagement" (2009, 18).

Berry's results mirror those of Krepps (1992) and Krepps and Caves (1994). According to Krepps (1992, 179), "as tribal control increases relative to BIA control, worker productivity rises, costs decline, and income improves. Even the price received for reservation logs increases."

Tribal versus Federal Protection of Culture

Federal trusteeship of Indian land and resources does not comport with fiscally optimal federalism in almost all dimensions. It takes the control of resource use decision out of local hands where information about the value of output and production techniques is greatest and removes the incentive for innovative management by local leaders. Moreover, by putting control at the federal level, trusteeship raises the cost of holding the trustee accountable to the beneficiary as *Cobell v. Salazar* clearly illustrates. All of these reasons – information, incentives, and accountability – call for devolving resource decisions to a lower level of governance, perhaps even to the individual resource owner in the form of complete privatization.

One dimension on which trusteeship may benefit tribes is through its restraint on alienability. Typically economists view restraints on alienation as a limit on the potential to gain from trade. Because trust lands cannot be alienated, parcels cannot be sold to producers who might value it more, consolidated to take advantage of scale economies except through leasing, or used as collateral in capital markets.

These restraints on alienation, however, do come with a benefit not captured in individual trades, because restraints on alienation may help preserve customs and culture. Consider, for example, zoning rules that limit alienability for certain uses. Though such rules may disallow more valuable land uses, they can preserve the character of community. Without them, individual owners would be faced with the "prisoner's dilemma."

In the context of American Indians, McChesney (1992, 120) puts it this way: "*A priori*, the individual Indian owner of land may be in a prisoner's dilemma, the dominant strategy being to sell, even though all would be better off agreeing not to sell to preserve an Indian way of life." If an individual Indian sold his or her land to a non-Indian who did not share the same cultural norms, the costs of tribal collective action could rise. If cultural assets – preserving the "Indian way of life" – have value, that value is best assessed at the tribal level where local information can give a more accurate measure of the cultural asset's value and where collective agents can be better held accountable optimizing that value.

McChesney (1992) points out that preservation of the "Indian way of life" may explain restricting alienation to non-Indians, but that it does not explain why alienation should be restricted on all reservations by the federal government rather than leaving that decision to local tribal governments who better understand the costs and benefits of alienation. A proposal by Canadian First Nations to change the Indian Act would let individual bands decide if they want out of Canadian federal trusteeship so that bands can decide for themselves to what degree they want collective ownership or private ownership. Under such self-determination, bands could decide if they want to limit alienation to non-band members (see Flanagan et al. 2010).

GETTING FROM HERE TO THERE

When the U.S. Supreme Court placed Indian relations in the hands of Congress in the 1830s, the prospects for optimal systems of federalism for Indians greatly diminished. Rather than optimizing the locus of collective action by balancing the benefits of scale economies through collective action with information and agency costs, Indian policy has mainly been determined by Congress and its agencies with too little input from the Indian people.

This top-down control stifles the possibility of building on a long history of *de facto* bottom-up federalism within most tribes. American Indian history is a history rich in property rights and governance institutions consistent with customs and culture and compatible with the resource constraints they faced. For example, in pedestrian times, bison hunting tribes were organized into larger groups necessary to achieve the scale economies necessary to drive bison into surrounds or over jumps. When the horse arrived on the scene, the efficient size of the group was reduced as a few proficient horsemen could supply bison to smaller family and clan units (see Anderson 1995). Once confined to reservations but before allotment, American Indians were proving they could adapt their institutions and be productive with the resources at hand (Carlson 1981).

Even if the best of intentions are attributed to the reformers who championed the Allotment Act of 1887, namely to assimilate Indians into non-Indian culture and empower their productivity through the incentives inherent in private ownership, the passage of that Act raised the costs of bottom-up fiscal federalism on reservations. As Roback (1992, 23) concludes:

> The allotment policy did not institute private property among the Indians; instead it overturned a functioning property rights system that was already in place ... Allotment failed because it privatized the land among individuals without understanding the existing family and tribal structure or the property rights structure that accompanied it.

In other words, allotment failed to understand a key principle of fiscal federalism, namely that local knowledge is a strong argument in favor of local control.[32]

Allotment perpetuated the guardian–ward relationship between

---

[32] See Frye and Parker (2016) for a recent discussion of the benefits of local, tribal control versus non-local federal control. They provide evidence that tribes who opted into more federal control through the Indian Reorganization Act (IRA)

American Indians and the federal government, leaving tribes with little opportunity for finding an optimal balance between local governmental control and top-down bureaucratic management. To be sure, perpetual trusteeship has prevented the transfer of even more land from Indian Country to non-Indians and thus helped to preserve local culture, but that benefit has come at a high cost. To whit, the literature described here suggest that returns from land and natural resources are lower than they would have been.

American Indians have called for self-determination for decades, but a heavy hand from the top down has limited opportunities. When such opportunities have arisen, as in the case of forest management, tribes have proven they can do it themselves. Moreover, true self-determination includes the freedom to voluntarily give up sovereignty, which may encourage business with non-tribal companies and customers as the evidence of increased income growth under P.L. 280 presented here suggests. However, there remain questions about what it really takes for a tribe to credibly limit its own sovereignty, and the ability of individual tribes to select into or opt out of P.L. 280 in piecemeal ways has been constrained by state governments which have too often offered tribes all-or-nothing choices. Either they fully commit to a completely sovereign tribal law enforcement and court system that matches tribal norms and customs but raises the costs of doing business with non-Indians, or they accept state jurisdiction which facilitates contracting with non-Indians, but does not match tribal customs and norms, particularly with respect to criminal law enforcement.

The principles of fiscal federalism offer a blueprint for how tribal governments should think about the importance of their sovereignty and the necessary limits on it. Should Indian lands and other natural resources remain under the trusteeship of the federal government? Should tribes limit alienation of land to non-Indians? Should tribes seek to transfer ownership of individual trust land to the tribe? Should legal disputes on reservations remain the domain of tribal courts or be transferred to larger nodes of government? Should the sovereign power to tax or regulate non-Indians on reservations be limited? Answering these and other questions regarding the appropriate level of governmental control is what fiscal federalism and self-determination are all about.

---

of 1934 have had slower average income growth since the 1930s when compared to tribes that chose non-IRA, local governance.

REFERENCES

Akee, Randall. 2009. "Checkerboards and Coase: The Effect of Property Institutions on Efficiency in Housing Markets." *Journal of Law and Economics* 52(May): 395–410.

Alesina, Alberto, and Enrico Spolaore. 2003. *The Size of Nations*. Cambridge, MA: MIT Press.

Anderson, Terry L. 1995. *Sovereign Nations or Reservations? An Economic History of American Indians*. San Francisco: Pacific Research Institute.

Anderson, Terry L. 2012. "At Last, Some Bright Spots in Indian Country." *Wall Street Journal* (weekend), March 24–25.

Anderson, Terry L., and Dean Lueck. 1992. "Land Tenure and Agricultural Productivity on Indian Reservations." *Journal of Law and Economics* 35(2): 427–454.

Anderson, Terry L., and Dominic P. Parker. 2008. "Sovereignty, Credible Commitments, and Economic Prosperity on American Indian Reservations." *Journal of Law and Economics* 51 (November): 641–666.

Berry, Alison. 2009. "Two Forests under the Big Sky: Tribal v. Federal Management." *PERC Policy Series*, 45. Bozeman, MT: Property and Environment Research Center.

Besley, Timothy, and Maitreesh Ghatak. 2006. "Public Goods and Economic Development." In *Understanding Poverty*, Abhijit Banerjee, Roland Behabou, and Dilip Mookherjee, eds. Oxford, UK: Oxford University Press, 285–302.

Brown, James R., J. Anthony Cookson, and Rawley Heimer. 2015. "Law and Finance Matter: Lessons from Externally Imposed Courts." Working Paper.

Carlson, Leonard A. 1981. *Indian, Bureaucrats, and Land: The Dawes Act and the Decline of Indian Farming*. Westport, CT: Greenwood Press.

Carlson, Leonard A. 1992. "Learning to Farm: Indian Land Tenure and Farming before the Dawes Act." In *Property Rights and Indian Economies*, Terry L. Anderson, ed. Lanham, MD: Rowman & Littlefield, 67–83.

Cookson, Anthony J. 2010. "Institutions and Casinos on American Indian Reservations: An Empirical Analysis of the Location of Indian Casinos." *Journal of Law and Economics* 3(4): 651–687.

Cookson, Anthony J. 2014. "Economic Consequences of Judicial Institutions: Evidence from a Natural Experiment." Working Paper.

Cooter, Robert D., and Wolfgang Fikentscher. 2008. "American Indian Law Codes: Pragmatic Law and Tribal Identity." *American Journal of Comparative Law* 56: 29–74.

Cornell, Stephen, and Joseph S. Kalt. 2000. "Where's the Glue? Institutional and Cultural Foundations of American Indian Economic Development." *Journal of Socio-Economics* 29: 443–470.

Dimitrova-Grajzl, Valentina, Peter Grajzl and A. Joseph Guse. 2014a. "Jurisdiction, Crime, and Development: The Impact of Public Law 280 in Indian Country." *Law and Society Review* 48(1): 127–160.

Dimitrova-Grajzl, Valentina, Peter Grajzl, A. Joseph Guse and Richard M. Todd. 2015. "Consumer Credit on American Indian Reservations." *Economic Systems* 39: 518–540.

Dixit, Avinash. 2003. "Trade Expansion and Contract Enforcement." *Journal of Political Economy* 111 (December): 1293–1317.

Flanagan, Tom, Christopher Alcantara, and Andre Le Dressay. 2010. *Beyond the Indian Act: Restoring Aboriginal Rights.* McGill University Press: Montreal, Canada.

Frye, Dustin and Dominic P. Parker. 2016. "Paternalism versus Sovereignty: The Long Run Economic Effects of the Indian Reorganization Act." In *Unlocking the Wealth of Indian Nations.* T.L. Anderson, ed. Lanham, MD: Rowman and Littlefield.

Getches, David H., Charles Wilkinson, and Robert A. Williams Jr. 1998. *Cases and Materials on Federal Indian Law.* St. Paul, MN: West Group.

Goldberg, Carole. 2010. "In Theory, in Practice: Judging State Jurisdiction in Indian Country." *Colorado Law Review* 81: 1027–1065.

Goldberg, Carole, and Heather Valdez Singleton. 2008. "Final Report: Law Enforcement and Criminal Justice under Public Law 280." U.S. Department of Justice, Washington, D.C. Document # 222585.

Goldberg-Ambrose, Carole. 1997. *Planting Tail Feathers: Tribal Survival and Public Law 280.* Los Angeles, CA: University of California.

Haddock, David D., and Robert Miller. 2006. "Sovereignty Can Be a Liability: How Tribes Can Mitigate the Sovereign's Paradox." In *Self-Determination: The Other Path for Native Americans,* T. L. Anderson, B. L. Benson, and T. E. Flanagan, eds. Stanford, CA: Stanford University Press, 194–213.

Harring, Sidney L. 1994. *Crow Dog's Case: American Indian Sovereignty, Tribal Law, and United States Law in the Nineteenth Century.* Cambridge: Cambridge University Press.

Krepps, Matthew B. 1992. "Can Tribes Manage their Own Timber Resources: The 638 Program and American Indian Forestry." In *What Can Tribes Do? Strategies and Institutions in American Indian Economic Development,* Stephen Cornell and Joseph P. Kalt, eds. Los Angeles, CA: University of California, 179–203.

Krepps, Matthew B., and Richard E. Caves. 1994. "Bureaucrats and Indians: Principal–Agent Relations and the Efficient Management of Tribal Forest Resources." *Journal of Economic Behavior and Organization* 24: 133–151.

Kuhn, Peter and Arthur Sweetman. 2002. "Aboriginals as Unwilling Immigrants: Contact, Assimilation and Labour Market Outcomes." *Journal of Population Economics* 15(2): 331–355.

Listokin, David, Robin Leichenko, and Juliet King. 2006. *Housing and Economic Development in Indian Country: Challenge and Opportunity.* New Brunswick, New Jersey: Center for Urban Policy Research.

McChesney, Fred S. 1992. "Government as Definer of Property Rights: Indian Lands, Ethnic Externalities, and Bureaucratic Budgets." In *Property Rights and Indian Economies,* Terry L. Anderson, ed. Lanham, MD: Rowman & Littlefield, 109–146.

McKinnon, Ronald, and Thomas Nechyba. 1997. "Competition in Federal Systems: The Role of Political and Financial Constraints." In *The New Federalism: Can the States Be Trusted?* John Ferjohn and Barry R. Weingast, eds. Stanford, CA: Hoover Institution Press, 3–58.

McLish, Thomas. 1988. "Tribal Sovereign Immunity: Searching for Sensible Limits." *Columbia Law Review* 88: 173–193.

Melton, Ada Pecos, and Jerry Gardner. 2000. "Public Law 280: Issues and Concerns for Victims of Crime in Indian Country," Albuquerque: American Indian Development Associates.

Morishima, Gary S. 1997. "Indian Forestry: From Paternalism to Self-Determination." *Journal of Forestry* 95(11): 4–9.

North, Douglass C. 1981. *Structure and Change in Economic History*. New York: Norton & Co.

Oates, Wallace E. 1999. "An Essay on Fiscal Federalism." *Journal of Economic Literature* 37(3): 1120–1149.

Ostrom, Elinor. 1990. *Governing the Commons: The Evolution of Institutions for Collective Action*. Cambridge: Cambridge University Press

Parker, Dominic P. 2012. "The Effects of Legal Institutions on Access to Credit: Evidence from American Indian Reservations." Dept. of Agricultural and Applied Economics, University of Wisconsin.

Roback, Jennifer. 1992. "Exchange, Sovereignty, and Indian–Anglo Relations." In *Property Rights and Indian Economies*, Terry L. Anderson, ed. Lanham, MD: Rowman & Littlefield, 5–26.

Trosper, Ronald L. 1978. "American Indian Ranching Efficiency." *American Economic Review* 68(4): 503–516.

Voight, Stefan, Michael Ebeling, and Lorenz Blume. 2007. "Improving Credibility by Delegating Judicial Competence – The Case of the Judicial Committee of the Privy Council." *Journal of Development Economics* 82: 348–373.

Wilkins, David E. 2002. "Tribal–State Affairs: American States as "Disclaiming" Sovereigns." In *The Tribes and the States*, B. A. Bays and E. H. Fouberg, eds. Lanham, MD: Rowman & Littlefield, 1–28.

4. Do profits promote pollution? The myth of the environmental race to the bottom

Robert K. Fleck and F. Andrew Hanssen

The ability to vote a bad government out of office is enough —
Karl Popper[1]

INTRODUCTION

The prospect of a "race to the bottom" in environmental policy has a powerful hold on the public mind. The idea is this: Firms prefer low levels of environmental regulation. Residents want their jurisdictions (countries, states, cities) to attract firms because firms provide jobs. As a result, jurisdictions compete for firms by offering weak environmental standards. Firms invariably gravitate toward the jurisdiction with the *weakest* environmental standard. All jurisdictions, therefore, end up offering the weakest environmental standard, even though each jurisdiction would benefit if all jurisdictions set higher standards.

On the surface, the idea has appeal. The basic premise appears reasonable—firms prefer to operate where costs are lower, and complying with environmental regulations may be costly. Furthermore, environmental disasters have occurred in some of the countries to which capital has been flowing. Consider, for example, China, the current poster child for bad environmental policy. Chinese environmental standards are appallingly lax and multinational firms have been flocking to China. Ergo, China suffers from an environmental race to the bottom.

Yet most economists demur, instead arguing that neither theory nor evidence supports the existence of a race to the bottom in environmental policy. Are economists simply turning a blind eye to competition's

---

[1] Popper (2012).

harmful effects, as they are often accused of doing? Maybe, but let us think a bit further. Consider China once again. Nearly all serious economists agree that environmental conditions in many parts of China are appalling, and that many Chinese suffer greatly as a result. But have China's bad environmental policies been motivated by a "race to the bottom" to attract multinational firms? The answer is no. Rather, the culprit is something altogether different—the fact that the Chinese government is freely able to enact policies counter to the desires and interests of its own people.

In this chapter, we will explain why economists find the idea of an environmental race to the bottom so implausible (even with respect to badly polluted countries like China). We will then show that at the root of most environmental problems, one finds not a race, but rather a government that is able to ignore the wishes of its people. Our goal is to convince readers that anyone concerned about the environment should focus not on combating apocryphal races (which are simply not happening), but rather on pushing governments to take the interests of their citizens into account when enacting environmental (and other) policies.

While persuading unrepresentative governments to engage in representative policy making is an ambitious task, the payoff—in reduced environmental degradation and increased social well-being—is potentially enormous. We cannot, of course, provide any simple recipes. However, we will outline a framework which can be used to think about the problem.

OVERVIEW AND ANALYSIS OF THE "RACE TO THE BOTTOM" ARGUMENT

The race to the bottom argument turns critically on the assumption that environmental standards are of paramount importance in firm location decisions. In fact, environmental standards matter less to most firms than do such things as taxes, quality of infrastructure, distance from suppliers and customers, and, especially, the quality of the workforce. Of course, environmental standards may matter greatly to certain firms—specifically, highly polluting firms (toxic waste disposal units, giant hog farms) for whom complying with environmental regulations is very costly. But highly polluting firms are not what most jurisdictions wish to attract, and the prospect of drawing a giant hog farm (for instance) is unlikely to spark a race to the bottom.[2]

---

[2] Competition among jurisdictions to *avoid* these kinds of businesses often leads to a race to the top (also known as NIMBY—"not in my backyard").

By contrast, the quality of the workforce is almost always critical— labor is by far the most costly input for the average firm.[3] And the need for a high quality workforce will directly influence what type of location a firm chooses. Quite obviously, workers prefer clean, beautiful settings to polluted, ugly ones. Consequently, a firm will find it easier to attract good workers if it locates in a clean, beautiful place.[4] Firms thus have a strong incentive to choose locations with good environmental conditions.

This is not a new phenomenon. During the Industrial Revolution, firms operating in unpleasantly dirty cities had to pay wages higher than those paid by firms located in the cleaner, more pleasant countryside.[5] In the mid-20th century, the impetus to clean up Pittsburgh, the most notoriously polluted U.S. city at the time, came not from environmental groups, but from firms (including those in the steel industry) who found it difficult to hire good managers given Pittsburgh's dirty condition.[6] Not surprisingly, scholars analyzing modern data find that people place great value on living in a clean environment.[7]

In short, firms are *not* inexorably drawn to locations with weak environmental standards. Quite the contrary: firms have a clear, profit-motivated reason to seek stringent environmental standards if stringent standards are what prospective employees prefer. In other words, firms need not be enlightened (or have any concern other than for profits) in order to care about the condition of the environment. In well-governed countries,

---

Interestingly, some states have, in response to local opposition to unpleasant but necessary activities (e.g., landfills), adopted laws allowing the state to override local efforts to prohibit such activities (Fischel 2001, 179–81). This is, of course, the antithesis of regulation by higher levels of government being necessary to prevent a race that induces a local lowering of environmental standards.

[3]   Compensation of employees is the largest component of input costs for the economy as a whole, and particularly for some of the most important sectors of the economy—private goods-producing industries, private services-producing industries, and information/communications/technology-producing industries (see Howells, Barefoot, and Lindberg 2006).

[4]   The idea that people value attractive settings very highly is, of course, something widely recognized and emphasized by environmentalists. Notably, the "wealth of nature" literature suggests that communities should treat the natural beauty of their locations as economic assets that can generate wealth (e.g., Rasker, Tirrell, and Kloepfer 1992; Power 1996).

[5]   See, e.g., Williamson's (1982) calculations of the degree to which higher infant mortality in cities required employers to pay higher wages in order to attract workers.

[6]   See, e.g., Fischel (2001, 167–70).

[7]   See, e.g., Chay and Greenstone's (2005) estimates of how much home buyers value air quality.

workers can freely change both place of residence and employer, and will do so in order to pursue more attractive working conditions. Workers' desires thus influence firms' desires, and if workers strongly prefer a clean environment, so, for the most part, will firms.

A REVIEW OF ECONOMIC MODELS

The preceding discussion suggests that environmental races to the bottom may be less plausible than they first appear.[8] We can be more precise if we turn to economic theory. A number of economic models have been developed to analyze races to the bottom (and related issues). Taken as a whole, these models predict that environmental races to the bottom are unlikely *unless citizens are poorly represented by their governments*. We will now review three of the most relevant of these models.

Charles Tiebout's (1956) model illustrates how the fact that individuals can move to new places when confronted by policies they do not like helps promote the optimal set of public policies. To take a simple example, suppose there are two people, one of whom values public parks while the other does not. As long as the two people are *mobile* (able to move between jurisdictions)—a central assumption of Tiebout's model—both can obtain the policy they wish. The person who values parks moves to a jurisdiction with more parks and higher tax rates (in order to maintain the parks). The person who does not value parks moves to a jurisdiction with no parks and lower tax rates (because no parks need be maintained).

Tiebout's model is quite straightforward, but nonetheless elucidates two very important phenomena. First, when residents are mobile, jurisdictions

---

[8] It is worth noting that economists have established the plausibility of races to the bottom in other policy arenas, simply not with respect to *environmental* policy. For example, when setting welfare policy, jurisdictions often face an incentive to establish ungenerous standards, so as to encourage welfare recipients to move to other jurisdictions (and to discourage potential welfare recipients from moving in). This was an important issue in the 1996 debate over welfare reform (e.g., Rosen 2005, 176). However, environmental policy differs in a crucial way from welfare policy: while ungenerous welfare standards *benefit* the residents of the jurisdiction enacting the standards (by lowering welfare expenses and thus taxes), lax environmental standards *harm* the residents of the jurisdiction enacting the standards (by making the air or water dirtier). The fact that residents suffer directly from the harm caused gives them a strong incentive to oppose excessively low environmental standards. (Indeed, as mentioned earlier, residents often have a NIMBY incentive to set *high* local environmental standards in order to shift pollution to other jurisdictions.)

either offer the desired mix of policies or lose people to alternative jurisdictions that do. Second, because people differ in the policies they desire, not every jurisdiction need offer the *same* policies (the same environmental standards, for example). Indeed, the "sorting" described by Tiebout is likely to lead to different environmental standards being enacted in different places, each with the support of its citizens.[9] This is quite contrary to the idea of a race.

William Fischel (1975) extended Tiebout's analysis to take the location decisions of firms into account. In the Fischel model, when firms manufacture goods, they create pollution which falls entirely within the jurisdiction where the firm is located and affects all residents equally. Firms are willing to pay a jurisdiction for the right to locate and pollute within its borders.[10] No jurisdiction will allow a firm to pollute unless the firm pays a fee at least equal to the environmental damage it causes.

Sorting then ensues: jurisdictions with residents who value environmental quality highly will allow few polluting firms and receive little in payments, while jurisdictions with residents who care relatively little about environmental quality will accept many polluting firms and receive more in payments. Both sets of residents end up with the (differing) policies they prefer. As in the original Tiebout model, the fact that residents can move to other jurisdictions if made unhappy ensures enactment of the desired policies. The fact that different jurisdictions enact different policies enables a larger number of people (with differing policy preferences) to be made happy.

The assumption that residents are mobile is central to the results of the Tiebout and Fischel models, and to the fact that in neither model is there a race to the bottom. By contrast, Wallace Oates and Robert Schwab (1988) assume that residents *cannot* move between jurisdictions. In this case, a race to the bottom *can* ensue.

In the Oates and Schwab model, a firm employs the residents of the jurisdiction in which it locates, so that residents receive higher wages if a firm chooses to locate in their jurisdiction. Jurisdictions compete for firms by setting taxes and environmental standards. A jurisdiction makes its residents best off if it competes for firms by lowering taxes, not by lowering environmental standards. However, if a jurisdiction decides to establish higher tax rates regardless, it must compensate the firm by

---

[9] Tiebout's model thus makes it clear that the existence of different environmental standards in different places is not *prima facie* evidence that one place (e.g., the locale with the weaker standard) has gotten it wrong.

[10] In the context of the race to the bottom arguments, one could interpret the "payment" as a certain number of jobs.

enacting environmental standards below the level preferred by its residents (or else the firm will choose a lower-tax location). Why would a jurisdiction choose higher taxes if it must then establish an environmental policy that residents like less than the higher tax revenues? A plausible reason is that policy makers benefit from the taxes even though residents do not. At the extreme, what Oates and Schwab call a tax might be termed a bribe.

Thus, competition for firms may indeed lead to overly lax environmental standards, as the Oates and Schwab model demonstrates, but only if the two following conditions hold: 1) policy makers do not act in the interest of their citizens; and 2) the citizens cannot easily move to another jurisdiction. If residents can either leave or "throw the rascals out," policy cannot differ by too much from what the residents desire. But when residents can neither leave nor replace self-serving government officials, bad policies—including sub-optimal environmental standards— are likely to follow. The root cause of the Oates and Schwab race is bad (unrepresentative) government, and bad government can persist only if people are unable to leave.[11]

UNREPRESENTATIVE GOVERNMENT AND BAD ENVIRONMENTAL POLICY

Consider what is perhaps the most obvious example of bad/unrepresentative government in recent history: the Soviet Bloc. The Soviet Union and its communist "allies" were notorious both for their undemocratic ways and for their aggressive attempts to prevent people from leaving. The two went hand in hand—the communist governments treated their citizens so badly that only walls and machine guns prevented a mass exodus.[12] If ever one would predict bad environmental policy, it would be in these circumstances, and communist countries had disastrous environmental records. Given that these were centrally planned economies, competition for firms—i.e., a race to the bottom—certainly does not explain the communists' appalling environmental record.[13]

---

[11] More generally, the ability of people to move to a well-governed country prevents their rulers from governing too badly (Fleck and Hanssen 2006).

[12] See, for example, Hirschman (1993, 179), who points out that East Germany lost *15 percent* of its population to West Germany between 1949 and 1961, before finally investing—massively—in devices intended to prevent emigration (including the Berlin Wall).

[13] On environmental problems in the Soviet Bloc, see, e.g., Sachs (1995). On the economics of central planning, see, e.g., Kornai (1992).

A large number of systematic empirical analyses have come to the same conclusion: Bad/unrepresentative governments implement bad environmental policies. One of the first researchers to test this idea was Roger Congleton (1992). He writes:

> The essential difference between authoritarian regimes and democracies is their decision-making procedure. Democracies make policy by counting the votes of ordinary citizens or their elected representatives. Authoritarian regimes only take account of the "votes" of an unelected elite, in the limit the "vote" of a single ruler. (413)

Because an authoritarian regime need consider only the wishes of an unelected elite (in the limit, a single ruler), it can get away with allowing far more pollution than the broader public would choose. Congleton analyzes a sample of 118 countries, and finds that more authoritarian countries are significantly more likely to establish weak environmental standards, and substantially less likely to sign international environmental treaties. Congleton concludes, "The empirical results support the contention that political institutions largely determine environmental regulation, rather than technological aspects of pollution control or market structure" (421).

Barrett and Graddy (2000) examine the relationship between civil and political liberties and several pollution measures in a number of countries. The authors write:

> As nations become richer, their citizens demand that the non-material aspects of their standard of living be improved. But if this reasoning is correct, then the observed levels of environmental quality will depend on more than a nation's prosperity. They will depend also on citizens being able to acquire information about the quality of their environment, to assemble and organize, and to give voice to their preferences for environmental quality; and on governments having an incentive to satisfy these preferences by changing policy, perhaps the most powerful incentive being the desire to get elected or re-elected. In short, they will depend on civil and political freedoms. (434)

Barrett and Graddy find that increases in civil and political liberties improve environmental performance, though the results vary somewhat with the particular pollution measure being investigated.[14]

Finally, unrepresentative governments tend to do a poor job of establishing

---

[14] There is similar evidence with respect to corruption. In their study of 63 countries, Fredriksson and Svensson (2003) find that more corruption is significantly associated with lax environmental regulations.

and protecting property rights (rulers may arbitrarily confiscate land, for instance). The poor enforcement of property rights creates the incentive to use natural resources inefficiently, and environmental degradation may follow. Consider logging. In countries where ownership of land and trees is insecure, there is an incentive to log immediately (while one can obtain the lumber) rather than waiting until the optimal moment (by which time one may have lost control of the land or someone else may have cut down the trees). Similarly, there is little incentive to preserve a forest or to replant logged trees if one expects the land may be taken away suddenly. In his study of the causes of deforestation, Robert Deacon (1994, 414) writes:

> Many observers have attributed this shrinkage [of forest cover in some countries in recent years] to population growth, the process of economic development, and misguided government policies. Much of the economic literature on deforestation stresses different factors—the importance of property rights and the role of ownership security in promoting conservation of forests and other natural assets.

Deacon conducts a statistical analysis of 120 countries, relating deforestation to the security of property rights, population pressure, and income growth. He finds that both population pressure and insecure property rights cause deforestation, and that the effect of population growth is greatest where property rights are insecure.[15]

In short, a large body of evidence links the quality of the environment to the quality of government. Governments that fail to represent their citizens' interests enact lax environmental policy, for reasons that have nothing to do with a race to the bottom.[16]

---

[15]   There are a number of other studies that reach similar conclusions. For example, Southgate, Sierra, and Brown (1991) find that security of land tenure has a negative relationship to the rate of deforestation in Ecuador. Anderson and Lueck (1992) show how the productivity of land on Indian reservations depends on the type of tenure: in short, where a fuller set of property rights can be held by individuals (rather than by more bureaucratically controlled trusts), land use is more productive.

[16]   Norton (2002) makes a similar argument in his analysis of the potentially adverse effects of population growth, showing that economic institutions have a much bigger influence on environmental degradation than does population growth per se, and that good institutions (i.e., good government) serve to mitigate most negative consequences of population growth on the environment.

TOPICS FROM CURRENT POLICY DEBATE

A race to the bottom in environmental policy is thus unlikely in theory and undemonstrated in practice. Where extremely lax environmental policies are enacted, the root cause is primarily that government officials can ignore the wishes of their citizens. To drive this point home, we will discuss several policy issues where environmentalists mistakenly attribute poor environmental outcomes to races to the bottom when the real culprit is unrepresentative government.[17]

Movements of Capital to Pollution Havens

In recent years, environmentalists have focused attention on alleged "pollution havens"—countries that set very low environmental standards in order to attract investment. Pollution havens are the logical result of an environmental race to the bottom. Yet there is little evidence that pollution havens exist. Again consider China, the country most often called a pollution haven. As Dean, Lovely, and Wang (2005) show, firms from developed countries (Organisation for Economic Co-operation and Development) engaging in joint ventures with Chinese partners tend to locate in provinces with relatively strict environmental standards (because such places tend to have skilled workers). In other words, Western firms are attracted by *stringent* environmental standards. This holds true even for joint ventures involving highly polluting industries. Thus, although the different parts of China may compete against each other for foreign investment, setting low environmental standards is not the means by which they compete. Low environmental standards actually repel, rather than attract, firms from wealthy countries. The same phenomenon has been documented for other parts of the world—flows of capital are, at most, weakly attracted to low environmental standards.[18]

Again, we are not claiming that developing countries have only minor pollution problems—they often have major problems, but those problems do not arise from efforts to attract foreign investment. Indeed, it is easy to see why serious pollution problems would repel investment.

---

[17] To keep our discussion at manageable length, we restrict ourselves to issues that have received attention from mainstream environmentalists (all the following examples have been gleaned from the Sierra Club's websites).

[18] See, e.g., Dean, Lovely, and Wang's (2005) review of the literature and Smarzynska and Wei's (2004) analysis of 25 countries in Eastern Europe and the former Soviet Union. Also see Antweiler, Copeland, and Taylor (2001).

Most obviously, water pollution is a major cause of death in developing countries around the world. As the World Bank (2005, 10) reports:

> Lack of clean water and basic sanitation is the main reason diseases transmitted by feces are so common in developing countries. In 1990, diarrhea resulted in 3 million deaths, 85 percent of them among children. In 2000, 1.2 billion people still lacked access to a reliable source of water that was reasonably protected from contamination.

The presence of feces in drinking water clearly arises from something other than an effort to attract foreign capital and entrepreneurs. After all, entrepreneurs will generally prefer clean water for themselves and their (otherwise frequently ill) employees.

So why are pollution problems so often severe in rapidly growing economies such as China's? Because even when unrepresentative governments deliver jobs, they do not necessarily deliver the policies their citizens want. In China, most people have benefitted greatly from the country's economic growth (which has been possible only because China improved its economic policies).[19] But China's people would also benefit from the improved environmental policies that more representative government would bring. As the *Economist* (2004a) explains:

> China is using its natural resources to lift the living standards of its people as rapidly as possible—as the developed world did (and still does) ... the concern is political: in democratic countries, affluence leads to demands for a cleaner environment. In China, there is no mechanism for people's wishes to influence government policy directly, unless (and until) the Communist Party loses its grip on power.

International Trade

Many environmentalists have expressed concern that a race to the bottom will be spurred by international trade. Some of these arguments simply miss the point.[20] However, even where the environmental effects of trade are cause for concern, the problem is not a race.

---

[19]   China's earlier economic policies were, of course, disastrous. For example, the Great Leap Forward caused such a dramatic decline in food production that millions died from starvation between 1959 and 1961 (see, e.g., Li and Yang 2005).

[20]   For example, Stephen Mills (2004), who directs the Sierra Club's international programs, writes:

> Because the United States has been relatively successful in promoting conservation efforts at home, it has exported much of the environmental burden caused

Consider, for example, the widely expressed worry that international trade promotes deforestation in third-world countries. As explained earlier, forests tend to be over-harvested where property rights are poorly defined—even people who prefer standing forests may engage in logging (without replanting) if they believe that someone else will log the forest anyway. It is true that increased trade can sometimes make things worse— if property rights to trees are poorly defined, and international trade increases the rate at which forests in timber-exporting countries are being cut (by increasing the price exporters receive for timber), deforestation may follow. However, the root problem is not trade. Indeed, when property rights are secure, the higher price of exported timber brought about by trade gives loggers an additional incentive to *conserve*, to ensure the survival of their forests by not overharvesting and by planting new trees.[21]

Environmental problems also result from what economists term "externalities"—costs that are "external" to the decision maker, and therefore not taken into account.[22] In plain language, there will be too much pollution when those choosing the level of pollution do not weigh the full effects. Externalities may arise in the production of commodities; for example, upstream logging can affect downstream residents by increasing flooding and/or decreasing water quality, and the destruction of forests can reduce habitat for birds that migrate from different countries.

If an increase in international trade increases logging in the presence of externalities, the corresponding rise in environmental damage may more than offset the benefits from the increased trade. But to address the problem, it is again essential to recognize that the root cause is neither a race to the bottom nor international trade, but the fact that some of the costs are external to the decision maker.[23] In this instance,

---

by its high levels of natural-resource consumption to developing countries. These countries—and the communities within them—are less capable of resisting exploitation, which causes a race to the bottom to attract foreign investors regardless of their environmental or labor policies.

Note that Mills seems to imply that *high* standards in the U.S. cause a race to the bottom in other countries. But this makes no sense—the logic of the race to the bottom argument posits that higher standards in the U.S. *reduce* the pressure on other countries to lower their standards.

[21]   Chichilnisky (1994) provides a detailed analysis of how the failure to establish property rights to natural resources can influence trade patterns and lead to undesirable environmental outcomes.

[22]   Any good introductory microeconomics textbook will explain externalities (e.g., Landsburg 2005).

[23]   For a recent study of how property rights and international trade affect rates of deforestation in different countries, see Ferreira (2004).

the "unrepresentativeness" of the policy making is due to the fact that one jurisdiction can shift costs to another—the citizens of the polluting jurisdiction may fully support the policy (since they do not bear the costs).

Resolving problems arising from externalities requires mediating between populations with differing interests, something we will discuss in more detail in the next section. Simply attempting to reduce competition for firms or restrict trade can easily increase, rather than decrease, environmental degradation—prohibiting imports (or increasing tariffs) generally raises domestic production of the otherwise-imported goods, and domestic production may create greater environmental damage than would production elsewhere.[24] Indeed, perhaps the most careful study yet done on the link between trade and environmental conditions finds that free trade is good for the environment (Antweiler, Copeland, and Taylor 2001). Hence, restricting trade for a foolish reason (e.g., out of fear of a race to the bottom in environmental regulation) will likely worsen environmental conditions.

Role of Special Interests

Environmental problems may also occur when policies are enacted to favor special interests. Consider, for example, the promotion of exports. Environmentalists have expressed concern about export subsidies, and with good cause. Carl Pope (2002), executive director of the Sierra Club, provides a clear explanation of how environmental degradation can result from a free trade agreement that prohibits the payment of cash subsidies to producers of exports, but does not prohibit implicit subsidies through excessively lax environmental standards.[25] This is a valid concern, but one must think carefully about the real source of the problem.

Subsidizing exporters is generally a very poor—and unrepresentative—policy (benefitting the politically influential exporting industry at the cost of greater harm to the broader public), and for other countries to respond with subsidies of their own just makes things worse for their own people.

---

[24] In addition, restricting competition for capital will generally reduce the demand for labor in poor countries and, thus, harm workers in those countries.

[25] In Pope's words, "The WTO system is biased. It favors the least environmentally protective methods for countries seeking to increase the market share of their producers." (Pope 2002, 62–6, 63.) Note the parallel to the Oates and Schwab model, in which a government lowers environmental standards for a firm instead of reducing the tax rate on the firm. In the scenario described by Pope, a government lowers environmental standards for a firm because the government cannot subsidize the firm with cash.

Thus, the root of the problem is not a race, but a government that caters to special interests rather than representing the general interests of its citizens. The best response is, as Pope recommends, to prohibit export subsidies of all kinds.[26]

Just as promoting exports can harm the environment, so can restricting imports. For example, past protection of the U.S. automobile industry from (mostly Japanese) competition left American consumers not only paying more for cars (both domestic and imported), but buying cars that used more gasoline than the (Japanese) alternatives, thus harming the environment.[27] Ironically, one of the most vocal proponents of protectionist policies of this type was Congressman Richard Gephardt, whom some have lauded as an environmental hero.[28] Yet Gephardt obtained his fame by leading the charge against Japanese manufacturers of fuel-efficient cars, thereby preventing American drivers from buying automobiles that would better conserve gasoline. Those who truly value the environment should be skeptical of protectionist measures promoted under the auspices of a "blue-green" coalition; i.e., blue collar workers and green environmentalists (e.g., Pope and Wage 2001). An advocate of industry-friendly protectionism is no environmentalist, and true environmentalists should not allow their misplaced fears about trade-induced races to draw them into environmentally harmful alliances.

---

[26] Many other criticisms of international trade are voiced by environmentalists, and most rest on misunderstandings of basic economics. Frequently, the arguments are based on the premise exporting is desirable and importing is undesirable. This premise is plainly incorrect, as any good introductory economics textbook will demonstrate (e.g., Landsburg 2005). Note for example, that complaints about the harm that inexpensive imported corn does to Mexican farmers (e.g., Mills 2004) generally ignore the benefits of inexpensive corn to the many Mexicans who eat corn. In another example, the Sierra Club (1998) purports to explain "supply" and "demand" in the international timber market, but demonstrates only a complete misunderstanding of supply and demand models.

[27] For example, the so-called "Voluntary Export Restraints" (VERs) initiated in 1981 reduced imports from Japan, increased sales of American cars, and raised prices paid by consumers (see, e.g., Berry, Levinsohn, and Pakes 1999). The VERs also led to an increase in the horsepower and size of Japanese cars sold in the U.S. (see, e.g., Feenstra 1988).

[28] Writing in *Sierra Magazine*, McManus (2002) describes Gephardt as one of the "champions of environmental laws." Also see, e.g., Sierra Club (2001). *The Economist* (2004b) summed up Gephardt as follows: "For much of his career, Mr. Gephardt was America's foremost protectionist."

Pollution Standards in the United States

Concern is also expressed that races to the bottom may arise in purely domestic settings. Consider, for example, water pollution standards in the U.S. Should the federal government set national-level standards and/or establish guidelines for state-level policy? The answer depends on the nature of the problem—standards set solely by states may be too lax if some or all of the damage done by water pollution can be shifted to other states. For instance, residents of Oklahoma recently complained that waste from Arkansas chicken farms is fouling the Illinois River watershed, which is a major source of drinking water for Oklahoma.[29] Thus, Oklahoma would benefit from stronger environmental policies in Arkansas. However, the issue once again is not a race to the bottom, but rather the fact that the government of one state (Arkansas) weighs only some of the costs (i.e., only the *in-state* harm of pollution) when deciding how much pollution to allow. Society as a whole will gain if policy makers in Arkansas consider *all* the costs when setting policy, and this is true regardless of whether Arkansas is "racing" to attract firms (it would be true even if Arkansas were a hermit kingdom, completely isolated from the rest of the world except for its water flow).

What if water pollution remains entirely within state boundaries? Some environmentalists have worried that states will race to the bottom when setting pollution standards for "isolated, non-navigable intrastate waters."[30] However, if the bodies of water are located entirely within the state, the pollution will harm residents of the state that sets the policy. And if the harm from the pollution is large (and in many cases it may be), residents are likely to oppose allowing it. Only if residents are poorly represented—if elected officials can act counter to the wishes of their constituents—will federal policy be needed.

WHAT CAN BE DONE TO IMPROVE REPRESENTATION IN GOVERNMENTS?

We have argued that environmentalists should stop worrying about races to the bottom and, instead, focus their attention on improving the respon-

---

[29] See the *Economist* (2005).
[30] For example, Sierra Club, Maine Chapter (2005) states: "The CWA's [Clean Water Act's] federal floor 'levels the playing field' and prevents the proverbial 'race to the bottom' so that states that do act to protect their waters from pollution and destruction are not placed at a competitive disadvantage by those states who choose not to do so."

siveness of governments to the interests of the people. One key task is to increase the influence of the disenfranchised, especially in the developing world. Many environmental organizations already place great emphasis on this essential, albeit very difficult goal.[31] Those efforts deserve applause for many reasons—one of which is that they will improve environmental quality. Because we have little to add on that front, we will focus instead on a related (albeit more narrow) issue: the advantages and disadvantages of alternative ways of democratic decision making.

Economists and political scientists agree that the effective organization of government decision making requires balancing two needs: 1) encouraging politicians to represent their constituents; and 2) effectively managing externality problems. It would, of course, be nice if one could rely on democratic elections to choose politicians who act only in the general interest and set policy with all costs and benefits in mind, but that is an unrealistic expectation even for representative governments.[32] Thus, one must choose between imperfect alternatives when considering governing institutions. In balancing the two needs mentioned above, an important choice is the degree of decentralization in decision making. Because local levels of government are often better linked to constituent interests, while higher levels of government are typically better placed to address externalities, the optimal degree of decentralization depends on the nature of the problem: Is the concern poor representation of constituents at the national level, or is it local jurisdictions ignoring the costs they impose on other jurisdictions?[33]

These tradeoffs demonstrate why haphazardly blaming races to the bottom for environmental problems can be counter-productive. To take a concrete example, consider public forest land. Economists and environmentalists agree that the U.S. Forest Service has often badly mismanaged national forests (at times spending the public's money to cut down trees!).[34] Evidence amassed in several studies suggests that at least some

---

[31]   See, for example, Sierra Club (2005). It is important to note that even in democracies, those who do not vote will generally be less well represented than those who do—see Hamilton (1993) on the relationship between who votes and who bears the costs of hazardous waste facilities.

[32]   Even well-intentioned politicians must pay more attention to those within their jurisdictions than to those without (otherwise, the politicians will not be in office for long).

[33]   For more on this issue, see, e.g., Rosen's (2005) Chapter 20 or Oates (1999). See also Adler (2001), who examines wetlands protection and concludes that even when interstate externalities are present, state-level action may be sufficient to overcome them.

[34]   See, e.g., O'Toole (1988), Leal (1995), and Sedjo (2000).

state governments manage state forest land much better than the federal government manages federal forests.[35] It would be a big mistake if, out of misguided concern about a race to the bottom between states, control of state forests were transferred to the federal government. Of course, in cases where one state's policies affect another state's forests—such as in preserving habitat for migratory species or regulating airborne pollution—the federal government may indeed have a role to play (at a minimum, by providing a clear set of rules under which states can negotiate and enforce agreements to preserve habitat and prevent excessive pollution).

CONCLUSION

Environmentalists, politicians, and scholars often express concern about "races to the bottom" in environmental standards. In this chapter, we have argued that worries about environmental policy being too lax may be well founded, but not because of a race. Rather, the potential for overly lax environmental standards arises from governments failing to act in the interests of their people—that is, from unrepresentative government. Even if competing for firms, governments that are broadly representative of citizens' interests will not engage in environmental races to the bottom. By contrast, governments that pay little attention to citizens' interests often implement overly lax environmental standards, even if they are *not* competing for firms.

Focusing on root causes can help promote solutions that actually improve the environment. The need is certainly great—the world has a multitude of serious environmental problems, and each year many people die as a result of lax environmental policy. Blaming a race to the bottom pushes attention away from where it should be: on governments that fail to represent the interests of their citizens.

---

[35]   Leal (1995) compares the management of state forest land in Minnesota and Montana to the management of federal forests in those states and finds that the state forest lands are far better managed. State politicians have more reason to be concerned with bad policy in state forests, and the reason is straightforward. When it comes to, say, building excessive logging roads through forests, Montanans care far more about wasting Montanans' money in Montana forests than they care about wasting other taxpayers' money in Montana forests. This is not to say that state forests (or more generally state lands) are uniformly well managed, but it is clear that anyone concerned with the management of public lands should consider *both* the advantages and disadvantages of assigning management responsibility to more localized levels of government.

REFERENCES

Adler, Jonathan H. 2001. The Ducks Stop Here? The Environmental Challenge to Federalism. *Supreme Court Economic Review* 9: 205–41.

Anderson, Terry L., and Dean Lueck. 1992. Land Tenure and Agricultural Productivity on Indian Reservations. *Journal of Law and Economics* 35: 427–54.

Antweiler, Werner, Brian R. Copeland, and M. Scott Taylor. 2001. Is Free Trade Good for the Environment? *American Economic Review* 91: 877–908.

Barrett, Scott, and Kathryn Graddy. 2000. Freedom, Growth, and the Environment. *Environment and Development Economics* 5: 433–56.

Berry, Steven, James Levinsohn, and Ariel Pakes. 1999. Voluntary Export Restraints on Automobiles: Evaluating a Trade Policy. *American Economic Review* 89: 400–30.

Chay, Kenneth Y., and Michael Greenstone. 2005. Does Air Quality Matter? Evidence from the Housing Market. *Journal of Political Economy* 113: 376–424.

Chichilnisky, Graciela. 1994. North–South Trade and the Global Environment. *American Economic Review* 84: 851–74.

Congleton, Roger D. 1992. Political Institutions and Pollution Control. *Review of Economics and Statistics* 74: 412–21.

Deacon, Robert T. 1994. Deforestation and the Rule of Law in a Cross-Section of Countries. *Land Economics* 70: 414–30.

Dean, Judith M., Mary E. Lovely, and Hua Wang. 2005. Are Foreign Investors Attracted to Weak Environmental Regulations? Evaluating the Evidence from China. World Bank Policy Research Working Paper 3505. Washington, DC.

Economist. 2004a. No Economic Fire Without Smoke? Exaggeration of China's Environmental Problems Does Not Help to Resolve Them. July 8. Online: www.economist.com/books/displaystory.cfm?story_id=E1_NRJGJJD (cited June 2007).

Economist. 2004b. The Nearly Man. January 22. Online: www.economist.com/world/na/displaystory.cfm?story_id=E1_NPSPNJT (cited June 2007).

Economist. 2005. Watch that Bird's Rear. July 14. Online: www.economist.com/world/na/displaystory.cfm?story_id=E1_QTSQVVV (cited June 2007).

Feenstra, Robert C. 1988. Quality Change under Trade Restraints on Japanese Autos. *Quarterly Journal of Economics* 103: 131–46.

Ferreira, Susana. 2004. Deforestation, Property Rights, and International Trade. *Land Economics* 80: 174–93.

Fischel, William A. 1975. Fiscal and Environmental Considerations in the Location of Firms in Suburban Communities. In *Fiscal Zoning and Land Use Controls*, eds. Edwin S. Mills and Wallace E. Oates. Lexington, MA: Heath-Lexington Books, 119–74.

Fischel, William A. 2001. *The Homevoter Hypothesis: How Home Values Influence Local Government Taxation, School Finance, and Land-Use Policies.* Cambridge, MA: Harvard University Press.

Fleck, Robert K., and F. Andrew Hanssen. 2006. How Bad Can a Government Be? Potential Exit and the Quality of National Governments. Working Paper. Montana State University, Bozeman, Montana.

Fredriksson, Per G., and Jakob Svensson. 2003. Political Instability, Corruption and Policy Formation: The Case of Environmental Policy. *Journal of Public Economics* 87: 1383–405.

Hamilton, James T. 1993. Politics and Social Costs: Estimating the Impact of Collective Action on Hazardous Waste Facilities. *Rand Journal of Economics* 24: 101–25.

Hirschman, Albert O. 1993. Exit, Voice, and the Fate of the German Democratic Republic: An Essay in Conceptual History. *World Politics* 45: 173–202.

Howells, Thomas F., III, Kevin B. Barefoot, and Brian M. Lindberg. 2006. Annual Industry Accounts: Revised Estimates for 2003–2005. *Survey of Current Business* (December): 45–55. Online: www.bea.gov/scb/pdf/2006/12december/1206_indyaccts.pdf (cited March 2007).

Kornai, János. 1992. *The Socialist System: The Political Economy of Communism.* Princeton: Princeton University Press.

Landsburg, Steven E. 2005. *Price Theory & Applications*, 6e. Mason, OH: Thomson.

Leal, Donald R. 1995. Turning a Profit on Public Forests. PERC *policy series*, PS-4. Online: www.perc.org/perc.php?id=639 (cited May 2007).

Li, Wei, and Dennis Tao Yang. 2005. The Great Leap Forward: Anatomy of a Central Planning Disaster. *Journal of Political Economy* 113: 840–77.

McManus, Reed. 2002. Ten Reasons to Oppose the Fast Track. *Sierra Magazine* (March/April). Online: www.sierraclub.org/sierra/200205/lol3.asp (cited January 2007).

Mills, Stephen. 2004. The Sierra Club's Stance on Immigration. *Sierra Magazine* (November/December). Online: www.sierraclub.org/sierra/200411/sidebar2.asp (cited January 2007).

Norton, Seth W. 2002. Population Growth, Economic Freedom, and the Rule of Law. PERC *policy series* PS-24.

Oates, Wallace E. 1999. An Essay on Fiscal Federalism. *Journal of Economic Literature* 37: 1120–49.

Oates, Wallace E., and Robert M. Schwab. 1988. Economic Competition among Jurisdictions: Efficiency Enhancing or Distortion Inducing? *Journal of Public Economics* 35: 333–54.

O'Toole, Randal. 1988. *Reforming the Forest Service.* Washington, DC: Island Press.

Pope, Carl. 2002. Race to the Top: The Biases of the WTO Regime. Harvard International Review. *Environment* 23(4). Online: hir.harvard.edu/articles/957/1/ (cited May 2007).

Pope, Carl, and Robert Wage. 2001. *Green Growth: Agenda for a Just Transition to a Sustainable Economy.* Online: www.ourfuture.org/projects/next_agenda/ch9.cfm (cited April 2007).

Popper, Karl. 2012. *The Open Society and its Enemies.* London: Routledge.

Power, Thomas M. 1996. *Lost Landscapes and Failed Economies: The Search for a Value of Place.* Washington, DC: Island Press.

Rasker, Ray, Norma Tirrell, and Deanne Kloepfer. 1992. *The Wealth of Nature: New Economic Realities in the Yellowstone Region.* Washington, DC: Wilderness Society.

Rosen, Harvey S. 2005. *Public Finance*, 7th edn. Boston: McGraw-Hill.

Sachs, Jeffrey. 1995. Economies in Transition: Some Aspects of Environmental Policy. Environment Discussion Paper No. 1. Central and Eastern Europe Environmental Economics and Policy Project.

Sedjo, Roger A., ed. 2000. *A Vision for the U.S. Forest Service: Goals for Its Next Century.* Washington, DC: Resources for the Future.

Sierra Club. 1998. Responsible Trade: Don't Trade Away Our Forests. April 29. Online: www.sierraclub.org/trade/environment/pests.asp (cited April 2007).

Sierra Club. 2001. Responsible Trade: Stop Fast Track. December 6. Online: www.sierraclub.org/trade/fasttrack/fight.asp (cited April 2007).

Sierra Club. 2005. Environmental Justice. date. Online: www.sierraclub.org/policy/conservation/justice.asp (cited April 2007).

Sierra Club, Maine Chapter. 2005. Marine & Coastal Issues. Online: maine.sierraclub.org/marine_-_clean_water_act.htm (cited May 2007).

Smarzynska, Beata K., and Shang-Jin Wei. 2004. Pollution Havens and Foreign Direct Investment: Dirty Secret or Popular Myth. *Contributions to Economic Analysis & Policy* 3, No. 2, Article 8.

Southgate, Douglas, Rodrigo Sierra, and Lawrence Brown. 1991. *World Development* 19: 1145–51.

Tiebout, Charles. 1956. A Pure Theory of Local Expenditures. *Journal of Political Economy* 64: 416–24.

Williamson, Jeffrey G. 1982. Was the Industrial Revolution Worth It? Disamenities and Death in 19th Century British Towns. *Explorations in Economic History* 19: 221–45.

World Bank. 2005. *World View.* Online: www.worldbank.org/data/wdi2004/Section1–intro.pdf (cited April 2007).

5. Uncontrolled experiments from the laboratories of democracy: traditional cash welfare, federalism, and welfare reform

Jonah B. Gelbach[1]

> It is one of the happy incidents of the federal system that a single courageous state may, if its citizens choose, serve as a laboratory; and try novel social and economic experiments without risk to the rest of the country.
> —Justice Louis Brandeis, *New State Ice Co. v. Liebmann*, 285 U.S. 262, 311 (1932).

I. INTRODUCTION

The story of the rise and fall of traditional cash welfare in the United States is complex in some ways, but straightforward in others. For roughly six decades, the primary source of federal cash assistance to the non-elderly, non-disabled poor was the Aid to Families with Dependent Children (AFDC) program. While the details of the program's rules could be technical and complex, AFDC was basically a check-cutting program. It was one intended to do little more than its name suggested—provide assistance to (low-income) families with dependent children. For its first three decades, the AFDC program forged a relatively low profile. In the mid-1960s, though, benefit levels began to rise, perhaps as a result of a structurally expanded federal role in AFDC funding. Caseloads rose, too. And perhaps as a result, the seeds of a political backlash were planted.

By the period between the late 1980s and the mid-1990s, many policy makers at both the state and federal levels were chafing at the program's

[1] This chapter was substantially completed in 2012, and I have not sought to update it substantively since then. I am grateful to numerous co-authors and colleagues for many conversations over the years concerning welfare policy and empirical research. Any mistakes that remain are of course my own.

relatively rigid rules. The "laboratories of democracy" concept proved useful in organizing opposition to the existing system, with states like Wisconsin and Michigan asking for and getting waivers—permission to use federal funds to operate programs with important structural differences from the AFDC program. Bill Clinton's election in 1992 brought more openness to such changes among Democrats, and in 1996 President Clinton made good on his earlier campaign promise to "end welfare as we know it"[2] by signing the Personal Responsibility and Work Opportunity Reconciliation Act (PRWORA),[3] which eliminated the AFDC program formally. In its place is the Temporary Assistance for Needy Children (TANF) program, the block-grant umbrella covering a patchwork of state programs.

News accounts and political (and policy) discussions brim with what can be called the triumphalist consensus concerning welfare reform. For example, read current Brookings scholar Ron Haskins, who played an important role in shepherding PRWORA through Congress in his role as a congressional staff member. Toward the end of his ten-years-thence account of the fight to enact PRWORA, in a chapter subtitled "The Triumph of Work," Haskins writes that "[s]weeping reforms have produced sweeping effects."[4] One would expect to see this claim followed with a list of some of these sweeping "effects" that welfare reform has "produced." But what comes in Haskins's next sentence is not a causal claim at all. Rather: "The evidence that welfare use *has dropped*, that work and earnings *have increased* and that child poverty *has fallen* is overwhelming."[5]

A moment's reflection reveals that overwhelming evidence of a thing's occurrence is not even trivial evidence that the thing has happened for any particular reason. As the discussion below suggests, the evidence for the triumphalist consensus largely boils down to a claim of *post-welfare-reform-ergo-propter-welfare-reform*. Long before the reforms of the 1990s, scholars knew that there was little empirical evidence that

---

[2] A.L. May, Clinton Avoids Jackson, Pledges to "End Welfare," *Atlanta Journal and Constitution*, September 10, 1992.

[3] Public Law 104-193; see 110 Stat. 2105 for text.

[4] Ron Haskins, *Work Over Welfare*, The Brookings Institution (2006), at 362.

[5] Haskins ibid., at 362 (my emphasis). I do not mean to pick on Haskins, who is a serious and fair-minded scholar. One can find many declarations of victory from across the political spectrum. See, for example, virtually anything written on welfare policy by the Heritage Foundation's resident opponent of anti-poverty efforts, Robert Rector, or Will Marshall, "Welfare Nostalgia Won't Help Poor," Progressive Policy Institute, August 26, 2011, available at http://progressivepolicy.org/welfare-nostalgia-won%E2%80%99t-help-poor.

AFDC's incentive effects were all that substantial. And so it should not be much of a surprise that eliminating AFDC does not seem to have caused very much of the major changes in welfare use and labor market outcomes at the root of *post-hoc* triumphalism. Welfare reform did occur against the backdrop of a booming labor market, and it also occurred at a time when social stigma directed at welfare use seems to have greatly increased; perhaps these are alternative explanations for the trends observed after welfare reform. It will be worth keeping such possibilities in mind through the balance of this chapter.

In Part II of this chapter, I lay out the basic structure of the old AFDC program and the ways in which the state and federal reforms of the 1990s transformed federally funded cash assistance. I will not attempt a comprehensive review of the vast micro-econometric literature on the incentive effects of both the AFDC program and its post-reform successors.[6] But where appropriate, I discuss general conclusions and some specific findings on the behavioral effects of both the old and new programs. While empirical evidence certainly suggests the AFDC program had incentive effects, it hardly justifies the extremity of the negative views held by many. The program did not eliminate poverty, to be sure. But given its basic structure and funding levels, it is unreasonable to have expected it to. And while the increase in employment of low-skilled single mothers following welfare reform surprised many observers, the common refrain that welfare reform "worked" is built on notably shaky empirical ground, a point revisited in Part IV.

In Part III, I evaluate welfare reform from the perspective of Justice

---

[6]   There are many excellent reviews already. Among them are Robert Moffitt, Incentive Effects of the U.S. Welfare System: A Review (1992) 30(1) *Journal of Economic Literature* 1; Hilary Williamson Hoynes, Work, Welfare, and Family Structure: What Have We Learned?, in *Fiscal Policy: Lessons From Economic Research*, ed. Alan Auerbach, MIT Press (1997), 101–46; Robert A. Moffitt, ed., *Welfare, the Family, and Reproductive Behavior: Research Perspectives*, Committee on Population, National Research Council (1998); and Robert Moffitt, The Temporary Assistance for Needy Families Program, in *Means-Tested Transfers in the U.S.*, ed. R. Moffitt (2003). For reviews focusing on the effects of welfare reform, see Rebecca M. Blank, Evaluating Welfare Reform in the United States (2002) 40(4) *Journal of Economic Literature* 1105, 1106; Jeffrey Grogger and Lynn A. Karoly, *Welfare Reform: Effects of a Decade of Change*, Harvard University Press (2005); Rebecca Blank's chapter, What We Know, What We Don't Know, and What We Need to Know about Welfare Reform, in James P. Ziliak, ed., *Welfare Reform and its Long-Term Consequences for America's Poor*, Cambridge University Press (2009); and Janet M. Currie, *The Invisible Safety Net: Protecting the Nation's Poor Children and Families*, Princeton University Press (2008).

Brandeis's laboratories metaphor, taking an atypically jaded view of the devolution of the 1990s. Given the vast array of differences in state welfare plans, the reforms of the 1990s might best be thought of as uncontrolled experimentation, undermining the Brandeisian notion of states as useful laboratories.

In Part IV, I present some empirical evidence from Connecticut's Jobs First welfare reform plan, which was initially implemented as an AFDC waiver and subsequently formed the core of Connecticut's post-PRWORA welfare system. This evidence suggests that the nuts and bolts of welfare reform—actual programmatic differences—had surprisingly little to do with the late-1990s increase in employment among the disadvantaged. Moreover, Connecticut's welfare reform reduced income for at least some women, which implies that one's assessment of whether welfare reform "worked" is unavoidably normative. While I do not imagine that policy makers are likely to reintroduce AFDC, I believe that evidence from Connecticut (and similar evidence from other states)—together with the absence of any evidence that welfare reform explains much of the drop in caseloads or increase in employment observed over the periods research-ers have studied—calls for a reassessment of just how important welfare program details were in driving the changes of the late 1990s and early 2000s.[7]

II.   A BRIEF HISTORY OF NATIONAL CASH WELFARE POLICY

Section 401 of the Social Security Act of 1935 established the Aid to Dependent Children (ADC) program "[f]or the purpose of ena-bling each State to furnish financial assistance, as far as practicable under the conditions in such State, to needy dependent children."[8] Sixty years later, President Clinton signed the Republican Congress's Personal Responsibility and Work Responsibility Act of 1996, eliminating ADC's successor program, AFDC, and replacing it with TANF. PRWORA's clearly stated purposes departed substantially from the check-cutting

---

[7]   That leaves the important question of what does explain these changes. The booming late-1990s labor market is one explanation, though the boom did end. Another possible explanation is hard-to-quantify cultural changes. Sorting out the relative contributions of these factors, if it is even possible, is far beyond the scope of this review.

[8]   Title IV of the Social Security Act of 1935, § 401 (accessed at http://www.ssa. gov/history/35activ.html).

objective of 1935's ADC program. Subsection (a) of 42 U.S.C.A. § 601 declares that

> The purpose of this part is to increase the flexibility of States in operating a program designed to—
> **(1)** provide assistance to needy families so that children may be cared for in their own homes or in the homes of relatives;
> **(2)** end the dependence of needy parents on government benefits by promoting job preparation, work, and marriage;
> **(3)** prevent and reduce the incidence of out-of-wedlock pregnancies and establish annual numerical goals for preventing and reducing the incidence of these pregnancies; and
> **(4)** encourage the formation and maintenance of two-parent families.

Thus, a program that started out with the simple purpose of delivering cash assistance became one with a mandate not only to provide that assistance—temporarily—but also to: end dependence, whether through work, job "preparation" or marriage; affect pregnancy; affect marriage; and affect household formation and structure. Lest anyone doubt PRWORA's decisive shift away from assistance as a matter of right, subsection (b) of 42 U.S.C.A. §601 trumpets that "This part shall not be interpreted to entitle any individual or family to assistance under any State program funded under this part."[9] Relatedly, it is no accident that TANF is not ANF: we will see that the "Temporary" qualifier does real work.

In section II.A, I begin by discussing the basics of the AFDC program, including a bit of the considerable programmatic history that transpired between the mid-1930s and the mid-1990s.[10] I also discuss empirical evidence on some important aspects of AFDC's behavioral effects. I offer some bigger-picture thoughts concerning AFDC in section II.B. In section II.C, I discuss some of the key reforms that state waivers and PRWORA introduced, relative to AFDC, and I also discuss empirical evidence on welfare reform's effects.

---

[9]   42 U.S.C.A. § 601(b).
[10]   This discussion is not meant to be exhaustive; I mean only to emphasize only some of the aspects of this history that seem most important from today's vantage point.

A.   The AFDC Program's Basic Features

1.   The individual level

At the individual level, the AFDC program can be thought of as a negative income tax (NIT) program with a categorical eligibility requirement.[11] I discuss the NIT part first and then turn to the categorical eligibility requirement.

a.   NIT aspects of AFDC   The simplest NIT program involves two parameters: a maximum grant amount, G_{AFDC}, and a benefit reduction rate, t_{AFDC}. A person with pre-tax-and-transfer earnings Y who faces this two-parameter NIT program will either receive a transfer payment from the government, or pay a tax to the government according to whether the quantity

$$P = GAFDC - tAFDCY \qquad (5.1)$$

is positive (transfer received) or negative (tax paid). It is conventional to use a name like "t" for the benefit reduction rate because it functions like an income tax by reducing the transfer payment P by t_{AFDC} dollars for every dollar of pre-transfer income earned. As such, a greater value of t_{AFDC} has all the same work disincentive effects of an income tax.

To visualize the incentive effects of an NIT program, consider panels (a) and (b) of Figure 5.1 below. The straight line in panel (a) shows the trade-off between hours of leisure, which are depicted on the horizontal axis, and post-tax-and-transfer consumption, which is depicted on the vertical axis, when there is no transfer program. For simplicity, I assume that there is a constant marginal tax rate at all possible earnings levels in this panel, so that its budget line has constant slope.

In panel (b), the solid line represents the budget line under an NIT program with maximum benefit level G_{NIT} and benefit reduction rate t_{NIT}. To the left of $H^{Breakeven}$, the person earns more than $Y^{Breakeven} = \frac{G_{NIT}}{t_{NIT}}$ and so she pays a positive tax to the government. To the right of $H^{Breakeven}$, the opposite is true, and so the worker receives a net transfer from the government. The amount of any tax or transfer is given by the height separating the solid and dashed lines.

Leaving aside categorical eligibility considerations to be discussed

---

[11]   For discussion of the NIT and U.S. welfare policy, see Robert A. Moffitt, The Negative Income Tax and the Evolution of U.S. Welfare Policy (2003) 17(3) *Journal of Economic Perspectives* (Summer, 2003), 119–40.

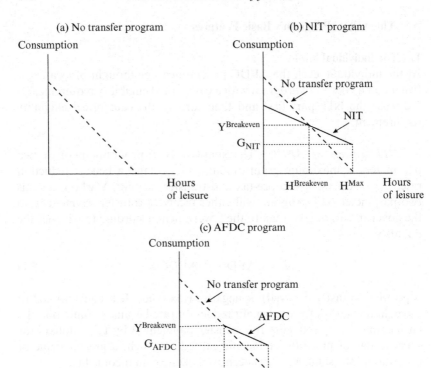

Figure 5.1 Simplified budget sets with no transfer program, with an NIT, and with AFDC

below, the AFDC program can be thought of as a modified version of the simple NIT program depicted in panel (b) of Figure 5.1. The first modification is that the AFDC program never actually required anyone to pay a tax back to the government.[12] Algebraically, this means the AFDC program involved a transfer payment equal to

---

[12] Of course, state and federal income tax systems might so require, but I am abstracting from those systems for purposes of this discussion. In practice, it is important to account for these systems, as well as the effects of various other means-tested transfer programs (e.g., Food Stamps, the EITC, housing assistance, Medicaid, and so on), but for simplicity I will not do so here. Detailed discussions of these issues appear in Gary Burtless and Jerry A. Hausman, The Effect of Taxation on Labor Supply: Evaluating the Gary Negative Income Tax Experiment (1978) 86(6) *Journal of Political Economy*, 1103–30; Michael Keane

$$P^- = \max[G_{AFDC} - t_{AFDC} \, Y, 0]. \tag{5.2}$$

Such a program transfers assistance to those with sufficiently low income—below the break-even level $Y^{Breakeven} = \frac{G_{AFDC}}{t_{AFDC}}$. Panel (c) of Figure 5.1 shows that the AFDC program results in the budget line given by the solid line when leisure hours are between H^{Max} and $H^{Breakeven}$, stapled onto the dashed line when leisure hours are less than $H^{Breakeven}$. The result is just the NIT program from panel (b) without the part of the NIT budget line to the left of $H^{Breakeven}$.

Notice that for a fixed value of t_{AFDC}, increases in the maximum grant G_{AFDC} cause $Y^{Breakeven}$ to rise. The more generous the maximum grant level, the greater the share of people who will be eligible for the program—and so also the share of people who will face work disincentives from the implicit tax t_{AFDC}. This effect is known as the "mechanical effect" on eligibility.[13]

Increases in t_{AFDC} reduce $Y^{Breakeven}$ and thus have the opposite effect on the share of people who will be program-eligible. While this reduces the mechanical effect, increases in t_{AFDC} also lead to greater work disincentives at the margin for those people who receive AFDC. This is a first type of behavioral effect of NIT programs: at the margin, they distort what labor economists think of as the labor–leisure decision.

A third type of effect is AFDC's so-called "entry effect." Consider panel (a) of Figure 5.2 below. A woman whose preferences are represented by an indifference map including the curve through point A optimally would choose not to participate in AFDC. Instead, she would work enough hours so that her labor income exceeds the breakeven level. By contrast, a woman whose indifference map includes the curve through point B optimally would choose to participate in AFDC, working few enough hours so that her labor income is below the break-even level.

No one with consistent preferences could have an indifference map containing both of these curves.[14] However, panel (b) illustrates the possibility that a woman's indifference map could contain a single indifference curve that is locally tangent to both points A and B. That means that

---

and Robert Moffitt (1998), A Structural Model of Multiple Welfare Program Participation and Labor Supply (1998) 39 *International Economic Review*, 553–89; and Moffitt (1992), *supra* note 6.

[13] See Orley Ashenfelter, Determining Participation in Income-Tested Social Programs (1983) 78(383) *Journal of the American Statistical Association*, 517–25.

[14] That is because, for people with consistent preferences, indifference curves never cross.

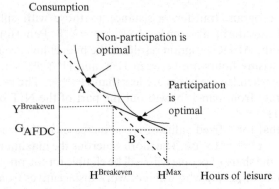

(a) Participation is Optimal, or Non-Participation is Optimal

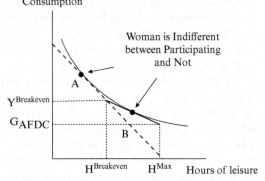

(b) Indifference between Participation & Non-Participation

Figure 5.2   Simplified budget sets with no transfer program, with an NIT, and with AFDC

such a woman would be exactly indifferent between choosing the leisure-consumption bundle at point A, which involves participating in AFDC, and choosing the leisure-consumption bundle at point B, which does not involve welfare participation. A woman whose indifference curve through point B is rotated slightly up and to the right would instead have a unique optimum that involved participation in AFDC. One whose indifference curve through point B is rotated slightly down and to the left would strictly prefer not to participate in AFDC. This example illustrates how the budget line non-linearity that AFDC creates will induce some people to reduce income in order to become eligible for welfare assistance. That is the entry effect.

Under AFDC, the federal government set the benefit reduction rate

t_{AFDC}, and states had no discretion to modify it. The benefit reduction rate was 100 percent from the program's inception until 1967, at which point it was reduced to 67 percent.[15] In 1981, Congress restored the benefit reduction rate to 100 percent.[16]

Under AFDC, states had wide discretion to set the maximum benefit level. Table 5.1 below shows state-specific maximum benefit levels for a family of three in 1996. Even in Alaska, whose $1,425 monthly maximum benefit level[17] was greatest among all states, the maximum benefit level is quite small in absolute terms—just 70.8 percent of the official federal poverty line for a family of three. The median monthly maximum benefit level in 1996, $625, was less than 40 percent of the federal poverty line. Mississippi's value of $200, which was the minimum across states, was less than one-eighth of the poverty line.

Maximum benefit levels were not always so low in relative terms. Panel (a) of Figure 5.3 shows the 10th percentile, the median, and the 90th percentile of the distribution of state monthly maximum benefit levels for a family of three for selected dates between 1970 and 1996, in constant 2010 dollars. The 90th percentile in 1996 was $802, far below the 90th percentile for 1970, which was $1,430. Both the median and the 10th percentile also fell substantially over this quarter-century period— from $985 to $541 for the median, and from $557 to $278 for the 10th percentile.

These reductions in monthly maximum benefit levels at these three points in the cross-state distribution were different in absolute-dollar levels, but of course the three points in the distribution start out at different absolute levels. In panel (b) of Figure 5.3, I scale each of the three time series so that its 1970 level equals 100. The resulting graph shows that trends in the three points in the cross-state distribution tracked each other closely in relative terms. By 1996, each of the three percentiles had lost between 40 and 50 percent of its real 1970 value. Thus, AFDC maximum benefit levels fell throughout the cross-state distribution.

b.   Effects on labor supply and welfare participation   As Justice Brandeis surely would have appreciated, the substantial variation of benefit levels across states and over time formed the backbone of the literature on AFDC's incentive effects. As noted above, basic labor supply theory

---

[15]   See Moffitt (2003), *supra* note 11, at 131.
[16]   Ibid.
[17]   All dollar figures are expressed in 2010 dollars, using CPI-U to inflate, unless stated otherwise.

Table 5.1   Maximum benefit for a family of three, 1996

State	Nominal 1996 Dollars[a]	Real 2010 Dollars[b]	As Share of Poverty Line[c]
Minimum	*120*	*200*	*11.5*
Median	*377*	*625*	*37.3*
Maximum	*923*	*1,425*	*70.8*
Alabama	164	270	15.7
Alaska	923	1,425	70.8
Arizona	347	581	33.3
Arkansas	204	343	19.6
California	596	983	58.2
Colorado	356	600	40.4
Connecticut	636	1,030	61.0
Delaware	338	566	32.4
DC	415	705	40.3
Florida	303	506	29.1
Georgia	280	459	26.8
Hawaii	712	1,194	59.4
Idaho	317	531	30.4
Illinois	377	575	36.1
Indiana	288	481	27.6
Iowa	426	688	40.8
Kansas	429	691	41.1
Kentucky	262	456	25.1
Louisiana	190	325	18.2
Maine	418	731	40.1
Maryland	373	625	35.8
Massachusetts	565	905	54.2
Michigan*	459	782	44.0
Minnesota	532	863	51.0
Mississippi	120	200	11.5
Missouri	292	475	28.0
Montana	438	732	40.7
Nebraska	364	605	34.9
Nevada	348	567	33.4
NH	550	852	52.7
NJ	424	678	40.7
NM	389	652	37.3
NY**	703	955	55.3
NC	272	413	26.1
ND	431	719	41.3
Ohio	341	585	32.7
Oklahoma	307	528	29.4
Oregon	460	785	44.1

Table 5.1   (continued)

State	Nominal 1996 Dollars[a]	Real 2010 Dollars[b]	As Share of Poverty Line[c]
Pennsylvania	421	714	40.4
RI	554	878	53.1
SC	200	335	19.2
SD	430	664	41.2
Tennessee	185	314	17.7
Texas	188	314	18.0
Utah	426	692	40.8
Vermont	633	988	62.9
Virginia	354	570	33.9
Washington	546	892	52.3
WV	253	434	24.3
Wisconsin	517	857	49.6
Wyoming	360	542	34.5

Note: *For Wayne County only. **Excluding Suffolk County.

Sources:
a   ACF, *Aid to Families with Dependent Children: The Baseline*, June 1998, Table 5.7 http://aspe.hhs.gov/hsp/afdc/baseline/5benefits.pdf.
b   Ibid., Table 5.7, with CPI adjustments based on CPI index values of 156.9 for 1996 and 218.056 for 2010 (downloaded from ftp://ftp.bls.gov/pub/special.requests/cpi/cpiai.txt).
c   Ibid., Table 5.9 http://aspe.hhs.gov/hsp/afdc/baseline/5benefits.pdf.

suggests that a more generous maximum benefit level should lead to more welfare participation and less paid work.[18] Moffitt's (1992) review of the empirical evidence on this question suggests that the literature finds statistically significant effects, but that they are not large. Crucially, he reports that estimated entry effects are sufficiently small so that "most AFDC women would, apparently, be poor even in the absence of the AFDC program."[19] Indeed, estimates in Moffitt (1983) imply that characteristics like age and education are more important predictors of labor market and welfare participation outcomes than are welfare program parameters like the benefit reduction rate; he writes that "virtually all of

---

[18]   My discussion of welfare's effects on labor supply here is necessarily brief; for more details, see, e.g., Robert A. Moffitt, "Welfare Programs and Labor Supply," Chapter 34 in 4 *Handbook of Public Economics*, A.J Auerbach and M. Feldstein, eds (2002).
[19]   Moffitt (1992), *supra* note 6, at 56.

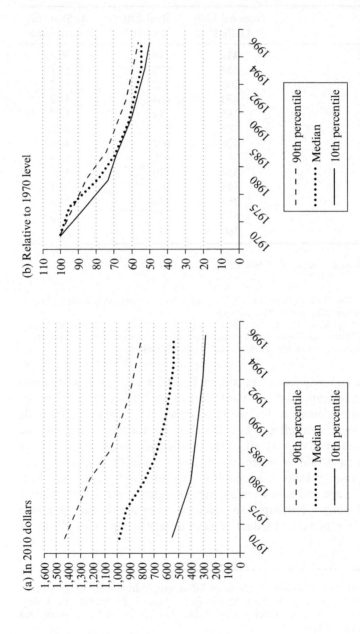

Source: ACF, *Aid to Families with Dependent Children: The Baseline*, June 1998, Table 5.6, http://aspe.hhs.gov/hsp/afdc/baseline/5benefits.pdf, provides benefit levels in real 1996 dollars. I adjusted these to 2010 dollars using CPI-U numbers from ftp://ftp.bls.gov/pub/special.requests/cpi/cpiai.txt.

Figure 5.3   Trends in real maximum benefit levels for family of three, 1970–1996

these nonprogram changes have a far greater effect on labor supply than the program changes that have been the focus of the analysis."[20]

Given the relatively small labor supply effects of the welfare system, it is natural to wonder what does explain most of the variation over time in AFDC use. One alternative explanation is the mechanical one I discussed in connection with Figure 5.2. There are many disadvantaged people—in labor economics terms, people with low marginal products—and even in the absence of the welfare system, many of them would work little, or they would earn little despite working considerably more than a little. The expansion of the AFDC system would have made many of these people eligible for public assistance even without affecting their behavior much. If this explanation is largely correct, then the AFDC program induced only small economic costs (over and above the costs of raising the tax revenue needed to fund the program).

A second explanation is that welfare use is sensitive to labor market conditions. There is compelling evidence from some high-quality studies that this is true.[21] By itself, though, this explanation does poorly in explaining long run trends. As Figure 5.4 shows, the annual average of the number of monthly AFDC recipients rose sharply during the boom of the late 1960s, leveled off during the macroeconomic slowdowns of the 1970s, stayed roughly constant throughout the 1980s, and then began to increase in the late 1980s. Of course, there is no reason why one should seek only a single explanation for a decades-long trend in welfare use, and a combination of the mechanical and labor market explanations seems more promising than either explanation on its own.

A third explanation involves what economists would call endogenous preferences and other social scientists might call cultural change. Moffitt (1992) notes, somewhat skeptically, that "It is ... sometimes argued that there was a reduction in the stigma of welfare receipt over [the late 1960s and early 1970s] as AFDC came to be viewed as a 'right.'"[22] Supreme Court decisions protecting eligibility for AFDC are one potential source,

---

[20]   Robert Moffitt, An Economic Model of Welfare Stigma (1983) 73(5) *American Economic Review* 1023, 1033.

[21]   See, for example, Hilary Williamson Hoynes, Local Labor Markets and Welfare Spells: Do Demand Conditions Matter? (Aug. 2000) 82 *Review of Economics and Statistics* 351; Jacob Alex Klerman and Steven J. Haider, A Stock-Flow Analysis of the Welfare Caseload (2004) 39 *Journal of Human Resources* 865.

[22]   Moffitt (1992) *supra* note 6 at 8.

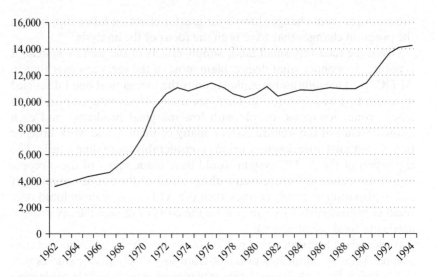

Source: Number of welfare recipients: my tabulations from Table 2.1 of ACF,
Aid to Families with Dependent Children: The Baseline, http://aspe.hhs.gov/hsp/afdc/
baseline/2caseload.pdf.

*Figure 5.4   Annual average of monthly number of AFDC recipients,
1962–1994 (in 1000s)*

or perhaps only a reflection, of such a reduction in stigma that should be
familiar to legal scholars.[23]

The culture explanation might do some useful work in the more recent
period of retrenchment in government's commitment to assisting welfare
families. President Reagan made potent use of the "welfare queen"
symbol, and by the 1990s supporting welfare was the sort of thing political

---

[23]   For example, see *Goldberg v. Kelly,* 397 U.S. 254, 264 (1970) (holding
that procedural due process requires an in-person pre-termination evidentiary
hearing before welfare benefits may be discontinued, because "termination
of aid pending resolution of a controversy over eligibility may deprive an
eligible recipient of the very means by which to live while he waits"); *Shapiro
v. Thompson,* 394 U.S. 618 (1969) (holding that states may not deny welfare
applications solely on the basis of an applicant's having resided in-state for
less than one year); *King v. Smith,* 392 U.S. 309, 314 (1968) (finding invalid on
statutory grounds an Alabama regulation, which deemed a man a "substitute
father" of a mother's children if they engaged in "'frequent' or 'continuing'
sexual relations"—defined variously as weekly or possibly only semi-annually,
and which would have prevented AFDC eligibility by dint of the "substitute
father's" presence in the household unit).

consultants might equate with proposing cuts in military spending: some politicians did it, but those with ambitions outside of safely liberal districts did so at their peril. AFDC had been a favorite target among those on the right at least since Charles Murray's 1984 book *Losing Ground*, and the program had become a political pinata by the time of the 1994 Republican Congressional victories.[24]

Evaluations of President Clinton's political success often pay homage to his choice to sign PRWORA. The legislation was both the product of a Republican Congress and far outside what would have been considered politically viable, say, ten years before—which itself was a time when Republicans controlled both the White House and the Senate. There is no question that American politics turned sharply against welfare over this period, and so it is not unreasonable to speculate that American culture might have as well. Such an "outward shift in welfare stigma" would provide an additional reason for the large reduction in caseloads, over and above changes in welfare programs' incentive and entitlement structure and the boom of the 1990s. Unfortunately, the extent of stigma and its impact on behavior are difficult to measure except in the most indirect ways,[25] so this hypothesis may be untestable as a practical matter.

c. Categorical eligibility and effects on family structure Before PRWORA, maximum benefit levels in all states increased when the number of people in the AFDC family unit did. Table 5.2 below shows

---

[24]   As a mark of just how far against the traditional welfare system politics had swung, then-House Speaker Newt Gingrich proposed removing the children of welfare recipients from their families and placing them in orphanages. Katharine Q. Seelye, "Republicans Plan Ambitious Agenda in Next Congress," *New York Times*, November 15, 1994. Careful readers might detect a certain tension between this proposal and PRWORA's focus, see above and below, on the importance of children's living in stable families with their own parents. Interestingly, as part of his 2012 presidential campaign, Speaker Gingrich has recently suggested that janitorial work in schools would constitute effective job preparation. Maggie Haberman, "Newt: Fire the Janitors, Hire Kids to Clean Schools," *Politico*, November 18, 2011 8:15PM EST, downloaded from http://www.politico.com/news/stories/1111/68729.html on February 12, 2012. The Speaker has not indicated whether he envisions using orphanages and custodial training as complements or substitutes.

[25]   See Moffitt (1983) *supra* note 20, for an attempt. One potential criticism is that "stigma" in Moffitt's model is essentially any source of model specification error. Thus, for example, the value of Medicaid benefits, on which Moffitt does not have data, contributes to his estimates of stigma. That definition of stigma differs from what I mean to capture here.

Table 5.2   Real incremental maximum benefit for increasing family size from two to three persons, 1996

State	Two Persons[a]	Three Persons[b]	Difference
Minimum	*133*	*167*	*33*
Median	*434*	*541*	*100*
Maximum	*1,141*	*1,283*	*204*
Alabama	190	228	38
Alaska	1141	1283	142
Arizona	382	482	100
Arkansas	225	284	58
California	666	828	163
Colorado	389	495	106
Connecticut	713	884	171
Delaware	375	470	95
DC	453	577	124
Florida	335	421	86
Georgia	327	389	63
Hawaii	785	990	204
Idaho	349	441	92
Illinois	386	524	138
Indiana	318	400	82
Iowa	502	592	90
Kansas	489	596	107
Kentucky	313	364	51
Louisiana	192	264	72
Maine	434	581	147
Maryland	406	518	113
Massachusetts	659	785	126
Michigan*	516	638	122
Minnesota	607	739	132
Mississippi	133	167	33
Missouri	325	406	81
Montana	485	609	124
Nebraska	407	506	99
Nevada	402	484	82
NH	668	764	96
NJ	448	589	142
NM	431	541	110
NY**	801	977	177
NC	328	378	50
ND	463	599	136
Ohio	388	474	86
Oklahoma	331	427	96
Oregon	549	639	90

Table 5.2   (continued)

State	Two Persons[a]	Three Persons[b]	Difference
Pennsylvania	459	585	126
RI	624	770	146
SC	221	278	57
SD	528	598	69
Tennessee	197	257	60
Texas	227	261	35
Utah	475	592	117
Vermont	741	880	139
Virginia	409	492	83
Washington	612	759	147
WV	279	352	72
Wisconsin	612	719	107
Wyoming	445	500	56

Note: *For Wayne County only. **Excluding Suffolk County.

Sources:
a   ACF, *Aid to Families with Dependent Children: The Baseline*, June 1998, Table 5.7, http://
    aspe.hhs.gov/hsp/afdc/baseline/5benefits.pdf, based on CPI index values of 156.9 for
    1996 and 218.056 for 2010 (downloaded from ftp://ftp.bls.gov/pub/special.requests/cpi/
    cpiai.txt).
b   Ibid.

the incremental benefit received in 1996 when the AFDC unit increased
from two to three persons. Measured in 2010 dollars, the incremental
maximum benefit level ranged from $33 per month for Mississippi to
$204 for Hawaii, with the median being $100.[26] The policy of increasing
benefits for additional family members came under heavy attack in the
years leading up to PRWORA, with critics arguing that even the rather
meager incremental benefit levels that appear in Table 5.2 were enough
to induce sizable added fertility. Thus did New Jersey introduce one of
the highest-profile state waiver programs: a so-called "family cap" that
prevented benefit payments from rising with additions to the family
unit.[27]

---

[26]   Incremental maximum benefit levels were generally similar for families
having other sizes; for more details, see ACF, *Aid to Families with Dependent
Children: The Baseline*, June 1998, Table 5.7, http://aspe.hhs.gov/hsp/afdc/
baseline/5benefits.pdf.

[27]   Family cap policies were especially controversial in the 1990s, in part due
to some observers' concerns that they would increase abortions. See, e.g., Jennifer

Categorical eligibility refers primarily to the requirement that a parent either be dead, continuously absent from the home, unable to work due to a disability, or unemployed. Leaving aside unemployment for the moment, these criteria meant that most family units that received AFDC assistance were headed by single mothers. This fact elicited little concern in the program's early years, because the whole point was to provide support either for orphans or for widows so that single mothers would not have to work.[28]

Subsequently, though, many critics of the AFDC program pointed to the categorical eligibility requirement as a cause of the growth in female-headed households and out-of-wedlock child bearing, which they saw as an important social ill.[29] If AFDC's categorical eligibility requirement were empirically important, then one would have expected that as real welfare benefit levels fell, marriage rates would rise and divorce rates would fall. Yet trends reported in Blank's review show that both marriage rates *and* divorce rates fell steadily after the early 1980s.[30] In addition, the birth rate among all unmarried women aged 15–44 increased steadily after the mid-1970s, slowing down around 1990 and peaking around 1994, before most major welfare reforms took hold.[31] Thus the theory advanced by AFDC's critics fits the time series trends rather poorly.[32]

Simple time series evidence can be only the jumping-off point for a phenomenon as complex as fertility and marital behavior, of course. But the micro-econometric literature also shows little reason to believe that welfare programs caused much of the changes in family structure with which AFDC's opponents charged the program. Moffitt (1992) has written that "the econometric estimates of family structure effects are not large enough to explain long-run declines in marriage rates and, in any case, are incapable of explaining recent upward trends in female headship because

---

Preston, Births Fall and Abortions Rise under New Jersey Family Cap, *The New York Times*, November 3, 1998.

28   See Robert A. Moffitt, Four Decades of Antipoverty Policy: Past Developments and Future Directions (2007) 25(1) *Focus*, 39–44, at 41.

29   Ibid.

30   Rebecca Blank (2002), *supra* note 6, at 1154, Figure 5.

31   Blank notes that the early-1990s slowdown "in the nonmarital birth rate is evident among both black and white women, and among teens and older women," ibid.

32   Whatever the causal impact of the requirement of parental deprivation, one result of this debate was the creation of the AFDC-Unemployed Parent program in 1990. I do not discuss this aspect of AFDC in detail here, because it involved a relatively small share of the caseload. For details, see, e.g., Hilary Williamson Hoynes, "Welfare Transfers in Two-Parent Families: Labor Supply and Welfare Participation under AFDC-UP" (1996) 64(2) *Econometrica* 295–332.

welfare benefits have been declining."[33] Further, "the welfare system does not appear to be capable of explaining most of the long-term trend or any of the recent trend of increasing numbers of female-headed families in the United States."[34] And work done after Moffitt's 1992 review showed, as Hilary Williamson Hoynes has put it, that estimates aren't even statistically significant once one controls for state and/or individual fixed effects (so that the benefit level variation identifying the estimates is not the result of permanent differences across states or individuals).[35]

One paper that does appear to find substantial welfare-induced fertility effects is by Mark Rosenzweig.[36] Rosenzweig uses a different measure of welfare generosity than most other authors in this literature. Most authors had used the state maximum monthly benefit variable for the year in which a woman was observed, Rosenzweig uses the average maximum benefit level, for a woman with two children, over the nine-year period when a woman was aged 12–20.[37] Rosenzweig's rationale for using this measure of benefit generosity, rather than the contemporaneous year-specific maximum benefit level, is that the average value better captures the benefit available over the long run, which should be more relevant than year-to-year values for a woman evaluating the level of support she can expect from public assistance over the extended period it takes to raise a child.[38] His data, from the National Longitudinal Survey of Youth,

---

[33]   Moffitt (1992), *supra* note 6, at 56–7.

[34]   Ibid., at 57.

[35]   See Hoynes, *supra* note 6, at 129. One additional influential paper is David T. Ellwood and Mary Jo Bane, *The Impact of AFDC on Family Structure and Living Arrangements*, 7 Research in Labor Economics, ed. by Ron G. Ehrenberg, JAI Press (1985). Ellwood and Bane were among the first to investigate the relationship between family structure and welfare benefits while using state fixed effects to control for unmeasured state-level differences in culture or economic conditions. As Bane and Ellwood (1994) describe on p. 111 of their book, they find that:

> welfare's impact inversely is proportional to the significance of the event. There is little observed impact of welfare on births out of wedlock. There is a larger impact on the decision of women to divorce. Impacts are particularly sizable on the decision of a woman who is already a single parent to live in her parent(s)' home.

[36]   Mark R. Rosenzweig, Welfare, Marital Prospects, and Nonmarital Childbearing (1999) 107 *Journal of Political Economy* S3.

[37]   Ibid., at S7.

[38]   Given that Rosenzweig includes fixed effects, his identifying variation comes from state-level *changes* in average benefit generosity. Taking changes in averages will tend to focus estimator attention on changes in persistent benefit levels, rather than changes in year-to-year benefit levels. For further discussion of issues related

include information on overlapping birth cohorts—those from 1958–1965—so Rosenzweig is able to control for state fixed effects as well.[39]

Rosenzweig uses a multinomial logit model that groups women's combined marriage and fertility outcomes, over the period when they are aged 14–22, into categories involving: (i) no births; (ii) only marital births; or (iii) any premarital births, defined as a birth that occurred more than six months before the woman got married, if she did. His key regressor is the average maximum benefit level variable discussed above. He then uses his multinomial logit coefficient estimates to predict the change in the share of sample members who would wind up in each of categories (i), (ii), and (iii) had the AFDC maximum benefit level been $130 lower (measured in 1985 dollars). Leaving aside some technical details that can be glossed over for purposes of my discussion, Rosenzweig finds that this reduction in benefit generosity would reduce the share of his overall sample that ever has a premarital birth from 0.104 to 0.073—a reduction of 30 percent.[40] Among those in Rosenzweig's low-parental income subsample, the corresponding change is from a baseline of 0.170 to 0.096, which is a drop of 44 percent.[41]

Rosenzweig's estimates suggest considerably larger effects than do others in the literature. Perhaps this is because they are identified from life-cycle rather than noisy year-to-year variation, as Rosenzweig argues. But mis-specification is a plausible alternative explanation. As I noted above, (i) Rosenzweig's measure of long run welfare benefits is the (unweighted) average state maximum benefit level during the period when the sample member is aged 12–20, and (ii) his measure of pre-marital fertility is a dummy equal to one for sample members who have any pre-marital births in the period when they are 14–22. I see three potential problems with this approach.

The first problem has to do with what one means by a long run benefit measure. Even assuming that women know the *contemporaneous* benefit level in their states, as virtually all authors implicitly do, it is not obvious

---

to long run versus year-to-year changes in a regressor, see Terra G. McKinnish, Model Sensitivity in Panel Data Analysis: Some Caveats about the Interpretation of Fixed Effects and Differences Estimators, unpublished and undated paper, available at http://stripe.colorado.edu/~mckinnis/fe053100.pdf.

[39] Rosenzweig's sample contains women born at different times in any given state, and real state maximum benefit levels vary over time. Cohort-based differences in state-specific average maximum benefit levels provide the variation in benefits necessary to both: (i) use the average maximum benefit level a woman faces as a regressor; and (ii) include state fixed effects. He also includes birth cohort dummies.

[40] Rosenzweig, *supra* note 36, at S21, Table 5.

[41] Ibid.

that sample members know the benefit levels their state would have years later. In other words, does it make sense to assume that they have perfect foresight? If sample members just assume—however wrongly—that the current year's benefit level will persist forever, then the contemporaneous benefit level is the right one in any given year, and Rosenzweig's model is mis-specified. Thus, Rosenzweig's econometric model, and thus his empirical results, seem to hinge importantly on an unstated but hyper-informed expectational model. One alternative would be to model expectations of future benefit levels using an adaptive expectations framework. In such a framework, expectations of future benefit levels would be a function of the sequence of past benefit levels, with declining weight placed on those benefit levels further in the past. Yet Rosenzweig includes only two lags from the perspective of a 14-year-old sample member, since no maximum benefit levels are included before the sample member turns 12. Moreover, in forming his average, he puts the same weight on all years' benefit levels.

The second problem has to do with which years' maximum benefit levels are missing from Rosenzweig's measure of maximum benefit levels. Rosenzweig excludes maximum benefit levels from the years when a sample member is aged 21 and 22, yet fertility behavior in those years is part of his dependent variable. Thus the way he defines his welfare benefit measure has the very odd property that it involves assuming women (i) have perfect foresight concerning future benefits at the same time that (ii) in two of the nine years he studies, they completely ignore contemporaneous benefit levels.

The third issue is Rosenzweig's choice to aggregate fertility behavior over a lengthy, nine-year period. A more reasonable approach would have been to estimate a discrete-time hazard model. In such a model, each woman has a separate observation each year that she is at risk of having a pre-marital birth (and those who have already had such a birth exit the sample once they do). This approach would certainly be no less econometrically correct than Rosenzweig's aggregate approach.[42] With regard to my first specification criticism above, a discrete-time hazard model would have forced Rosenzweig to consider explicitly what model

---

[42] Indeed, that statement is a bit charitable. The nine-year aggregate behavioral outcome is the result of nine individual years of behavior. It is not clear what year-by-year model would result in Rosenzweig's nine-year-aggregate model. Of course, every model has its unrealism. But it is not clear why Rosenzweig could not have estimated a year-by-year hazard model; for an example, see Jeff Grogger and Stephen G. Bronars, The Effect of Welfare Payments on the Marriage and Fertility Behavior of Unwed Mothers: Results from a Twins Experiment (2001) 109 *Journal of Political Economy* 529–45.

to use for sample members' expectations concerning long run maximum benefit levels. With regard to my second criticism, this approach would have made it obvious that—whatever model of expectations Rosenzweig used—excluding the contemporaneous benefit level cannot be justified.

In sum, it is difficult to know what to make of Rosenzweig's empirical results. I certainly agree with his basic point—that long run variation in welfare benefits should matter more in determining fertility decisions than should year-to-year variation. But the problems with his econometric implementation raise the possibility that his results hinge importantly on measurement and specification choices that both (i) are difficult to justify and (ii) plausibly drive his results. I do not think Rosenzweig's paper importantly changes the basic conclusion from the pre-existing literature on welfare and family structure—that there were likely relatively small effects in general. And note again that time series patterns show increases in non-marital fertility at the same time as real welfare benefit levels were falling (see Figure 5.3). From the perspective of understanding trends in non-marital fertility, then, sizable welfare program effects on fertility and family structure would simply increase the scope for non-welfare sources of change.

d.   Other features   I have glossed over many details in how the AFDC program worked from the perspective of beneficiaries; I will mention some of these here in the interests of completeness. A number of other safety net programs interacted with AFDC. The two most notable are Food Stamps[43] and Medicaid. AFDC participation often brought automatic eligibility for the Food Stamps program, which also operated like an NIT program with no possibility of paying positive tax.[44] Let G_{fs} be the Food Stamps maximum grant and let t_{fs} be the Food Stamps benefit reduction rate. The Food Stamps program "taxed" AFDC benefits in the sense that it treated AFDC payments as income for Food Stamps benefit-computation purposes. Thus, an AFDC family's total payment from the two programs, assuming it was positive, equaled

$$P_{total}^{+} = G_{fs} + (1 - t_{fs})\,[G_{AFDC} + (1 - t_{AFDC})Y], \qquad (5.3)$$

and setting $t_{AFDC} = 1$, this turns into

---

[43]   This program has been renamed and is now called the Supplemental Nutrition Assistance Program, or SNAP.

[44]   See Committee on Ways and Means (1994), *Green Book*, Chapter 10 (available at http://aspe.hhs.gov/94gb/sec10.txt). Takeup was very high, with 87.3 percent of AFDC units also receiving Food Stamps payments in 1992; see Table 10-27.

$$P_{total}^- = G_{fs} + (1 - t_{fs}) G_{AFDC}. \tag{5.4}$$

Thus, given that the Food Stamps benefit reduction rate, t_{fs}, equaled 30 percent, the total benefit package equaled the maximum Food Stamps benefit plus 70 percent of the maximum AFDC benefit payment. Because Food Stamps benefits were substantial by comparison to maximum AFDC benefits, even for relatively generous states, the Food Stamps part of the benefit was an important part of the traditional welfare system's transfer payment. For example, the maximum monthly food stamps allotment for a family of three in 1996 was $435 when measured in 2010 dollars.[45] The median real AFDC benefit for a family of three in 1996 was New Mexico's $541. Thus, a family of three in New Mexico could receive as much as $813 per month in 1996.[46]

Because the Food Stamps benefit is uniform in the (contiguous) United States, Food Stamps benefits greatly increased the net value of participating in AFDC in states with very low AFDC benefits. For example, the lowest maximum monthly AFDC benefit level for a family of three in 1996 was Mississippi's $167. A Mississippi family receiving this benefit would receive an AFDC benefit payment of $167 plus a Food Stamps payment of $385, for a total of $552. For this family, the Food Stamps benefit accounts for approximately 70 percent of the total benefit payment from the two programs. On the other end of the spectrum, consider a family in Vermont, whose 1996 maximum monthly AFDC benefit of $912 was the highest value in the (contiguous) United States. A family that received this payment would have received a Food Stamps benefit of only $161, which would have constituted only about 15 percent of the $1,073 total benefit payment from the two programs. These calculations show that the relative contribution of the Food Stamps program to AFDC families' resources varied dramatically according to the states in which the families lived.

Hoynes and Schanzenbach (2012) have recently studied the labor

---

[45] According to Table 16.6 of the 1996 *Green Book*, the maximum monthly allotment was $313 for a family of three persons living in the contiguous United States (allotments were higher in Alaska, Hawaii, Guam, and the Virgin Islands). Multiplying $313 by the 2010 CPI-U index number of 218.056 and dividing by the 1996 CPI-U index number of 156.9 yields $435.

[46] This is the result of adding the food stamps maximum allotment of $435 to the maximum AFDC maximum benefit of $541 and then subtracting 30 percent of the latter benefit.

supply effects of introducing the Food Stamps program.[47] While some of their estimates are imprecise, they find very large labor supply responses. For example, their Table 2 (on p. 157) shows that among single-parent households, the average annual number of hours worked by the household head falls by 183. Scaling this effect to account for the fact that not all women in this group participated in Food Stamps, their results imply a reduction of 505 hours of work per year, nearly half the total of 1,068 annual hours worked among heads of single parent households in Hoynes and Schanzenbach's estimation sample. On the other hand, average earnings by the head of these households fell by only $533 (in 2005 dollars), or $1,472 after scaling to account for the Food Stamps participation rate.

But even the scaled drop represents only a 10 percent reduction relative to mean earnings in the sample, which were $14,194. A 50 percent drop in hours can be associated with a 10 percent drop in earnings only if the group of people reducing hours worked has especially low wages. To verify this observation, I divide the $1,472 drop in earnings implied for Food Stamps participants by the corresponding drop in labor supply of 505 hours. The result is $2.91 per hour, suggesting that while the Food Stamps program may have entailed large disincentives in hourly terms, these effects must have been concentrated among precisely those workers for whom the distortion would have been especially inexpensive in the sense of reducing income from the labor market.[48,49]

---

[47] The food stamps program was introduced over time on a county-by-county basis between 1963 and 1975. To estimate the effects of introducing the program in new counties, Hilary Williamson Hoynes and Diane Whitmore Schanzenbach, 'Work Incentives and the Food Stamp Program' (2012) 96(1) *Journal of Public Economics* 151–62 use labor market outcomes data covering the period 1967–1978 from the Panel Study on Income Dynamics. Their Figure 1, on p. 153, shows that roughly 40 percent of counties already had food stamps programs in 1967, with 100 percent of counties having them by 1974.

[48] In 1973, the monthly maximum food stamps benefit level for a family of four was $114 (see data file posted by Robert Moffitt at www.econ2.jhu.edu/people/moffitt/datasets.html and documented at www.econ2.jhu.edu/people/moffitt/ben_doc.pdf). Converting to 2005 dollars for comparability with Hoynes and Schanzenbach's figures, this amounts to $501 (I used the CPI calculator at www.bls.gov/data/inflation_calculator.htm to do the conversion). This is considerably greater than the monthly earnings reduction corresponding to a drop in annual earnings of $1,472. Another way to put all this is to observe that the hourly wage corresponding to mean earnings of $14,194 and mean hours of 1,068 is $13.29—far in excess of the implied average wage for women whose labor supply was importantly affected by the introduction of the food stamps program.

[49] For earlier work on the labor supply effects of the food stamps program, see Thomas Fraker and Robert Moffitt, The Effect of Food Stamps on Labor Supply: A Bivariate Selection Model (1988) 35 *Journal of Public Economics* 25–56; and

AFDC participation also brought automatic eligibility for Medicaid for both parents and children in the AFDC family unit. Given the rising cost of health care, this was another important part of the welfare system, especially for people with predictably high medical costs for either adults or children in the AFDC family unit. Thus, the threat of losing Medicaid eligibility served as a deterrent to leaving welfare. Beginning in the 1980s, Congress changed the Medicaid rules to allow states to provide eligibility to children even in the absence of AFDC participation.[50] These "Medicaid expansions," which have continued to the present time, thus reduced the work disincentive caused by Medicaid eligibility for families receiving welfare.[51]

The AFDC program also allowed certain expenses to be "disregarded" from income for benefit-computation purposes. So-called earnings disregards existed for work expenses like transportation as well as for child care costs.[52] In addition, the Family Support Act of 1988[53] included both work and training requirements.[54]

2. The federal–state relationship in AFDC

AFDC and its predecessor ADC were always joint federal–state programs. Under ADC, the federal government would reimburse states for one-third of benefit payments made, up to \$18 per month for the first child in a home and up to \$12 per month for each additional child.[55] Thus, the

---

Michael Keane and Robert Moffitt, A Structural Model of Multiple Welfare Program Participation and Labor Supply (1998) 39 *International Economic Review* 553–89.

[50] See Aaron Yelowitz, The Medicaid Notch, Labor Supply, and Welfare Participation: Evidence from Eligibility Expansions (1995) 110(4) *Quarterly Journal of Economics* 909–39; Jonathan Gruber, "Medicaid," in *Means-Tested Transfer Programs in the United States*, ed. Robert A. Moffitt, University of Chicago Press (2003); and Janet Currie, *The Invisible Safety Net: Protecting the Nation's Poor Children and Families*, Princeton University Press, (2008), for further details on Medicaid expansions. See Bitler & Zavodny, this volume, for a discussion of Medicaid and federalism.

[51] Other programs interacting with AFDC included child care subsidies and both state and federal EITC programs.

[52] Some authors have treated these disregards as if they reduce the effective benefit reduction rate. However, this is appropriate to do only if the expenses in question are per se valued by welfare recipients. This seems plausible for high-quality child care, but not obviously for, say, bus fares.

[53] Public Law 100-485.

[54] See 1996 *Green Book*, at 388.

[55] According to data posted by the St. Louis Federal Reserve Bank at http://research.stlouisfed.org/fred2/data/CPIAUCNS.txt, the current price index for urban consumers was 13.7 in July 1935 and 225.922 in July 2011. Dividing the 2011 figure by the 1935 figure yields a ratio of 16.49. Multiplying this by \$18 and

net cost to states of the first dollar of assistance was 67 cents but rose to a full dollar when benefit payments exceeded the match cap.

Section 411 of the Social Security Act of 1965,[56] which created the Medicaid program, radically altered this system in two ways. First, the 1965 Act allowed states to use matching rates from the newly created Medicaid program (formally, the "Federal medical assistance percentage"), rather than one-third, as the federal matching rate for reimbursement of state AFDC expenditures.[57] This was an important difference because the 1965 Act's language ensured that the Medicaid matching rate would never be less than 50 percent and could be as high as 83 percent.[58] As of 1996, the match rates varied between 50 and 78 percent,[59] with the match-rate formula set so that states with lower per capita incomes received greater matching rates.[60] Second, the 1965 Act eliminated the cap on the amount of benefit payments that the federal government would match.[61]

The net effect on the federal–state relationship of these 1965 changes, then, was to convert the AFDC program from one with a capped match at a rate of one-third to an uncapped match at a rate of at least one-half, and possibly as high as five-sixths. The Food Stamp program came into being at roughly the same time. To see why these changes matter, consider the first two columns of Table 5.3, which report the cost to a state of providing a dollar of assistance in the pre-1965 period and the period between 1965 and PRWORA's enactment in 1996.

The table's first row considers a state whose pre-1965 maximum benefit level was less than the federal cap for matching purposes. To increase an AFDC family's income by one dollar cost the state 67 cents, since the federal government would contribute one-third of the one dollar of benefits paid. The second row considers a state whose maximum benefit level exceeded the federal cap for matching funds. This state would bear the full cost of providing another dollar of assistance.

Now consider the situation between 1965 and 1996, for states using the

---

$12 yields $297 and $198, which are nontrivial figures relative to contemporary benefit levels.

[56]   Public Law 89-98, § 411, available at 79 Stat. 423.
[57]   To take advantage of this option, states had to start a Medicaid program. Ibid.
[58]   Ibid., § 1905(b)(1), at 352.
[59]   House Ways and Means Committee Prints: 104–14, 1996 *Green Book*, §8, at 454, available at http://frwebgate.access.gpo.gov/cgi-bin/getdoc.cgi?dbname=104_green_book&docid=f:wm014_08.pdf.
[60]   Ibid.
[61]   Public Law 89-98, § 411, available at 79 Stat. 423.

Table 5.3   State cost of providing another dollar of assistance to recipient family

Maximum Benefit Level	Pre-1965	1965–1996	1996 and later
State with Match Rate of 50 Percent			
Less than federal match cap	0.67	0.71	1.43
Greater than federal match cap	1.00	0.71	1.43
State with Match Rate of 80 Percent			
Less than federal match cap	0.67	0.29	1.43
Greater than federal match cap	1.00	0.29	1.43

Medicaid match rate. Since such states faced no cap, figures in the top two rows of Table 5.3 are the same, which concern states whose match rates were 50 percent, as was the case for 11 states plus the District of Columbia in 1996.[62] Recall that the federal Food Stamp program, which was born in 1965, implicitly taxes welfare benefits at 30 percent. Thus, after 1965, an AFDC family would have to receive $1/0.7 = $1.43 in welfare payments to increase its resources by one dollar. States with a 50 percent Medicaid match rate had to bear only half of this cost, or about 71 cents.

For states whose pre-1965 maximum benefit level was less than the cap for federal matching, the combined effect of introducing the Food Stamp program and switching to the Medicaid match rate was minor— an increase in the price of providing assistance from 0.67 to 0.71. But for states with maximum benefit levels above the cap for federal matching, the combined effect was a substantial reduction in the price of providing assistance, from 1.00 to 0.71. Moreover, by eliminating the cap altogether, the 1965 Act gave states with maximum benefit levels below the pre-existing cap an incentive to increase their maximum benefit levels. For states with Medicaid match rates above 50 percent, these effects could be magnified considerably. The bottom two rows of Table 5.3 show that a state with a Medicaid match rate of 80 percent would have had a price per dollar of assistance equal to just 29 cents between 1965 and 1996.

It is interesting to consider the effects these changes might have had on state benefit levels. The obvious prediction is that relatively more generous states, and states with greater federal match rates, would have increased their maximum benefit levels considerably. To my knowledge, there is no

[62]   1996 *Green Book, supra* note 59, at 888.

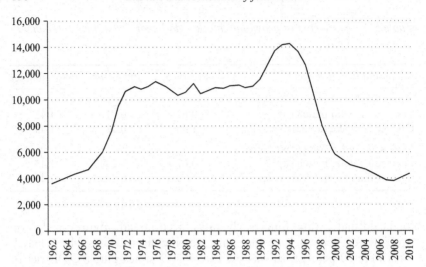

Sources: My tabulation from federal government data. For 1962–1996, data come from Table 2.1 of ACF, *Aid to Families with Dependent Children: The Baseline*, http://aspe.hhs. gov/hsp/afdc/baseline/2caseload.pdf. For later years, data come from excel files downloaded from www.acf.hhs.gov/programs/ofa/data-reports/caseload/caseload_recent.html, www.acf. hhs.gov/programs/ofa/data-reports/caseload/caseload_current.htm, and www.acf.hhs.gov/ programs/ofa/data-reports/caseload/caseload_archive.html.

Figure 5.5   *Annual average of monthly number of AFDC recipients (in 1,000s)*

systematic empirical evidence as to whether these predictions were borne out. But the question is intriguing, because, as Figure 5.5 shows, AFDC caseloads began to take off not long after the 1965 changes. (I discuss other features of Figure 5.5 in further detail below.)

I turn now to one of the least notorious aspects of PRWORA: its radical alteration of states' marginal cost of providing assistance to welfare recipients. PRWORA did not just allow states to implement the changes in the relationship between individual behavior and eligibility/benefit levels discussed above. It also converted the cash welfare system from a federal–state partnership with matching at the margin into a simple block grant.[63] States are not only allowed to design their programs largely as they please—they are also on the hook to pay for the marginal costs of program generosity. The final column of Table 5.3 illustrates the role of this change in welfare program structure. Since the federal Food Stamp

---

[63]   See §103 of PRWORA, 110 Stat. 2113.

program continues to exist for TANF recipients,[64] its implicit taxation of cash assistance payments continues as well. Thus, a one-dollar increase in cash assistance delivers only 70 cents of additional disposable income to the recipient family. To deliver a full dollar at the margin thus requires $1/0.7=$1.43 in additional state spending. Table 5.3's final column thus shows that PRWORA's block-granting of federal TANF funds doubled the price of providing cash assistance for a state with a 50 percent match rate, while quintupling it for a state with an 80 percent match rate.

All of this is especially notable because states are allowed to spend large amounts of their TANF block grant funds on things other than direct benefit payments. As a consequence, the TANF program is, roughly speaking, a system in which the federal government hands lump sums to the states and tells them to do as much or as little cash assistance as they please.[65] Under TANF, states are allowed to spend block-grant funds on a variety of non-transfer purposes, including child care, transportation, and job training.[66] Between these structural changes and time limits, it should come as no surprise that cash assistance payments have plummeted since PRWORA. Figure 5.6 shows the steep decline in real cash payments under TANF that began following PRWORA. By 2009, less than a third of all payments made under the TANF program were made in the form of cash transfers to recipients.[67]

There is a sizable literature concerning the determinants of state

---

[64] Among its non-AFDC-related aspects, PRWORA greatly restricted Food Stamp eligibility for able-bodied adults without children; see 7 U.S.C. 2015(o)(2), added by §824(a) of PRWORA, 110 STAT. 2323, which places a three-month time limit on SNAP receipt, during any 36-month period, for adults aged 50 or younger who do not satisfy state work requirements. For more discussion, see, e.g., Betsey A. Kuhn, Michael LeBlanc, Craig Gundersen, The Food Stamp Program, Welfare Reform, and the Aggregate Economy (1997) 79(5) *American Journal of Agricultural Economics*, Proceedings Issue (Dec.), 1595–9. These restrictions were temporarily lifted by §101(e) of the American Recovery and Reinvestment Act of 2009; see 123 STAT. 121.

[65] Section 103 of PRWORA, 110 Stat. 2113, codified at 42 U.S.C. 609, does penalize states for failing to "maintain certain level[s] of historic effort." In addition, states can always use their own funds to pay benefits to time-limited people, though they bear the full marginal cost of providing such benefits.

[66] See section III.C.2 for more on diversion.

[67] Given that the monthly caseload fell roughly 60 percent over the period between 1996–2009, this change is not too surprising. It is an interesting fact about the block-granting of federal payments under PRWORA that, while inflation worked out to about 39 percent over this period, the federal government transfers the same number of nominal dollars to states even as caseloads have fallen 60 percent.

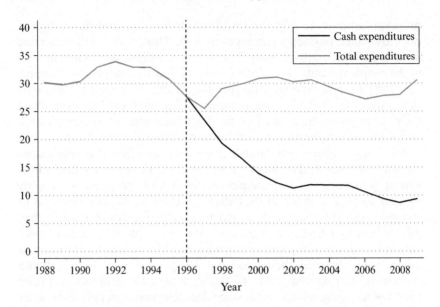

Source: Author's tabulations using data from Table 5 of Marianne P. Bitler and Hilary
W. Hoynes, The State of the Social Safety Net in the Post-Welfare Reform Era, Brookings
Papers on Economic Activity, Fall 2010. Data downloaded from www.brookings.edu/~/
media/Files/Programs/ES/BPEA/2010_fall_bpea_data/Bitler_Hoynes.zip.

Figure 5.6   *Total and cash-only expenditures under AFDC/TANF,
1988–2009 (billions of 2009 dollars)*

maximum benefit levels. An excellent paper in this literature is David
Ribar and Mark Wilhelm's.[68] Their main objective is to estimate state-
level price and income elasticities of providing cash assistance. Here,
the price of providing cash assistance is defined as the product of (i)
the state share of each dollar of assistance provided[69] and (ii) the share
of the state population that receives AFDC. Income is defined as per
capital total annual personal income.[70] Ribar and Wilhelm review earlier
work, which they characterize as producing "an unacceptably wide
range of estimates."[71] They argue that this wide range is the result of

    [68]   D. Ribar and M. Wilhelm, The Demand for Welfare Generosity (1999) 81
Review of Economics and Statistics, 96–108.
    [69]   This share is one minus the federal match rate discussed above; see Ribar
and Wilhelm ibid., at 97.
    [70]   See ibid., at 101, Table 2.
    [71]   Ibid., at 96.

mis-specification, and they present evidence that specification problems are solved when one includes state fixed effects, year fixed effects, and state-specific linear trends. Their own results suggest price elasticities, of −0.14 to 0.02, and income elasticities that are generally small, though with confidence bounds "extending from 0.11 to 0.82."[72] They conclude that "welfare generosity is much less sensitive to economic changes than many analysts had previously supposed."[73]

A number of papers have shifted attention away from estimating conventional demand functions. For example, Moffitt (1999) studies the factors that led to the state and federal welfare policy contractions discussed in this chapter,[74] writing from an explicitly public choice-oriented point of view that focuses on interactions between voter preferences, the labor market, and demographic change. He concludes that:

> plausible arguments can be made that welfare reform in the U.S. in the 1990s was strongly influenced by increases in public expenditures on welfare in the late 1980s and early 1990s, just before the major contractionary reforms; by reductions in real incomes and wages of the poor, and their employment rates as well, over the 1980s; and changes in the characteristics of welfare recipients and the poor, particularly the rise in unmarried single motherhood.[75]

Another collection of papers has focused on estimating the spillover effects of states' welfare policies onto other states, an issue of obvious interest from a federalism perspective. Examples include Figlio, Kolpin and Reid (1999) and Saavedra (2000).[76] Figlio, Kolpin and Reid (1999) report estimates that suggest states' benefit levels move in tandem with their neighbors' benefit levels, with own benefits rising and falling roughly dollar-for-dollar as neighbors' rise and fall. In addition, Figlio *et al.* present results (in their Table 3, at 450) suggesting that states pay more attention to reductions in their neighbors' benefits than to increases, so that "states are more concerned about being 'left ahead' in welfare benefit levels than they are about being 'left behind.'"[77] Saavedra (2000) estimates

[72]   Ibid.
[73]   Ibid., at 107.
[74]   Robert A. Moffitt, Explaining Welfare Reform: Public Choice and the Labor Market (1999) 6 *International Tax and Public Finance*, 289–315.
[75]   Ibid., at 291.
[76]   D. Figlio, V. Kolpin, and W. Reid, Do States Play Welfare Games? (1999) 46(3) *Journal of Urban Economics* 437–54; Luz Amparo Saavedra, A Model of Welfare Competition with Evidence from AFDC (2000) 47 *Journal of Urban Economics* 248–79.
[77]   Figlio et al., ibid., at 453.

a model constructed by Wildasin (2000)[78] and reports results that "suggest states behave strategically when they set AFDC benefits. The estimated slope parameter of the reaction function is positive and significantly different from zero, indicating that AFDC benefits in any given state are positively affected by the AFDC benefits in neighboring states."[79,80]

This topic of state fiscal competition is intimately bound up with the issue of welfare migration, which itself is an especially important topic in the federalism context. If migration is relatively inexpensive, then states that provide generous welfare benefits will find themselves attracting would-be beneficiaries. Such welfare magnetism would raise two important concerns. First, it suggests the possibility of a "race to the bottom" in benefit setting.[81] Second, since many estimates of welfare policy's behavioral effects on non-migration outcomes are identified primarily from variation in state-level welfare policy variables, endogenous location raises the possibility that much of this literature is subject to a serious endogeneity problem. Simply put, if state benefit levels are an important determinant of where people choose to live, then these benefit levels are choice variables that cannot be treated as exogenous. In this section, I briefly discuss both theoretical and empirical issues related to this so-called "welfare magnet" problem.

In the leading theoretical treatment of welfare migration, Charles Brown and Wallace Oates construct a two-jurisdiction general equilibrium model that has both poor and non-poor agents who can choose the jurisdiction in which to live.[82] They show that the welfare magnet problem can be conceived as a garden variety externality, because each jurisdiction in a decentralized welfare system can offload some of its poor residents onto the other jurisdiction by reducing its welfare benefit level. A "race to the bottom" might occur, resulting in a lower equilibrium benefit level in

---

[78]   David E. Wildasin, Income Redistribution in a Common Labor Market, (Sep., 1991) 81(4) *American Economic Review* 757–74.

[79]   Saavedra (2000) *supra* note 76, at 250–51.

[80]   Katherine Baicker, "The Spillover Effects of State Spending" (2005) 89(2–3) *Journal of Public Economics* 529–44, at 532, argues that neighbors' benefit variables, and other sources of variation, in Figlio et al. (1999), Saavedra (2000) and similar papers may "suffer from the absence of plausibly exogenous variation." She studies the effects of mandated increases in neighbors' Medicaid spending on states' own increases and argues that such mandates can be treated as exogenous.

[81]   As a corollary, such attractor states would have to levy higher taxes than repellor states, which will drive away better-off citizens, which would cause the tax base to shrink and exacerbate the problem.

[82]   Charles C. Brown and Wallace E. Oates, Assistance to the Poor in a Federal System (1987) 32 *Journal of Public Economics* 307.

each jurisdiction than there would be if (i) no one could migrate, or (ii) the benefit level were set centrally.

There are several potential system-design responses to this negative externality. One is to simply run a centralized system—as with, say, Medicare or Social Security. A second approach is to use the kind of hybrid system the U.S. had under AFDC's federal match of state benefit payments, with federal subsidies counteracting the race to the bottom incentives. Third, one might restrict migration's usefulness to the migrant in securing cash assistance. Brown and Oates note that the English Poor Laws took this approach: under the Law of Settlement and Removal of 1662, "church wardens and overseers were directed to remove to his 'home' parish any newcomer likely to become a burden to his adopted parish unless the new arrival could give surety that he would not become indigent or rented property of the value of ten pounds per year or more."[83]

Interestingly, attempts to restrict the welfare eligibility of people who move across state lines have been rebuffed twice by the U.S. Supreme Court. In *Shapiro v. Thompson*,[84] the Court struck down Connecticut, Pennsylvania and District of Columbia statutes that imposed a one-year waiting period before in-migrants could receive welfare benefits. Justice Brennan's opinion for the *Shapiro* Court discusses at length the state defendants' concerns related to the long-run burdens of serving as welfare magnets.[85] Nonetheless, the Court held that migration across state lines is a constitutional right[86] and observed that "we do not perceive why a mother who is seeking to make a new life for herself and her children should be regarded as less deserving because she considers, among others factors, the level of a State's public assistance."[87]

In *Saenz v. Roe*,[88] the Court confronted a California statute that limited the welfare payment an in-migrant could receive to the payment in her previous state of residence, when that payment would be less than California's, during the in-migrant's first year of California residence. The Court held that such a limitation was impermissible in light

---

[83] Ibid., at 323–4 (citing Derek Fraser, ed., *The New Poor Law in the Nineteenth Century*, St. Martin's Press (2008).

[84] *Shapiro v. Thompson*, 394 U.S. 618 (1969).

[85] Ibid., at 627–9.

[86] Ibid., at 631 ("freedom to travel throughout the United States has long been recognized as a basic right under the Constitution") (citing *United States v. Guest*, 383 U.S. 745, 757–8 (1966) (quotation mark removed).

[87] Ibid., at 632.

[88] *Saenz v. Roe*, 526 U.S. 489 (1999).

of the 14th Amendment's Privileges or Immunities clause,[89] and that PRWORA's explicit authorization of such a policy was unavailing, since "Congress may not authorize the States to violate the Fourteenth Amendment."[90]

Of course, a race to the bottom needs state runners. The Figlio *et al.* (1999), Saavedra (2000), and Baicker (2005) papers discussed above do suggest that states pay attention to their neighbors' benefit levels. Moreover, Baicker (2005, at 540) reports empirical evidence consistent with the view that "the states with the greatest potential in-migration are those that are most concerned with staying in line with their neighbors' spending."

A different angle from which to approach the race to the bottom question is to ask whether there is so much welfare-induced migration that informed and rational state policy makers *would* adjust benefit levels substantially. The literature on the extent of welfare-induced migration spans many decades and can usefully be divided into roughly three waves. Moffitt 1992 characterizes the first wave, which used data from the late 1960s to early 1970s as finding "rather weak or inconsistent effects of benefits on migration."[91] But as he notes, this literature was "severely hampered by a high level of data aggregation and by a consequent inability to disaggregate by individual characteristics, often even by female headship and AFDC receipt."[92]

The second wave of welfare migration studies used micro-data and typically found "positive and significant effects of welfare on residential location and geographical mobility."[93] But Moffitt 1992 notes that these studies face their own methodological challenges. For example, they tend to take initial location as given, even though this location itself is the result of choice. Bruce Meyer has further noted that conditioning on welfare

---

[89]   Ibid., at 503 (citing also, at 502, to both the majority and dissenting opinions in the *Slaughter-House Cases*, 16 Wall. 36 (1872), for the proposition that "the right of the newly arrived citizen to the same privileges and immunities enjoyed by other citizens of the same State ... is protected not only by the new arrival's status as a state citizen, but also by her status as a citizen of the United States").

[90]   Ibid., at 507.

[91]   Moffitt (1992), *supra* note 6, at 34.

[92]   Ibid.

[93]   See Moffitt (1992), *supra* note 6, at 35, Table 10. Two additional papers published after Moffitt's review are María E. Enchautegui,Welfare Payments and Other Economic Determinants of Female Migration (1997) 15(3) *Journal of Labor Economics* 529–54; and Phillip B. Levine and David J. Zimmerman, An Empirical Analysis of the Welfare Magnet Debate Using the NLSY (1999) 12 *Journalof Population Econo*mics 391–409.

receipt or poverty status when choosing study samples may introduce another important source of bias.[94]

The final wave of welfare migration studies consists of several that have tried to use either special geographic or lifecycle features to identify effects. Terra McKinnish has written two important papers on welfare migration. Both of these papers take advantage of the facts that (i) welfare benefit levels are set at the state level, while (ii) it will be cheaper to move from a low-benefit to a bordering high-benefit state when a woman lives near the border than when she lives far from it. Using county-level AFDC expenditures as her dependent variable, McKinnish (2005) finds that a $100 reduction in a bordering state's welfare benefit level is associated with a 4.9 percent drop in AFDC expenditures in a state's own county when the own county lies within 25 miles of the bordering state, relative to counties that are further from the bordering state.[95] In McKinnish (2007), she uses micro data to re-do this analysis; the resulting estimates are consistent with the existence of welfare migration, though they are not generally statistically significant.[96]

In my own paper, "Migration, the Life Cycle, and State Benefits: How Low Is the Bottom?"[97] I pointed out that the incentive to move to a higher-benefit state is much greater for women with younger children, since they can expect to have more years of future welfare eligibility. For example, under AFDC rules, a woman whose youngest child is newborn would have 18 years of remaining eligibility, whereas a woman whose youngest child is 17 would have just one year. The incentive to move for greater benefit levels is much stronger in the former case.

Moreover, I also pointed out that previous studies on welfare migration had tended not to use valuable information from the welfare dynamics literature. This literature shows that AFDC could be thought of as two very different programs stapled together. The first program was a temporary assistance program for women who had recently experienced a financially adverse event—typically a divorce, lost job, or new birth outside of

---

[94]   Bruce D. Meyer, Do the Poor Move to Receive Higher Welfare Benefits? Unpublished paper, September 14, 2000 (available at http://harrisschool.uchicago. edu/faculty/articles/meyer_do_the_poor.pdf).

[95]   Terra McKinnish, Importing the Poor: Welfare Magnetism and Cross-Border Welfare Migration (Winter 2005) 40(1) *Journal of Human Resources* 57–76, at 72. McKinnish defines a county to be a border county if it is within 25 miles of the bordering state in question; see 72.

[96]   Terra McKinnish, Welfare-induced Migration at State Borders: New Evidence from Micro-data (2007) 91 *Journal of Public Economics* 437–450, at 438.

[97]   Jonah B. Gelbach, Migration, the Life Cycle, and State Benefits: How Low Is the Bottom? (2004) 112(5) *Journal of Political Economy* 1091–130.

marriage. These women would participate for relatively short periods of time until they got back on their feet. The second program embedded in AFDC was a long-term income support program, which provided assistance to single mothers as long as they had minor children.

Once one views the issue of welfare migration from a dynamic perspective, it becomes clear that migration incentives are likely to matter only for those women affected by the second, more permanent type of AFDC support. Because data sets do not include an explicit "how-long-would-you-spend-on-welfare" variable, researchers have no choice but to find proxies for such a variable, and many used high school dropout status as an indicator of attachment to the welfare system. But dropout status is a coarse filter for these purposes, as in Mary Jo Bane and David Ellwood's 1994 book *Welfare Realities: From Rhetoric to Reform*,[98] which shows considerable heterogeneity according to whether high school dropouts have ever been married.

Bane and Ellwood report simulation results suggesting that, among those who ever have a spell on welfare, never-married high school graduates and ever-married high school dropouts would receive cash welfare for roughly six years over a 25-year window. By contrast, never-married high school dropouts would spend an average of at least ten years on welfare, while an ever-married high school graduate would spend just four years on welfare over this period.[99] And these figures mute the long run differences, since both dropout and never-married status are positively associated with the event of commencing a welfare-use spell in the first place. Thus, there is considerable value in focusing on never-married dropouts when trying to measure the effects of welfare benefit levels on migration choices, given the very important role of expected future program use in this decision.

I reported results from 1980 and 1990 Census microdata samples. For the 1980 sample, I found that single mothers' out-migration from a state between 1975 and 1980 is quite sensitive to states' own benefit levels, with the sensitivity greatest among those who are most likely to make extensive

---

[98]   Mary Jo Bane and David T. Ellwood (1994), *Welfare Realities: From Rhetoric to Reform*, Harvard University Press. While dated, this book is chock full of stimulating analysis and facts. Of special interest is the lucid discussion of welfare use dynamics in Chapter 2, including the fascinating facts, collected from a single data set, that (i) about a third of current welfare recipients had been receiving welfare for 24 consecutive months or less, (ii) half of all completed welfare spells, defined as consecutive time on welfare, were shorter than 24 months, (iii) fewer than 15 percent of all current welfare recipients would be on welfare for a total of 24 months or less, and (iv) nearly half of all current welfare recipients would be receiving welfare ten years later; see p. 29.

[99]   Ibid., at 52, Table 2.6.

use of the welfare system. These results are consistent with the existence of lifecycle welfare migration, though results for the 1990 sample are too unclear to draw any conclusions.

An additional contribution of my paper was to construct a metric that allows one to assess the magnitude of any welfare migration effects. Previous work had tended to focus on measures like the share of migration that was caused by cross-state welfare benefit differentials. Such measures do not map into answering the question of how much an impact welfare migration could have on (either optimal or actual) state benefit levels. To answer this question, I constructed a simple model in which each state chooses its benefit level to maximize an objective function that depends positively on transfers to the poor, positively on non-welfare government expenditures, and negatively on taxes. I then show how to compare the state's optimal welfare benefit level in the world where state-to-state welfare migration is allowed to the optimal welfare benefit level in the world where it is not (i.e., in the latter world, states may and do simply disallow migrants from receiving welfare benefits). If there is substantial welfare-induced migration in this metric, the optimal welfare benefit level would be much greater in the no-welfare migration world than in the actual world.

I show theoretically that one can write the approximate percentage increase in the optimal benefit level in the no-welfare migration world, relative to the optimal benefit level in the real world, as the ratio of two effects. The numerator of this ratio is the "welfare migration effect," which captures the increase in welfare-related spending that occurs when benefits are increased. The denominator is the "constant-population effect," which captures the change in welfare spending that occurs because an increase in generosity causes the state to pay more benefits to welfare participants who would have lived in the state regardless of the benefit change. I then use my empirical estimates as inputs to a simulation procedure meant to approximate these welfare migration and constant population effects. My results suggest that optimal welfare benefit levels in Illinois and Wisconsin—a representative medium- and high-benefit state—would be no more than 10 percent greater if there were no welfare migration.[100] In sum, my results suggest that, even accounting for previously neglected lifecycle considerations, the amount of welfare migration is probably too small to have large effects on optimal state welfare benefit levels, at least for relatively high-benefit states.[101]

---

[100]   See Gelbach (2004), *supra* note 97, Table 6, at 1116.

[101]   For Mississippi, a very low-benefit state, the results are sensitive to assumptions I discuss in detail in the paper; alternative point estimates suggest that

B.   Summary Thoughts on the Incentive Effects of AFDC

In general, careful studies did tend to show causal effects of AFDC on behavior. As Robert Moffitt concluded in his widely respected review of the literature through the early 1990s, there was "unequivocal evidence of effects on labor supply, participation in the welfare system, and on some aspects of family structure," though "the importance of these effects is limited in many respects."[102] Given this evidence, the ultimate policy consensus in favor of eliminating AFDC seems to be out of any real proportion to the evidence.

AFDC had some negative behavioral effects, to be sure, and AFDC certainly did not eliminate poverty. But how could it, given the maximum benefit levels? In 1996, the official poverty line for a family of three was $1,053 per month.[103] As the final column of Table 5.1 shows, no state had an AFDC maximum monthly benefit level close to this level. Given the 100 percent statutory benefit reduction rate, the maximum monthly benefit level is an effective ceiling on income. Thus, AFDC could hardly reduce officially measured poverty as a general matter.

Note that Food Stamps payments are not included in income for purposes of computing official poverty statistics,[104] so this feature of the programs would not change the conclusion in the previous paragraph. But even if Food Stamps benefits had been counted in measuring official

---

optimal welfare benefit levels might be only 2.1 percent greater in the absence of welfare migration, but they might also be as great as 36.5 percent greater; see ibid. Why would Mississippi's optimal benefit level be a function of welfare migration, given that Mississippi's low benefit level should operate to repel in-migration? Because when welfare migration does occur, Mississippi can convince some of its poor residents to leave by reducing its welfare benefit level.

[102]   Moffitt (1992) *supra*, note 6, at 56.

[103]   According to the Poverty Thresholds table at www.census.gov/hhes/www/poverty/data/threshld/thresh96.html, the annual poverty threshold was $12,641 for a family with three persons, of whom two are related children. Dividing this annual figure by 12 yields $1,053 per month.

[104]   See, e.g., Carmen DeNavas-Walt, Bernadette D. Proctor, and Cheryl Hill Lee, U.S. Census Bureau, Current Population Reports, P60-231, *Income, Poverty, and Health Insurance Coverage in the United States: 2005*, U.S. Government Printing Office (2006), at 45. For a discussion of shortcomings in the official approach to measuring income and poverty, see Kathleen S. Short, "The Supplemental Poverty Measure: Examining the Incidence and Depth of Poverty in the U.S. Taking Account of Taxes and Transfers," June 3, 2011, available at www.census.gov/hhes/povmeas/methodology/supplemental/research/WEA2011.kshort.071911_2.rev.pdf (associated tables appear at www.census.gov/hhes/povmeas/methodology/supplemental/research/tabspm2009revised.pdf).

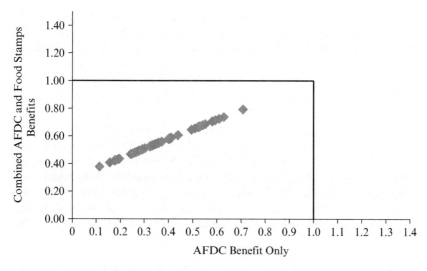

*Figure 5.7   1996 monthly maximum benefit levels as share of federal
             poverty line*

poverty, Figure 5.7 shows that it would make no difference. The figure
plots each state's maximum combined AFDC and Food Stamps benefit
as a share of the federal poverty line (vertical axis) against the maximum
AFDC benefit alone (horizontal axis). It shows that even the combined
program benefit in 1996 was below the poverty line—and far below it for
many states.

Thus, one could scratch one's head bald at the thought that the AFDC
program *could* have reduced, much less eliminated, officially measured
poverty. That is simply not what the program was built to do. That said,
AFDC did transfer a nontrivial amount of dollars to poor households, and
the failure of the poverty rate to indicate this fact is simply a measurement
problem. The poverty rate is just the sum of a dummy variable that equals
one for those with income below the threshold and zero for everyone else.
Thus, transfers of income across from those above the line to those below
the line do not affect the poverty rate unless the transfers are sufficient to
raise some people above the line.

In retrospect, one remarkable feature of the micro-econometric
literature on welfare policy is just how little attention was paid to the
benefits side of the equation. To be sure, it is substantially easier to
measure a transfer program's efficiency costs, in the form of incentive
effects, than it is to measure benefits; this is especially true because the
benefits often involve highly normative judgments related to distributive

justice. Perhaps as a consequence, economists tend to spend most of our time estimating the costs of running welfare programs. But there are alternatives. For example, we could ask and try to answer questions like, how many dollars of the marginal taxpayer's would have to be equivalent to an additional dollar in the hands of a low-income person in order for a welfare program's incentive costs to be worth bearing?

Moreover, some forms of benefit can be measured more directly. Gruber (2000) estimates the effects of AFDC in smoothing consumption following a divorce.[105] He finds that AFDC benefits do not crowd out other means of consumption smoothing (e.g., support from relatives or earnings); see Gruber (2000) at 157. This finding suggests that AFDC was a particularly effective form of consumption insurance, at least against the risks associated with divorce.[106] Empirical evidence also suggests that

---

[105]   Jonathan Gruber, Cash Welfare as a Consumption Smoothing Mechanism for Divorced Mothers (2000) 75 *Journal of Public Economics* 157–82.

[106]   There might be disagreement concerning the desirability of reducing the negative consumption shocks associated with divorce. For example, consider the allegorical Pennsylvania couple Harold and Phyllis whom Charles Murray discusses in his book *Losing Ground*. Charles A. Murray, *Losing Ground: American Social Policy, 1950–1980*, Basic Books (1984). Murray discusses whether the couple would marry after Harold gets Phyllis pregnant. Before the welfare policies Murray opposes, he believes Harold would have married Phyllis, and that that would have been a good thing. But after these policies take effect, Murray argues, they will not marry, because it makes no economic sense to do so. Murray criticizes this result as an example of "incentives to fail" that "maximiz[e] short term gains" (the chapter in which he discusses Harold and Phyllis is titled, "Incentives to Fail I: Maximizing Short Term Gains"). In a review of *Losing Ground*, "How Poor Are the Poor?", *The New York Review of Books*, May 9, 1985, Christopher Jencks contests Murray's suggestion that Harold and Phyllis's marriage would be an unequivocal social good, even granting some of Murray's premises concerning Harold and Phyllis, like whether Harold would necessarily have Phyllis her before the welfare policies Murray decries. Jencks writes:

> Shorn of rhetoric, then, the "empirical" case against the welfare system comes to this. First, high AFDC benefits allow single mothers to set up their own households. Second, high AFDC benefits allow mothers to end bad marriages. Third, high benefits may make divorced mothers more cautious about remarrying. All these "costs" strike me as benefits.

It seems unlikely that Murray would agree with that last sentence; thus it seems equally unlikely that he—or those who viewed *Losing Ground* as a call to action—would approve of AFDC's role in smoothing divorce-induced negative consumption shocks.

by helping allow mothers of infants time out of the labor force, AFDC increased breastfeeding rates.[107]

Recent evidence also suggests that the introduction of the Food Stamps program led to increased birth weight, especially among those babies born at lower birth weights. Given the close relationship between the Food Stamps and AFDC programs that I discussed in section II.A.1.d, both in terms of eligibility and in terms of program structure, this finding provides more evidence that income support like that provided by AFDC has real benefits.[108] So while we do not have much quantifiable evidence on the benefits of the old welfare system, especially compared to the evidence on incentive costs, it is unlikely that that is because there weren't any such benefits.

C. Welfare Reform: Waivers and PRWORA

Before the wave of waivers and PRWORA, states had very little control over program details. They could set benefit levels. And because they administered their own AFDC programs, they could choose the levels of efficiency, bureaucracy, and, within limits, harassment of participants they wanted to use.[109] As mentioned above, AFDC's structural inflexibility began to give way under various waivers to the AFDC rules. Approved under authority of Section 1115 of the Social Security Act,[110] these waivers first were allowed in the Reagan administration and really took off under President Clinton. I discuss the details of programmatic reforms in subsection 1 and then turn in subsection 2 to the empirical evidence on these reforms' effects. Much of my discussion in section 1 draws from Rebecca M. Blank's excellent 2002 review in the *Journal of Economic Literature*, Evaluating Welfare

---

[107]   See Steven J. Haider, Alison Jacknowitz and Robert F. Schoeni, Welfare Work Requirements and Child Well-Being: Evidence from the Effects on Breast-Feeding (Aug., 2003) 40(3) *Demography* 479–97, who write that their results show that "if welfare reform had not been adopted, national breast-feeding rates six months after birth would have been 5.5% higher than they were in 2000."

[108]   See Douglas Almond, Hilary W. Hoynes, and Diane Whitmore Schanzenbach, Inside the War on Poverty: The Impact of Food Stamps on Birth Outcomes (May 2011) 93(2) *Review of Economics and Statistics* pp. 387–403.

[109]   For a theoretical argument showing that bureaucratic hassles and other "ordeals" can be efficient, because they deter applications from less needy people when the level of neediness can't be observed, see Albert L. Nichols and Richard J. Zeckhauser,Targeting Transfers through Restrictions on Recipients (1982) 72(2) *American Economic Review* (Papers and Proceedings) 372–7.

[110]   Codified at 42 U.S.C. 1315.

Reform in the United States,[111] while subsection 2 is drawn almost entirely from Jeffrey Grogger and Lynn A. Karoly's impressive book, *Welfare Reform: Effects of a Decade of Change*.[112]

1. What welfare reform entailed

By the time of PRWORA's enactment, 27 states had implemented major waivers operating statewide.[113] These waivers, which required federal approval, changed many aspects of existing AFDC programs. Under the federal rules, AFDC was an entitlement for anyone who met both federal categorical eligibility conditions and a state's means test. Thus, depending on the spacing of a woman's births and her income, she could in principle retain AFDC eligibility for decades (though I am aware of no empirical work suggesting this was a common occurrence).

To illustrate the differences between AFDC and TANF programs that PRWORA allowed, one need only consider Connecticut's TANF program, itself begun as a waiver called Jobs First. This program included a *lifetime* time limit of 21 months on assistance.[114] Oddly, Jobs First wields this rattan cane alongside the dangling carrot of a liberalized NIT structure, which allows welfare participants to earn substantial incomes while retaining program eligibility.[115] Time limits and liberalized benefit reduction rates were only two of the potentially important changes states incorporated into their waiver programs. Other examples include family caps that eliminated the generally meager increase in benefits states had provided following birth of another child (see section II.A.1.c, above); work requirements; substantial sanctions for failing to participate in required work activities; more generous treatment of earned income and child support in benefit determination; more generous child care and Medicaid assistance; and novelty features like required drug testing.[116]

---

[111]   Blank (2002), *supra* note 6.

[112]   Grogger and Karoly (2005), *supra* note 6.

[113]   Blank (2002), *supra* note 6, at 1106.

[114]   The Jobs First program rules include provisions allowing exemptions from and extensions to the time limit. Evidence suggests both that the time limit does bind for some participants and also that exemptions and extensions are sometimes granted. See Dan Bloom, Susan Scrivener, Charles Michalopoulos, Pamela Morris, Richard Hendra, Diana Adams-Ciardullo, Johanna Walter, with Wanda Vargas, *Jobs First: Final Report on Connecticut's Welfare Reform Initiative*, at 4–12, Manpower Demonstration Research Corporation, February 2002, available at www.mdrc.org/publications/90/full.pdf, at 56.

[115]   I discuss the details further below.

[116]   See Corinne A. Carey, Crafting a Challenge to the Practice of Drug Testing Welfare Recipients: Federal Welfare Reform and State Response as the Most

PRWORA is sometimes thought of as basically changing default rules, so that now there is a presumption in favor of state flexibility.[117] This is true in some regards, and as I discuss below, state TANF rules certainly do vary widely. On the other hand, the PRWORA regime has its own rigidities. For example, states are required to impose lifetime time limits on TANF receipt of no greater than 60 months,[118] and PRWORA required that by 2002, at least half of families receiving TANF-funded aid be engaged in qualified work activities.[119]

States responded to PRWORA by creating programs with the same kinds of diversity seen in the waiver programs. They adjusted benefit reduction rates, created welfare-to-work programs, implemented various sanctions to punish recipients who fail to follow work-activity requirements, and imposed time limits. In addition, they took advantage of the elimination of the entitlement to cash assistance by developing "diversion" programs to encourage applicants not to take up cash welfare in the first place.[120] Some states also increased work-support subsidies, including for child care, transportation, and various types of wage subsidies.[121]

2. Evidence on the effects of welfare reform

The literature on welfare reform's effects is enormous. Grogger and Karoly's book *Welfare Reform: Effects of a Decade of Change* [122] has separate *chapters* on welfare reform's effects on each of the following topics: welfare use and payments; employment, labor supply and earnings; income

---

Recent Chapter in the War on Drugs (1998) 46 *Buffalo Law Review* 281, 297 ("South Carolina, the recipient of one such waiver, became the first state to make drug testing part of its welfare program.").

[117] See, e.g., Blank (2002), *supra* note 6 1106 (stating that the block granting of TANF "essentially removed almost all federal eligibility and payment rules, giving states much greater discretion in designing their own cash public assistance programs. This also eliminated a federal entitlement to cash assistance. States could choose which families they supported.").

[118] See, e.g., ibid.; note also that "[s]tates could exempt up to 20 percent of their caseload from this limit, could set shorter time limits if they chose, or could continue funding assistance to families entirely out of state funds after sixty months."

[119] Ibid. Note that PRWORA treated caseload reductions and work as perfect substitutes for this purpose: caseload reductions were credited toward the work activity requirement, so that "a state that reduced its caseload by 50 percent would meet its work requirement, regardless of how many current or former recipients were actually employed."

[120] According to Blank, 30 states used some sort of diversion program. Ibid., at 1114.

[121] Ibid.

[122] Grogger and Karoly (2005), *supra* note 6.

and poverty; family structure; and child outcomes. Grogger and Karoly report that most of the reforms considered in the papers they reviewed led to increases in employment.[123] Some policies, like financial work incentives, increased welfare use. Others, like time limits and sanctions for non-compliance with program rules, reduced welfare use.[124] Overall, the studies Grogger and Karoly reviewed vary as to the effects of reform on income.[125]

None of the studies Grogger and Karoly reviewed find evidence that welfare reform increased poverty, while several of the estimates they reviewed suggest that reform programs actually reduced poverty.[126] In principle this set of results is in line with the labor supply theory discussed above. Since maximum benefit levels were substantially less than the poverty line, even wholesale elimination of welfare eligibility would not increase the official poverty rate. On the other hand, if there are large entry effects, then providing AFDC could have caused increases in the officially measured poverty rate by causing women who would earn more than the poverty threshold in the absence of the AFDC program to forgo paid work in favor of the combination of lower consumption and zero/fewer work hours. Thus, it is theoretically possible that eliminating AFDC altogether might reduce the number of women whose income falls below the official poverty line. To the extent that welfare reform eliminated welfare eligibility for some women, it fits within this analysis.

But the evidence that welfare reform reduced poverty tends to come from studies evaluating programs that involved generous financial incentives to work,[127] which are present only in some states. Thus I am dubious of claims that reductions in the poverty rate attributable to welfare reform were the per se result of eliminating AFDC's labor supply disincentive. Rather, at least some of these reductions in poverty were due to the more active role that government played in subsidizing those who work. This fact should be no surprise to anyone familiar with the literature on federal (and state) EITC programs.[128]

In general, Grogger and Karoly found mixed results on marriage and childbearing, with some studies showing effects in each direction and relatively few showing statistical significance.

---

123 See ibid., Figure 10.1 and text at 231–3.
124 See ibid., Figure 10.2 at 232.
125 Ibid.
126 See ibid., Figure 10.2 at 232 and Figure 10.5 at 247.
127 See ibid., text at 234.
128 For a recent discussion of the federal EITC, see Nada Eissa and Hilary Hoynes, Redistribution and Tax Expenditures: The Earned Income Tax Credit (June 2011) 64(2/2) *National Tax Journal* 689–730.

Finally, note that much of the evidence reviewed by Grogger and Karoly —whether on poverty or other outcomes—comes from state-time periods when time limits did not yet apply.[129] Once the time limit binds for a given woman, her state's welfare program essentially has been eliminated for her.[130] At this point, any positive effects on work, income and other outcomes that result from more active state involvement in the woman's case can be expected to disappear, or at the least attenuate substantially. As a result, it is unclear whether reforms built on states' active labor market involvement will persist in the long run.[131] Unfortunately, we do not have the kind of variation in programs necessary to distinguish between short -and long-run effects.[132]

Grogger and Karoly conclude that the evidence "is generally consistent with the outcomes about which" their (quite standard) behavioral model "makes the clearest predictions."[133] They note, though, that a number of outcomes—including poverty, marriage, childbearing, and child

---

[129] See Grogger and Karoly (2005), *supra* note 6, text at 247 (noting the fact that results in their Figure 10.5 "represent the effects of reform as a bundle during the pre-time limit period. Post-time limit evidence is very limited, and most studies summarized in this figure cover time periods prior to when recipients could have exhausted their benefits."). Also, note that only some of the randomized experiments from which Grogger and Karoly's evidence on detailed aspects of welfare programs is drawn involved time limits.

[130] If states do not share data, then as many have noted, time-limited recipients could migrate to avoid time limits; see Gelbach (2004), *supra* note 97, and, e.g., Hal W. Snarr and Mark L. Burkey, A Preliminary Investigation of Welfare Migration Induced by Time Limits (2006) 36(2) *Journal of Regional Analysis and Policy* 124–39.

[131] This discussion recalls the point from section III.A.2, concerning the two programs—one providing transitory help and one providing more or less permanent assistance—implicitly embedded in AFDC. Almost by definition, the women most likely to be in need of long run labor market help are those served by the long run AFDC program. Thus, these are the women most likely to benefit from welfare reform's carrots—which PRWORA eliminates when these women reach the time limit.

[132] There is plenty of individual-level data, to be sure. But as I argue in section III below, cross-state variation in state program rules no longer is the simple source of identifying variation that it was in the pre-welfare reform era. That leaves researchers to use within-state designs, but without random assignment experiments, it is difficult to separately identify the effects of infrequent policy changes—like introduction of a state's time limit together with active labor market involvement—from effects of unrelated labor market variables, like labor demand. Finally, random assignment studies tend to be relatively short, with at most a few years of follow up, which makes it difficult to use them to assess effects over more than the medium-to-long run.

[133] Grogger and Karoly, *supra* note 6, at 248.

well-being—have been understudied.[134] In addition, they point out that most of what we know about the causal effects of welfare reform comes from relatively short follow-up periods,[135] whereas, as I note just above, an assessment of whether welfare reform "worked" or didn't really involves long run impacts. While I have the utmost respect for the job that Grogger and Karoly did describing and assessing an overwhelming amount of research, I have argued elsewhere that one drawback of their book is that it does not attack the question of "just how much welfare reform 'worked,' and how much of the work was due to other factors (including those that may have interacted with welfare reform, as noted by GK[)]."[136] This is not an easy question, though I do take a partial crack at it below.

For other discussions and reviews of the evidence, as well as some research conducted after Grogger and Karoly's publication, I refer readers to the following sources:

- Rebecca M. Blank, Evaluating Welfare Reform in the United States (2002) 40 *Journal of Economic Literature* 1105.
- Robert A. Moffitt, The Temporary Assistance for Needy Families Program, Chapter 5 of Robert A. Moffitt, ed., *Means-Tested Transfer Programs in the United States*, University of Chicago Press (2003).
- James P. Ziliak, ed., *Welfare Reform and its Long-Term Consequences for America's Poor*, Cambridge University Press (2009).
- Janet M. Currie, *The Invisible Safety Net: Protecting the Nation's Poor Children and Families*, Princeton University Press (2008).

II.   WELFARE REFORM AND THE LABORATORIES OF DEMOCRACY ANALOGY

In this section, I discuss welfare reform through the lens of Justice Brandeis's laboratories of democracy metaphor. Without variation of one type or another, of course, nothing can be learned about the empirical world; but laboratories are only as good as the experiments their operators conduct. Early in the welfare reform process, the federal requirement that states conduct evaluation studies led to a number of high-quality evaluations

---

[134]   Ibid.
[135]   Ibid.
[136]   Jonah B. Gelbach, Review of Welfare Reform: Effects of a Decade of Change (2006) 44 *Journal of Economic Literature* 1056, 1058.

of welfare reform programs. A number of these involved random assignment, and public use data are available for several.[137] Even the best of these experiments provide somewhat limited guidance for future policy choices, as most of them stirred together multiple reforms, allowing experimental evaluation of only the resulting soup.[138] But the multi-faceted nature of post-PRWORA 1990s devolution was a considerably worse development from a laboratories' perspective. States introduced dozens of reforms at once, effectively destroying the capacity of even quite savvy researchers to extract clear signals from the data about the details of state welfare reform policies.

As I discuss in Part II.A above, there was relatively little structural variation in the AFDC system, with a consensus among empirical economists being that benefit level variation was far and away the most important source of cross-state program variation. But by the time the waiver-era and PRWORA dust settled, there were essentially 51 different welfare programs. To illustrate this point, consider the heroic efforts of the Urban Institute's "Assessing the New Federalism" (UI-ANF) project. This project produced hundreds of studies between the mid-1990s and 2007, focused on the design, implementation, and effects of the waivers and PRWORA.[139]

One part of the UI-ANF project was the "Welfare Rules Database" (WRD), wherein the Urban Institute undertook the herculean task of collecting and categorizing the various aspects of state welfare policies. There are 30 *categories* of variables included in the WRD! In alphabetical order, these categories are:

> Activities exemptions, Activities requirements, Activities sanctions, Asset test, Benefit computation, Child support, Child support sanctions, Components, Contracts and agreements, Countable income, Deemed income, Diversion, Dollar amounts, Earned income disregards, Eligibility by number/type parents,

---

[137] For example, the Manpower Demonstration Research Corporation (MDRC) posts a list of available files at www.mdrc.org/pudf_available.htm, with instructions on how to request them at www.mdrc.org/pudf_howto.htm.

[138] A notable exception is MDRC's evaluation of Minnesota's Family Investment Program, or MFIP. This random assignment evaluation included three study groups: the AFDC control group; the main MFIP program group, which faced work requirements and was provided financial incentives to work; and the MFIP-Incentives Only group, which received financial incentives to work but did not face work requirements. See Lisa A. Gennetian, Cynthia Miller, and Jared Smith, Turning Welfare into a Work Support: Six-Year Impacts on Parents and Children from the Minnesota Family Investment Program, MDRC, July 2005, available at www.mdrc.org/publications/411/full.pdf.

[139] As of February 12, 2012, the UI-ANF website lists 362 reports; see www.urban.org/center/anf/Reports.cfm, with the most recent dated August 3, 2007.

Eligibility of individual family members, Eligibility of pregnant women, Eligibility of two-parent families, Eligibility of units headed by minor parents, Family caps, Immunization and health screening policies, In kind income, Inclusion of non-citizens in the unit, Income and assets of children, Income eligibility tests, Minor parent activities and bonuses, School policies for dependent children, Time limits, Transitional benefits, and Treatment of Additional Adults in Household.

And remember: each of these 30 categories includes multiple variables that characterize a state's welfare program. As a result, the WRD contains hundreds of variables.[140] And even welfare reform did not change the fact that there are only 51 state-level jurisdictions. In other words, our system of state laboratories imposed more experimental treatments than there were experimental units.

Researchers interested in estimating causal effects of policy on behavior and outcomes have responded to this challenge in four primary ways. The first response is to use data from state-specific waiver evaluation studies, several of which used randomization of program assignment to assign welfare participants and applicants to either the old AFDC program or the state's waiver program. Examples of such work include various official reports that professional program evaluation groups such as Abt Associates, Mathematica, Manpower Demonstration Research Corporation (MDRC), and the Urban Institute produced under contract with states.[141] Other examples include journal articles using data from these experiments.[142]

---

[140]   While it is not obvious from the WRD's website how many variables the database contains, a simple lower bound can be discerned by searching the variable descriptions for those containing the word "the." This query (at http://anfdata.urban.org/wrd/query/WRDSearch_result.cfm?desc=the) returned 576 variables when I conducted it on November 19, 2011.

[141]   See, e.g., Erik Beecroft, Wang Lee, David Long, Pamela A. Holcomb, Terri S. Thompson, Nancy Pindus, Carolyn O'Brien, and Jenny Bernstein, The Indiana Welfare Reform Evaluation: Five-Year Impacts, Implementation, Costs and Benefits, Abt Associates, September 2003, available at www.abtassociates.com/reports/indiana_final_report.pdf; Thomas M. Fraker, Christine M. Ross, Rita A. Stapulonis, Robert B. Olsen, Martha D. Kovac, M. Robin Dion, Anu Rangarajan, The Evaluation of Welfare Reform in Iowa: Final Impact Report, Mathematica Policy Research, Inc., June 11, 2002, available at www.mathematica-mpr.com/publications/PDFs/iowawelreport.pdf; Dan Bloom, Susan Scrivener, Charles Michalopoulos, Pamela Morris, Richard Hendra, Diana Adams-Ciardullo, and Johanna Walter, with Wanda Vargas, Jobs First: Final Report on Connecticut's Welfare Reform Initiative, MDRC, February 2002, available at www.mdrc.org/publications/90/full.pdf.

[142]   Some examples include Jeffrey Grogger and Charles Michalopoulos, Welfare Dynamics under Time Limits (2003) 111(3) *Journal of Political Economy*

A second response to the too-much-variation problem is to apply non-experimental multi-variate methods to repeated observations on data from multiple states, with simplifying assumptions used to choose the treatment variables considered. One such approach is to compare state-year cells in which some form of welfare reform—waiver or TANF—is in effect to state-year cells in which no reform operates.[143] The resulting coefficient estimates are then interpreted as some sort of average impact of implementing the given reform (waiver or TANF) among implementing states. Because TANF implementation occurred over a brief, 16-month window, after which all states had TANF in effect, there is relatively little variation with which to identify its effects in this way. Moreover, if these effects vary over time, then all one can hope to identify concerning TANF are its short-run implementation effects.[144]

Another simplifying approach is to try to classify various welfare-plan characteristics into specific variables thought to be substantively interesting or important.[145] In one of the more ambitious such studies, Urban

530–54; Marianne P. Bitler, Jonah B. Gelbach, and Hilary W. Hoynes, What Mean Impacts Miss: Distributional Effects of Welfare Reform Experiments (2006) 96 *American Economic Review* 988; and Marianne P. Bitler, Jonah B. Gelbach, and Hilary Hoynes, Distributional Impacts of the Self-Sufficiency Project (April 2008) 92(3–4) *Journal of Public Economics* 748–65.

[143] Examples include, Rebecca Blank and Robert Schoeni, What Has Welfare Reform Accomplished? Impacts on Welfare Participation, Employment, Income, Poverty, and Family Structure, National Bureau of Economic Research Working Paper No. 7627, NBER. (March 2000); Marianne P. Bitler, Jonah B. Gelbach, Hilary W. Hoynes, and Madeline Zavodny, Welfare Reform, Marriage, and Divorce (2004) 41(2) *Demography* 213–36; Marianne P. Bitler, Jonah B. Gelbach, and Hilary W. Hoynes, Welfare Reform and Children's Living Arrangements (Winter 2006) 41(1) *Journal of Human Resources* 1–27; Marianne P. Bitler, Jonah B. Gelbach, and Hilary W. Hoynes, Welfare Reform and Health (2005) 40(2) *Journal of Human Resources* 309–34; Robert Kaestner and Elizabeth Tarlov, Changes in the Welfare Caseload and Health of Low-Educated Mothers (2006) 25(3) *Journal of Policy Analysis and Management* 623–44; Phillip Levine and Diane Whitmore, The Impact of Welfare Reform on the AFDC Caseload (1997) *National Tax Association Proceedings* 24–33; Jeffrey T. Lewis, The Impact of Welfare Reform on the Employment and Labor Supply of Female High School Dropouts (2007) 38 *New York Economic Review* 37–60.

[144] For a detailed discussion of what can be identified using the simple, any-reform-in-place approach, see Marianne P. Bitler, Jonah B. Gelbach, and Hilary W. Hoynes, Some Evidence on Race, Welfare Reform and Household Income (2003) 93(2) *American Economic Review* (Papers and Proceedings) 293–8.

[145] See, e.g., Jeffrey Grogger, The Effects of Time Limits, the EITC, and Other Policy Changes on Welfare Use, Work, and Income among Female-Headed Families (May 2003) 85(2) *Review of Economics and Statistics* 394–408; Jeffrey Grogger, Time Limits and Welfare Use (2004) 39 *Journal of Human Resources*

Institute researchers Signe-Mary McKernan and Caroline Ratcliffe examined the empirical relationship between poverty and 19 welfare policy variables.[146] Of these variables, the authors hypothesize that one should have an unambiguously positive effect on poverty and five should have an unambiguously negative effect, with the theoretical effects of the other 13 being ambiguous. Summing up their results, McKernan and Ratcliffe write that "[o]ur findings are generally consistent with our hypotheses," and I have no quarrel with that conclusion. Nor do I mean to criticize them for their serious and substantial efforts. Nonetheless, it is difficult to know quite what policy lessons to draw from a study that includes as regressors 19 inter-related policy variables, even as it excludes numerous others. One simply cannot tell whether these are the "right" variables, either in the sense that they are the most important from a policy perspective or in the sense that there are no important omitted policy variables that are correlated with, and thus proxied by, the included ones.

A third response to the too-much-variation problem is altogether to ignore the issues of cross-state policy variation and confounding factors, instead just comparing outcomes of interest before and after welfare reform occurred. This is the approach taken in an influential paper by Bruce Meyer and James Sullivan.[147] Meyer and Sullivan compare various measures of income and consumption before and after the welfare reforms of the 1990s,[148] finding no evidence of increases in material deprivation among single mothers.[149] They do find drops in a measure of well-being that places positive value on time spent in non-paid work activities, which is not surprising given the large increase in market work among single mothers over their study period.

A fourth approach is to try to use state program rules together with individual characteristics to measure the budget set facing each survey subject independently. One example of this approach is Fang and Keane

---

405–24; and James P. Ziliak, David N. Figlio, Elizabeth E. Davis, Laura S. Connolly, Accounting for the Decline in AFDC Caseloads: Welfare Reform or the Economy? (2000) 35(3) *Journal of Human Resources* 570–86.

[146] Signe-Mary McKernan and Caroline Ratcliffe, The Effect of Specific Welfare Policies on Poverty, Research Report, the Urban Institute, May 23, 2006 (available at www.urban.org/UploadedPDF/411334_welfare_policies.pdf).

[147] Bruce D. Meyer and James X. Sullivan, Changes in the Consumption, Income, and Well-Being of Single-Mother Headed Families (December 2008) 98(5) *American Economic Review* 2221–41.

[148] Specifically, Meyer and Sullivan (2008) consider various measures involving data that refer to the years 1993–2003.

[149] Ibid., at 2237.

(2004),[150] who painstakingly construct individual-specific budget constraints from the many dimensions along which state policies vary over time. They then exclude state and year dummies from their analysis, which amounts to assuming that their budget constraint measures capture every systematically important determinant of behavior across states and over time. While they regard this assumption as a feature, not everyone need agree.[151]

Francesca Mazzolari focuses primarily on time limits, rather than trying to code the entire budget constraint.[152] She uses data covering 1989–2003 from overlapping panels of the Survey of Income and Program Participation. Using panel data allows her to measure the remaining welfare program eligibility for each woman in her sample, rather than using only variables that quantify overall state policy.[153] Mazzolari finds that by 2003, time limits per se had reduced national caseloads by 25 percent.[154] Intriguingly, only about 5 of the 25 percent are explained by behavioral responses,[155] understood as women reducing their use of welfare in advance of the time limit in order to preserve future eligibility. The remaining 20 percentage points are the result of the mechanical effect that time limits eliminate eligibility once they bind. Thus, Mazzolari's paper suggests that very little of the large drop in welfare caseloads can be attributed to behavioral, as opposed to mechanical, changes related to time limits.

A final possible response to the too-much-variation problem is to simply stop trying to study the causal effects of welfare reform.[156] Judging

---

[150]   Hanming Fang and Michael P. Keane, Assessing the Impact of Welfare Reform on Single Mothers (2004) *Brookings Papers on Economic Activity* (1)1–116.

[151]   For an argument that this assumption is decidedly a bug, see Rebecca Blank's comments in the "Comments and Discussion" section of Fang and Keane (2004), starting especially at p. 97.

[152]   Francesca Mazzolari, Welfare Use when Approaching the Time Limit (2007) 42(3) *Journal of Human Resources* 596–618.

[153]   Such direct measurement is important because a woman who has used welfare for 59 months in a state with a 60-month time limit faces very different incentives from an otherwise-identical woman in the same state who has never used welfare.

[154]   Mazzolari (2007) *supra* note 152, at 616.

[155]   Ibid.

[156]   As a cheap-kill example (and one that I do not intend as a criticism of the Urban Institute or its many outstanding scholars and researchers), I note that the Urban Institute changed the name of the Assessing New Federalism project to the "Low-Income Working Families" project, whose stated *raison d'être* is no longer to "assess" welfare reform but rather to "appl[y] rigorous research methods

only by the numbers of papers I have received to referee and have seen on conference agendas—hardly a scientific measure, I readily concede—there seems to have been less focus on "traditional" cash welfare policy, at least in the economics research community, than there was either before or during the wave of 1990s reform. The attention paid to poverty and the problems of low-income people more broadly is focused now much more on other policy avenues like expansion of health coverage and EITC programs at the state or federal level. Of course, even if I am right about this drop in focus, perhaps it is simply the natural result of a public policy debate that has largely concluded. On this theory, we had a national conversation about how to get rid of traditional welfare policy, we pretty much got rid of it, and now there just isn't much of interest to discuss.[157]

But this seems too simple to me, because researchers do continue to study Medicaid, the EITC, unemployment compensation, various programs operating under the aegis of the Social Security Administration, and other social policies that have substantial effects on those with low incomes.[158] And if nothing else, graduate students need jobs and assistant professors need tenure. As such, I am convinced that if there were good variation to use, researchers would use it. Of course, the provision of good long run research opportunities was hardly the point of welfare reform. My point is simply that it shows. Welfare and welfare reform constitute a policy field where the evidence that exists largely followed the reforms, rather than providing the empirical inputs to a policy production function. And the reforms themselves have largely blocked information gathering. From a policy-design perspective, the story of welfare policy devolution is a cautionary tale concerning what can be learned from a simultaneous explosion of state-level experimentation. By my lights, anyway, welfare reform has been no exemplar of Justice Brandeis's laboratory.

---

to track families over time and to analyze the risks these families face." See www. urban.org/center/lwf/index.cfm.

[157]   Of course, former recipients of cash assistance might feel differently. But my sense was and continues to be that relatively little of the welfare policy debates focused on the desires of the recipients.

[158]   Indeed, Janet Currie has written a valuable book making the important point that these programs together constitute a safety net that is critical to the well-being of the disadvantaged—and that itself may come under the sort of political attack that felled AFDC. See Janet M. Currie, *The Invisible Safety Net: Protecting the Nation's Poor Children and Families*, Princeton University Press (2008).

III. DID WELFARE REFORM "WORK"? EXPERIMENTAL EVIDENCE FROM CONNECTICUT

Perhaps the most frequently discussed outcome variables in both academic and policy making circles are welfare caseloads and employment rates of single mothers. As Rebecca Blank has written, "[i]t remains very difficult in any of this literature to separate economic and policy effects. ... The combination of extremely strong economic growth with rapid policy change means that both effects were reinforcing each other."[159] Thus, Blank wrote, this important question "remains a difficult [one] to answer in an entirely credible manner."[160]

In this part of the chapter, I use experimental data from Connecticut, which conducted a high quality random assignment study of its Jobs First welfare reform.[161] Because it included arguably the sweetest carrot and biggest stick of reforms nationwide, I focus primarily on Connecticut's Jobs First evaluation. The evaluation involved a random assignment experiment of the state's waiver program, which subsequently formed the basis of Connecticut's TANF program. In section A of this part of the chapter, I review the facts and literature on caseloads and the economy. I then discuss the Jobs First program, and its differences from AFDC, in section B. In section C, I present results from Connecticut on welfare participation, employment, and income. I report analogous results from several other states' random assignment studies below.

A. Background on Caseloads and the Economy

As illustrated in Figure 5.5 above, the average monthly welfare caseload fell enormously—by more than half —after peaking at about five million cases in 1994. At the same time, employment rates for single mothers rose by a remarkable 10 percentage points, from about 68 to about 78 percent, between 1994 and 2000.

Many popular commentators and policy makers have concluded that

---

[159] Blank (2002), *supra* note 6, at 1136.

[160] Ibid.

[161] This section draws on an earlier working paper of mine, Jonah B. Gelbach, Much Ado about Relatively Little? Experimental Evidence on Welfare Reform, Caseloads, and Employment, typescript, December 8, 2004, available at http://gelbach.law.yale.edu/papers/caseloads-paper-dec-8-04.pdf. As that paper is unpublished and I have no plans to submit it for publication anywhere, I will use some of the text verbatim in the present chapter.

welfare reform caused these changes. As I discuss in Part II.C, above, economic theory suggests that most elements of reform should reduce caseloads and increase employment (though more generous earnings disregards should actually increase caseloads, other things being equal). However, I have noted that welfare reform was not the only change over the mid-to late-1990s. There were significant expansions in the EITC. And the traditional link between Medicaid coverage of children and AFDC participation was purposely broken, allowing many children to retain public health insurance even if their mothers left welfare. Such changes should also have caused reductions in welfare participation and increases in employment, as some literature suggests they did.

But the 800-pound gorilla in this literature is the remarkable economic boom that occurred throughout the latter part of the 1990s. The dashed line in the left panel of Figure 5.8 below plots the national caseload and national unemployment rate over the period between 1993 and 2000.[162] The figure shows that both variables fell steadily over this period. Of course, the unemployment rate is just one convenient example; virtually every measure of labor market conditions improved radically over this period. Without further evidence, one cannot rule out the possibility that the caseload and employment changes among the welfare population were due entirely to welfare reform, entirely to the economy, or (more likely) due to some combination of these factors. As noted above, numerous authors attempted to sift the data to answer this question.[163] The share of the caseload drop causally attributed to welfare reform in this literature ranged from a low of zero (or even a negative share, i.e., suggesting that welfare reform may have increased caseloads) to a high of about half.[164]

---

[162] All unemployment rates used in this section were downloaded from the Bureau of Labor Statistics (BLS) website and are seasonally adjusted by the BLS.

[163] Notable examples include Ziliak et al., (2000) *supra* note 145; Levine and Whitmore (1997), *supra* note 143; Robert Moffitt, The Effect of pre-PRWORA Waivers on Welfare Caseloads and Female Earnings, Income, and Labor Force Behavior, in *Economic Conditions and Welfare Reform*, ed. S.H. Danziger, W.E. Upjohn Institute of Employment Research (1999); Blank and Robert (2000), *supra* note 142; Rebecca M. Blank, What Causes Public Assistance Caseloads to Grow? (2001) 36(1) *Journal of Human Resources* 3–19.

[164] For example, results in James P. Ziliak et al. (2000), ibid., imply that two-thirds of the caseload drop is due to macroeconomic improvements, and that "in the absence of other influences, welfare reform would not have led to any decrease in aggregate caseloads," at 572, though they find that some specific types of waivers do reduce caseloads, holding constant other features of welfare reform. Blank (2001), ibid., finds that waivers in the 1990–94 period actually increased caseloads, while waivers in the 1994–96 period were responsible for 28 percent of the caseload drop over this period; similar findings appear in G.L. Wallace

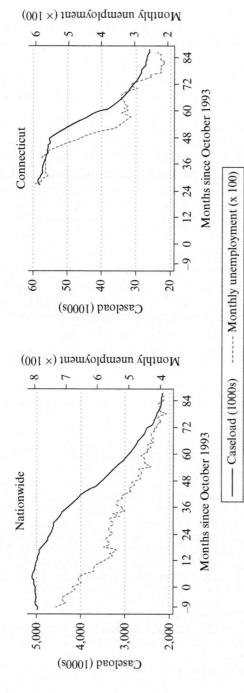

Source: Gelbach, *Much Ado about Relatively Little? Experimental Evidence on Welfare Reform, Caseloads, and Employment,* typescript, December 8, 2004, available at http://gelbach.law.yale.edu/papers/caseloads-paper-dec-8-04.pdf.

Figure 5.8   U.S. and Connecticut caseloads and unemployment rates, 1993–2000

The share of the caseload drop attributed to the economy ranges from zero to as much as two-thirds. In Rebecca Blank's words, "These estimates range widely across studies, and are highly affected by the years over which they are estimated and by the specification." As noted above, Blank concludes that "Despite evaluation and methodological problems, the bulk of the research literature suggests that the policy changes over the 1990s were important to the rapid caseload decline."[165]

On the other hand, Klerman and Haider[166] show that the county-specific monthly unemployment rate (and as few as two of its lags) explains half the decline in California's caseload over the period 1989–98, before California's TANF program was implemented. When they add variables measuring the levels and growth rates of the employment rate and retail earnings per capita, Haider, Klerman and Roth[167] show that 90 percent of the California caseload decline before 1998 can be explained by improvements in economic conditions. These two papers are notable not only because their findings suggest the possibility that welfare reform effects were limited, but also because they are based on internally consistent models of flow data. By contrast, most of the rest of the literature focuses on reduced form models of stocks, and Klerman and Haider show that those models are necessarily mis-specified.[168] Both of these papers emphasize that California's experience over the period before welfare reform may not have been representative of other states' experiences. For example,

---

and Rebecca M. Blank, What Goes Up Must Come Down? Explaining Recent Changes in Public Assistance Caseloads, in *Economic Conditions and Welfare Reform*, ed. S.H. Danziger, W.E. Upjohn Institute of Employment Research (1999) 49–89. Council of Economic Advisers (1997), Technical Report: Explaining the Decline in Welfare Receipt, 1993–1996, Working paper, CEA White Paper, finds that the share of the caseload drop due to waivers was 12–15 percent in 1993–96, while the share due to TANF implementation over 1996–98 was about 35 percent. J.E. O'Neill and M.A. Hill, Gaining Ground? Measuring the Impact of Welfare Reform on Welfare and Work, Working paper, Center for Civic Innovation, New York (2001). Civic Report 17 finds that welfare reform caused 12 percent of the caseload drop in 1992–96, and 49 percent in 1996–99. For more discussion of these papers, see Blank's (2002) review, *supra* note 6, 1105–66. Also, see Mazzolari (2007), *supra* note 152, and Jeffrey Grogger (2004), *supra* note 145, for work on how the introduction of time limits in particular was associated with caseload changes.

165   Blank (2002), *supra* note 6, at 1135.
166   Klerman and Haider (2004), *supra* note 21.
167   Steven J. Haider, Jacob Alex Klerman, and Elizabeth Roth, The Relationship Between the Economy and the Welfare Caseload: A Dynamic Approach (2003) 22 *Research in Labor Economics* 39–69.
168   Klerman and Haider (2004), *supra* note 21.

Klerman and Haider point out that "in comparing California to the rest of the nation, the 1990s recession was deeper, welfare reforms were passed later, and the reforms that were passed were weaker. Thus, the role for the economy may be greater in California than in other states."[169]

All of these papers—and most if not all of the literature seeking to disentangle policy from economic effects—use non-experimental data. These data characterize either individual employment and welfare use decisions or state-level welfare participation rates, employment rates, or caseload levels. Thus, the papers provide valid estimates of the contributions of policy and economic changes only when strong statistical assumptions are satisfied.[170] A random assignment experiment can avoid the need for these assumptions because women in both the treatment and control groups face identical economic conditions: the only reason the welfare programs facing these women are different is the randomized assignment of the women's effective program. Thus we can safely attribute differences in outcomes to the program itself, rather than other factors changing at the same time.

B.   Connecticut's Jobs First Program and Evaluation

Jobs First began operating in January 1996 as a waiver from AFDC rules,[171] and Connecticut subsequently adopted it as the state's TANF program.[172] For present purposes, the program had two key features.[173] First, as noted above, the program had a 21-month lifetime time limit,

---

[169]   Ibid., at 883 (citations omitted).

[170]   In co-authored work on welfare reform's effects on living arrangements, marriage and divorce, and health variables, I have made similar assumptions; see Bitler, Gelbach, Hoynes, and Zavodny (2004), *supra* note 142; Bitler, Gelbach, and Hoynes (2006), *supra* note 142; and Bitler, Gelbach, and Hoynes (2006), *supra* note 143.

[171]   See Dan Bloom, Laura Melton, Charles Michalopoulos, Susan Scrivener, and Johanna Walter, *Jobs First Implementation and Early Impacts of Connecticut's Welfare Reform Initiative*, at ES-1, MDRC, available at www.mdrc.org/publications/21/full.pdf.

[172]   See Connecticut Department of Social Services, *Jobs First – Background and History*, www.ct.gov/dss/cwp/view.asp?a=2353&q=305294.

[173]   It also made work activity mandatory for all women but those with a child younger than one year old; provided sanctions, which meant that the state would reduce benefit payments for violations of program rules; implemented a partial family cap; increased child care assistance; increased Medicaid assistance; and streamlined the rules governing how welfare recipients would receive whatever child support was paid on their children's behalf. For details on these and other aspects of the Jobs First program, see Bloom et al., *supra* note 114.

though participants who complied with other program requirements and had sufficiently low income could receive six-month extensions; others could receive exemptions with good cause.

Second, Jobs First allowed a 100 percent disregard of earned income up to the poverty line. To understand this provision, recall the modified NIT structure discussed in part II.A above, and ignore the interaction between the food stamps and welfare programs. For a woman with no non-labor income, a welfare program that disregards D dollars in earned income will pay a benefit equal to whatever is greater, zero or

$$P = G - t \times \max[0, Y - D], \tag{5.5}$$

so that benefits are reduced only if the participant earns more than D dollars.

Jobs First has the interesting feature that, in principle, the entire benefit payment is lost if the participant earns more than the disregard, D. This means that the benefit reduction rate t is locally infinite. For a less technical understanding of the program, consider Figure 5.9 below, which I have copied directly from Marianne P. Bitler, Jonah B. Gelbach, and Hilary W. Hoynes, *What Mean Impacts Miss: Distributional Effects of Welfare Reform Experiments.*[174] In the figure, the AFDC program is represented by the line connecting points A, C, and B (see Figure 5.2 above for discussion), while Jobs First is represented by the line connecting A and F. To understand the participation and labor supply effects of moving from AFDC to Jobs First, it helps to imagine that the same woman is trying to decide on her preferred labor supply and welfare participation separately under each program.

If the woman would participate on welfare when the welfare program she faces is AFDC, she either locates at point A or on the AFDC budget segment at some point between A and B, with point C being a generic example of this second location decision. Some women who would locate at A when they faced AFDC would also locate there when they faced Jobs First, while others would enter the labor force while still receiving in welfare, due to the increased return from combining work and welfare. Switching from AFDC to Jobs First will also cause a woman who would locate at a point like C to continue to combine work and welfare, so that she locates between A and F. Under the assumption of convex indifference curves, and that leisure is a normal good, the woman would increase work hours, i.e., wind up to the left of point C.

---

[174]   Bitler, Gelbach, and Hoynes, *supra* note 142.

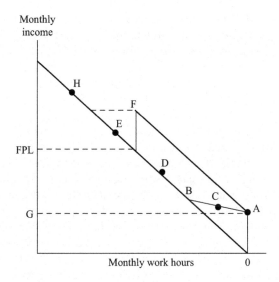

Figure 5.9   AFDC and Jobs First budget sets

Now consider a woman who would locate at point D under AFDC assignment. This woman would not participate in welfare if she faced AFDC
program rules. However, if we assume that leisure is a normal good, then
when she faced Jobs First program rules, this woman would participate in
welfare and reduce her work hours, locating on the line connecting A and
F, somewhere to the right of D. Next, consider a woman who would locate
at a point like E under AFDC assignment. This point involves consumption below 100 percent of the federal poverty line and entails more work
than is required to reach consumption equal to the poverty line under
Jobs First. That is, the woman can increase consumption and reduce
work hours by moving from E to F if she is assigned to Jobs First instead;
economic theory predicts she will take this opportunity. Finally, a woman
who would locate at point H under AFDC assignment might either stay
there under Jobs First assignment or move to point F, which entails both
less consumption and fewer work hours. Which she does will depend on
her willingness to exchange labor for consumption.

Putting all of this together yields an interesting and complex blend
of predictions. First, switching to Jobs First will have no impact on
hours worked or earnings for some of the women who would locate at
point A and points like H if AFDC were in effect. Second, switching to
Jobs First would increase hours worked and earnings for the rest of the
women who would locate at point A under AFDC assignment, as well
as those who would locate at points like C. Meanwhile, switching to

Jobs First would reduce hours worked and earnings for the rest of the women who would locate at point H under AFDC assignment, as well as all women who would locate at points like D and E. As for welfare participation, it will remain unchanged for women at point A and points like C under AFDC assignment, as well as some at points like H, but it will increase for those at points like D and E, and the rest of those at points like H.

Judging by Figure 5.9, then, a switch in program rules from AFDC to Jobs First would increase hours worked and earnings for some women, reduce these variables for others, and leave them unchanged for still others. The switch would cause some women to enter welfare participation, but it would not cause anyone to exit welfare. Of course, once the time limit became binding under the Jobs First program, there would be no available welfare program at all, and at that point welfare participation necessarily would fall.[175] My previous co-authored work shows that the basic predictions of static labor supply theory, augmented by observations related to the time limit, appear to be borne out by data from the Jobs First evaluation.[176]

In order to evaluate the performance of the Jobs First program, the state hired MDRC, to run a random assignment experiment. Details of the experimental evaluation appear in MDRC's final report,[177] but it will help to provide some basic facts here. Random assignment occurred between January 1996 and February 1997 in state welfare offices in New Haven and in Manchester.[178] Both new applicants and incumbent recipients in these offices were included in the experiment, with individuals assigned to each program with probability one-half. A total of 4,803

---

[175] This discussion shows that Jobs First is beset with what one might call multiple policy disorder: it encourages women to combine welfare and work, only to evict them from the welfare premises via time limits when they take the hint. This point has been made elsewhere. For example: "combining [the disregard expansion and time limit] complicates the program message: It is difficult to urge recipients both to leave welfare quickly in order to 'bank' their available months and to take advantage of a disregard by combining work and welfare." See D. Bloom, J.J. Kemple, P. Morris, S. Scrivener, N. Verma, and R. Hendra, *The Family Transition Program: Final Report on Florida's Initial Time-Limited Welfare Program*, Manpower Demonstration Research Corporation (2000).

[176] See Bitler, Gelbach, and Hoynes (2006), What Mean Impacts Miss, *supra* note 142.

[177] Bloom et al., *supra* note 114.

[178] The state implemented the Jobs First program rules for cases served through all other offices. Thus, beginning in January 1996, the experimental control group members were the only ones still facing AFDC program rules.

single-parent cases were included in the experiment,[179] of which 2,396 subsequently faced Jobs First program rules and the other 2,407 faced AFDC program rules. Experimental cases were followed for four years, with key post-random assignment data on monthly welfare benefit (including food stamps) payments and quarterly earnings coming from state administrative records. Some pre-random assignment data on benefit payments and earnings are available as well, and a baseline intake file includes information on some demographic variables. MDRC also did a detailed follow-up survey three years into the evaluation. Data from the evaluation have been used in numerous papers,[180] and public use files are available from MDRC for anyone who follows a simple request process.[181]

Look again at panel (b) of Figure 5.8, which shows the trend in Connecticut's statewide welfare caseload and unemployment rate during the experimental follow-up period. It shows that both variables fell steadily over this period, as with the nationwide time series for these variables. Thus, Connecticut's experience is broadly in line with the nationwide experience over the period of interest.

It also will be useful to compare the Jobs First experimental sample to the statewide and nationwide populations of welfare recipients. The first column of Table 5.4 below provides some basic summary statistics concerning the Jobs First experimental sample. The second and third columns provide information on the same variables for the Connecticut statewide and nationwide caseloads, which are based on my tabulations of 1993–97 AFDC Quality Control data.[182] Compared to those in the Jobs First experimental population, the statewide Connecticut caseload is more

---

[179] Of these, 30 cases are missing some data from the public use data set. Where appropriate, I exclude these cases in the analysis below.

[180] A list of MDRC publications related to "Family Well-Being and Child Development" appears at www.mdrc.org/area_publications_2.html; several Jobs First-related publications appear on this page. Scholarly publications using Jobs First evaluation data include Elizabeth Clark-Kauffman, Greg J. Duncan, and Pamela Morris, How Welfare Policies Affect Child and Adolescent Achievement (May 2003) 93(2) *American Economic Review* (Papers and Proceedings) 299–303; Susanna Loeb, Bruce Fuller, Sharon Lynn Kagan, and Bidemi Carrol, How Welfare Reform Affects Young Children: Experimental Findings from Connecticut—A Research Note (2003) 22(4) *Journal of Policy Analysis and Management* 537–50; Grogger and Michalopoulos (2003), *supra* note 142; and Bitler, Gelbach, and Hoynes (2006), *supra* note 142.

[181] See *supra* note 137.

[182] The AFDC-QC system was implemented to "ensure that the program's funds were going to people who were eligible, and to determine whether those who were eligible were receiving the amount to which they are entitled" (this quotation was taken from the Urban Institute's AFDC Data Archive

Table 5.4   Characteristics of Jobs First experimental sample compared to overall Connecticut and nationwide caseloads

Characteristic	Connecticut		National
	Jobs First Experiment	Quality Control	Quality Control
White	0.36	0.33	0.40
Black	0.37	0.30	0.34
Hispanic	0.21	0.35	0.18
Dropout	0.34	0.39	0.41
HS Diploma	0.56	0.51	0.44
More than high school diploma	0.06	0.10	0.15
At least 4 persons in case	0.22	0.30	0.33
Head younger than 25	0.29	0.29	0.30
Head aged 25–34	0.41	0.45	0.41
Head aged 35 or older	0.29	0.27	0.29
Recipient at time of random assignment	0.61	1.00	1.00
Current spell length 24 months or more	0.60	0.53	0.47
Number of observations	*4,773*	*4,227*	*181,295*

Hispanic, less black, less white, more likely to be dropouts, and living in households with larger cases. In general, then, the characteristics are reasonably similar across columns (leaving aside the fact that by construction, all Quality Control observations are current welfare recipients, whereas roughly 40 percent of Jobs First experiment observations are new applicants).

C.   Changes in Welfare Participation and Employment

Figure 5.10 below plots the shares of incumbent recipients included in the Jobs First treatment and AFDC control groups who received cash assistance in each of the 48 months after random assignment,[183] beginning

---

documentation page, available at http://afdc.urban.org/AFDocumentation. html).

[183] A very similar figure appears in the middle of Figure 3 of Bloom, Scrivener, Michalopoulos, Morris, Hendra, Adams-Ciardullo, Walter, and Vargas, *supra* note 114.

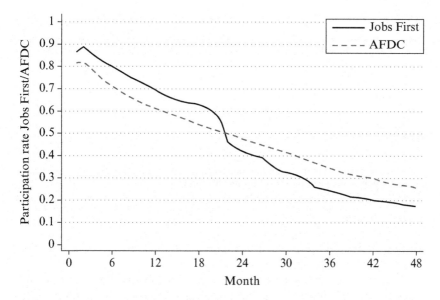

Figure 5.10   Post-random assignment welfare participation, by Jobs First program assignment

with the first month following random assignment.[184] Until month 22 after random assignment, the first month when the Jobs First time limit could bind for anyone in the experiment, the welfare participation rate was actually greater among Jobs First than AFDC group members. This is to be expected, given the discussion in part IV.B. In month 22, the Jobs First participation rate declines sharply, by about 11 points, which is strong evidence that the time limit was enforced for at least some women. For the

---

[184]   I use the first month after random assignment as the baseline. I would prefer to use the month of random assignment, of course, since the first month after random assignment will include some treatment effect (which explains why welfare participation is several percentage points greater for the Jobs First than the AFDC group—86.9 compared to 80.6 percent). However, the administrative data show that only 35 percent of new applicants in the Jobs First group, and 32 percent of those in the AFDC group, have positive cash assistance income in the month of random assignment. By the first month after random assignment, this share leaps 40 percentage points for the Jobs First group and 35 points for the AFDC group. This effect is clearly an artifact of delay in the dating of welfare payments related to approved applications, because welfare participation rates remain high in succeeding months. Thus the most reasonable approach is to use the first month after random assignment.

Table 5.5   Key results on welfare participation from Jobs First evaluation

	Jobs First Group		AFDC Group		Difference in Difference	Share Estimate
	Baseline‡	Change	Baseline‡	Change		
Full sample	86.9	−69.7*	80.6	−55.7*	−14.0*	20
Recipients only	95.6	−75.8*	94.2	−63.6*	−12.2*	21

Notes:
‡   Baseline is the first month after random assignment for the full sample and the month of random assignment for the recipients-only sample.
*   Differences are statistically significant with p values equal to 0 to three digits.
"Share Estimate" is the ratio of "Difference in Difference" estimate to Jobs First Group "Change" column.

rest of the period represented in Figure 5.10, the Jobs First participation rate is below the AFDC participation rate.

The first row and first column of Table 5.5 below shows that at baseline, 86.9 percent of Jobs First group members received cash assistance. The second column shows that this share fell by 69.7 percentage points over the 48-month follow-up period. But not all of this decline was caused by Jobs First—some of it would have happened even under AFDC due to the normal factors that induced women to leave welfare over time. Indeed, for the AFDC group, the welfare participation rate, which was 80.6 percent at random assignment, fell 55.7 percentage points over the 48-month follow-up period. Thus, the impact of the Jobs First program on the 48-month change in welfare participation rates was to reduce welfare participation by 14.0 percentage points (69.7 minus 55.7). This impact constitutes a 20 percent share of the Jobs First group's 69.7 percentage-point change.

The second row of Table 5.5 repeats this analysis for the subset of experimental subjects who were incumbent recipients at the time of random assignment (that is, this row excludes new applicants).[185] This group is of particular interest because the set of incumbent recipients at any point in time includes a larger share of those likely to spend a longer overall amount of time on welfare than does the set of new applicants.[186]

---

[185]   For the group of incumbent recipients, the data problem discussed in footnote 184 does not exist. Thus I use the month of random assignment as the baseline for this group.
[186]   For more on spell dynamics and the composition of cross-sections of current recipients, see, e.g., discussion in Chapter 2 of Bane and Ellwood (1994), *supra* note 98.

The results show that the Jobs First group's welfare participation rate fell by 12.2 percentage points more than the AFDC group's welfare participation rate did. Relative to the Jobs First group's drop of 75.8 percentage points, this amounts to only a 16 percent reduction.

Together, these results show that at most a fifth of the drop in welfare participation among those experiencing the Jobs First program is the causal result of welfare reform itself. This is a startling finding given the widely held view among policy makers, commentators, and some scholars that welfare reform was an important driver of the drop in caseloads. Yet here we have a random assignment experiment showing that 80 percent or more of the drop was caused by something else—perhaps the strong labor market, the EITC, or, possibly, the fact that AFDC participation was not a permanent condition for very many women who did use welfare.

One drawback of my approach in this analysis is that it captures only effects of Jobs First on program exit. There likely were also entry effects, i.e., changes in welfare participation among those who were not part of the group of women represented by the experimental study group. The steady state welfare participation rate under any set of program rules depends on both the probability that an incumbent recipient will exit and the probability that a non-recipient will enter welfare.[187] If Jobs First had a larger effect on program entry than it had on program exit, then my one-fifth results are underestimates of reform's overall relative contribution to the caseload drop.[188]

On the other hand, for women not yet facing a binding time limit, Jobs First actually encourages entry via the generous earnings disregard (see section B above). So it is possible that in the four-year period I study, accounting for entry effects would actually lead me to conclude that Connecticut's welfare reform caused even more of the caseload drop than Table 5.5 suggests.

The entry-effect problem is likely to be less pronounced in measuring the effects of welfare reform on employment than on welfare participation.

---

[187] For both accounting- and counterfactual simulation-based discussions of the important role that changes in entry rates appear to have played in changing welfare participation, see Jeffrey Grogger, Steven J. Haider, and Jacob Klerman, Why Did the Welfare Rolls Fall during the 1990's? The Importance of Entry (May 2003) 93(2) *American Economic Review* 288–92.

[188] Random assignment experiments have many advantages, but the inability of random assignment evaluations to measure entry effects is a serious shortcoming. It has been noted by a number of authors in the evaluation literature. See, James J. Heckman and Jeffrey A. Smith, Assessing the Case for Social Experiments (Spring 1995) 9(2) *Journal of Economic Perspectives* 85–110.

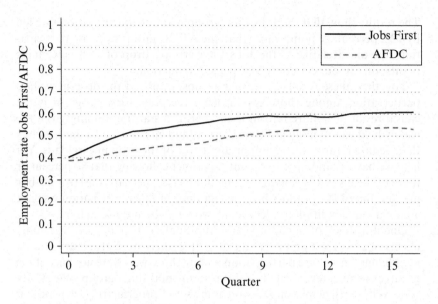

*Figure 5.11   Post-random assignment employment, by Jobs First program
assignment*

Thus, I will repeat the above analysis using employment rates as the outcome variable. Figure 5.11 plots the time series of employment rates, measured as the fraction of women with positive quarterly earnings, by program assignment group. It shows that employment increased more, and more quickly, among Jobs First group members than among those assigned to AFDC, though AFDC group members also increased their employment over the study period.

In Table 5.6 below, I quantify these trends. The table's top row shows that 39.1 percent of Jobs First group members had positive quarterly earnings at baseline.[189] This share increased by 21.0 percentage points over the 16 quarters following random assignment. AFDC group members had a baseline employment rate of 39.6 percent, which increased by 13.9 percentage points. The difference in these changes is 7.1 percentage points (21.0 minus 13.9). This difference represents only 34 percent of the 21.0 percentage-point increase in the post-random assignment employment rate for Jobs First group members.

---

[189]   I use the time of random assignment as baseline for both the full sample and the recipients subsample. This is appropriate because earnings data do not have the problem discussed in footnote 184.

Table 5.6   Key results on employment from Jobs First evaluation

	Jobs First Group		AFDC Group		Difference in Differences	Share Estimate
	Quarter of RA	Change	Quarter of RA	Change		
Full sample	39.1	21.0*	39.6	13.9*	7.1*	34
Recipients only	35.8	25.3*	34.6	18.3*	7.0*	28

Notes:
* Differences are statistically significant with p values equal to 0 to three digits.
"Share Estimate" is the ratio of "Difference in Difference" estimate to Jobs First Group "Change" column.

The table's bottom row shows that employment results were broadly similar for the subset of women who were receiving AFDC at the time of random assignment. Of these women, 35.8 percent of Jobs First group members had positive quarterly earnings at the time of random assignment, and this share increased by 25.3 percentage points over the 16 quarters following random assignment. AFDC group members had a baseline employment rate of 34.6 percent, which increased by 18.3 percentage points. The difference in these changes is 7.0 percentage points (25.3 minus 18.3). This difference is roughly the same as the difference for the full sample, and it represents only 28 percent of the 25.3 percentage-point increase in the post-random assignment employment rate for Jobs First group members who were receiving AFDC at the time of random assignment.

In the top two rows of Table 5.7, I repeat the same basic exercise for average quarterly earnings (measured in nominal dollars). In the quarter of random assignment, women in the Jobs First group had average earnings of $586, while those in the AFDC group had average earnings of $631. By the 16th quarter following random assignment, quarterly earnings among those assigned to the Jobs First program had risen dramatically, by $1,651. But the AFDC group saw nearly the same increase, with the $89 difference between these two increases amounting to just five percent of the increase in the Jobs First group's earnings. The same calculation shows that, of the equally impressive increase in quarterly earnings among incumbent recipients assigned to the Jobs First group, only six percent can be causally attributed to welfare reform. These results indicate that whatever factors caused the Jobs First group's earnings to increase so much had little to do with changes in welfare rules.

The next two rows of Table 5.7 analyze changes in transfer payments,

Table 5.7   Results on average quarterly earnings, transfers, and earnings plus transfers (in nominal dollars)

	Jobs First Group		AFDC Group		Difference in Differences	Share Estimate
	Quarter of RA	Change	Quarter of RA	Change		
Earnings						
Full sample	586	1,651*	631	1,562*	89i	5
Recipients only	479	1,615*	500	1,511*	103i	6
Transfers						
Full sample	1,579	−1,047*	1,433	−812*	−235*	22
Recipients only	2,057	−1,426*	1,947	−1,189*	−237*	16
Total Measured Income (earnings plus transfers)						
Full sample	2,165	603*	2,063	750*	−147**	−24
Recipients only	2,536	189***	2,447	323*	−134i	−71

Notes:
i   Differences not statistically significant from zero at conventional significance levels.
*   Differences are statistically significant with p values equal to 0 to three digits.
**   Difference is statistically significant with p value equal to 0.068.
***   Difference is statistically significant with p value equal to 0.003.

i.e., combined cash assistance and food stamps payments. In the random assignment quarter, Jobs First group members had average transfer payments of $1,579, compared to $1,433 for those in the AFDC group. For Jobs First group members, transfer payments dropped by $1,047 by the 16th quarter following random assignment, which was $235 more than the $812 decline for AFDC group members. Thus, 22 percent (100 percent times 235 ÷ 1,047) of the decline in transfer payments among Jobs First group members was caused by differences in welfare program rules. For incumbent recipients assigned to the Jobs First group, transfer payments fell by $237 between the quarter of random assignment and the 16th quarter following. This amounted to 16 percent of the $1,426 drop observed among Jobs First group members.

Next, consider the bottom two rows of Table 5.7, which compare changes in the sum of earnings and transfers—what I will call total measured income.[190] The figures in these rows show that Jobs First group members saw their quarterly total measured income rise by $603

[190]   Note that this measure of income excludes the value of the EITC, unreported earnings, transfers from family members or significant others (including child

between random assignment and the 16th quarter following. This is a substantial increase given their baseline total measured income of $2,165. However, total measured income rose by $750 for AFDC group members over the same period. Thus, the Jobs First program caused quarterly total measured income to fall by $147 over the follow-up period—which means that quarterly total measured income would have been 24 percent *greater* among Jobs First group members had they instead been assigned to the AFDC group. The same analysis shows that for incumbent recipients assigned to Jobs First, quarterly total measured income among these women rose by only $189 during the follow-up period. The difference-in-differences estimate in the final row of Table 5.7 shows that these women's increase in total measured income would have been $134—or 71 percent—greater still had they been assigned to AFDC.

At least for Connecticut, the results in Table 5.5–Table 5.7 constitute a striking rebuke to the triumphalist consensus, which holds that welfare reform is the primary cause of plummeting welfare use and spiking employment. These results show that reforms in the welfare rules were a relatively small factor in explaining either the drop in caseloads or the increase in employment observed over the period between 1996 and 2000. The results also show that differences in program rules explain essentially none of the very substantial growth in earnings among women in the Jobs First evaluation.[191] If these facts hold for other states as well, that would sharply contradict the view that changes in welfare program rules "were one of the primary causes behind falling caseloads, rising employment, and growing earnings among single mothers," as Rebecca Blank recently put it.[192] Changes in Connecticut's program rules may have been a factor, but they have certainly not been a "primary" one.

Moreover, the part of the caseload drop that is attributable to reform appears to be due entirely to the enforcement of Connecticut's time limit. Not even the most fervent devotees of evaluation methodology needed a

---

support), and so on. However, it is the only measure for which the Jobs First evaluation provides directly observed data.

[191] Given that welfare reform explains some of the observed employment growth, this necessarily means that working women in the Jobs First group are working fewer hours than AFDC group members, that they are working for lower wages, or both. Unfortunately, there is no source of administrative data in Connecticut that measures hours or wages (MDRC did collect such data in a follow-up survey, but that occurred only once, three years after random assignment).

[192] See Blank (2009), *supra* note 6, at 52.

random assignment experiment to know that welfare caseloads could be reduced by simply making many would-be participants ineligible.[193]

In addition, it is notable that most of the Jobs First-induced increase in employment occurred in the early quarters following random assignment. Indeed, employment rates in the sixth quarter after random assignment were 54.5 percent for the Jobs First group and 47.1 percent for the AFDC group, which amounts to a 7.4 percentage-point impact of the Jobs First program for that quarter. From this quarter until the end of the follow-up period, the two groups' employment rates increased by virtually identical amounts. Thus, Jobs First's entire treatment effect on employment had already occurred by the sixth quarter post-random assignment. Recall that no one could lose benefits as a result of the time limit before the end of the seventh quarter following random assignment. Thus, the quarters when Jobs First's impact on employment unfolded were also those when Jobs First's earnings disregard carrot would have been most effective. This finding suggests that much of the relatively small salutary impact of welfare reform on employment—as distinct from the upward trend that would have happened anyway—may be due to carrots rather than program-eliminating sticks.

D.   Did Welfare Reform "Work"? Final Thoughts Concerning Jobs First

The results just presented concern only welfare applicants or recipients from two offices in a single state. So a skeptic might accept the results above but refuse to believe they apply more generally. But there are several reasons not to be such a skeptic. First, Table 5.4 suggests that on a number of relevant demographic indicators, the Jobs First experiment's sample was not too different from the nationwide caseload. Second, in my working paper *Much Ado About Relatively Little*, I carried out the same type of analysis using data from experimental evaluations of reform programs not only in Connecticut, but also in Florida, Iowa, Minnesota, and Vermont.[194] Most of the estimates suggested that welfare reform explained relatively little of the caseload drop or employment increase observed among experimental treatment group members in these states. The primary exception was for Minnesota's MFIP program, for which I evaluated two reform programs. One of these had a generous earnings

---

[193]   On this point, again see Mazzolari (2007), *supra* note 152, on the issue of mechanical effects of time limits.

[194]   For details of the other states' reform programs, which vary substantially, I refer interested readers to Table 1 of my working paper, Gelbach (2004), *supra* note 161, and the discussion, at 8–9, surrounding it.

disregard reform, and one had the disregard as well as other changes, most notably including work requirements; neither program included a time limit. For these programs, the shares of employment changes attributable to reform approach or meet the 50 percent mark.

Thus, while Connecticut's experience with Jobs First surely was not identical to other states' experiences with their own pre-PRWORA evaluations, I believe the burden should shift. Triumphalists should be expected to justify their position with evidence other than post-welfare-reform-*ergo-propter*-welfare-reform. At least according to random assignment evaluation data, different programs in different states likely made very different contributions to observed changes in caseloads and employment. And in at least some of these, if not most, the contributions likely were considerably smaller than many seem to think. Finally, over the 48-month follow-up period, Jobs First caused a statistically significant drop in total measured income due to reductions in welfare payments that exceeded the Jobs First-caused increase in earnings.

So what does Connecticut's experience with Jobs First tell us about whether welfare reform worked? Even for welfare reform's cheerleaders, the answer is surprisingly far from an obvious yes. The evidence just discussed shows that trends in key outcome variables were more similar than not among AFDC-assigned and Jobs First-assigned women. Moreover, the reduction in total measured income appears to have been concentrated in the bottom part of the total measured income distribution.[195] Presumably this feature will have worsened over time, as the mechanical effects of time limits eliminate eligibility for welfare benefits over time. At least for Connecticut, experimental evidence suggests that radical welfare reform was not the triumph that some believe it to be.

IV. SUMMARY

In this chapter, I have discussed the basic elements of the AFDC program created by the Social Security Act of 1935, as well as the many differences between it and the state TANF programs that replaced it following PRWORA. I have discussed the basic economics of AFDC's incentive effects, as well as the ways in which TANF programs might be expected to alter those incentives, and thus behavior. I have argued that the empirical evidence on AFDC's behavioral impact was never nearly as

---

[195] See discussion at 1003–4, and Figure 8, of Bitler, Gelbach, and Hoynes (2006), *supra* note 142.

compelling, nor as sizable, as AFDC's critics maintained. Likewise, there is—at most—limited empirical evidence supporting what I have called the "triumphalist" position, that the wave of state and federal welfare reforms that took place in the 1990s play an important role in explaining the increase in employment among single mothers. Either the economic boom of the late 1990s, or some other difficult-to-measure change, appears to have played a more important role than welfare reform. What is more, the uncontrolled experimentation of the last two decades has left us with a crazy-quilt collection of state programs that do not lend themselves to the kind of empirical research that would be necessary to benefit from the Brandeisian idea of states as laboratories of democracy.

6. Medicaid

Marianne P. Bitler and Madeline Zavodny*

Medicaid is the public health insurance program for eligible low-income individuals and families in the United States. The program has grown considerably since it was created in 1965. Medicaid and the related Children's Health Insurance Program were projected to cover over 60 million people, almost one-fifth of the population, in fiscal year 2010 at a cost of $427 billion. These numbers will surely rise as a result of the Affordable Care Act (ACA), the health insurance reform law passed in 2010, which among other changes allows states to expand Medicaid eligibility for adults to 138 percent of the federal poverty guideline.[1]

Medicaid is jointly funded by the federal and state governments and is administered by states. States must follow certain federal mandates but also traditionally have had considerable leeway to determine eligibility and services. This creates cross-state variation that helps researchers identify the program's effects on people's behavior. Indeed, states are not even required to have a Medicaid program. Within the first year of its being created 26 states were offering Medicaid and 23 others plus the District of Columbia joined over the next few years. The holdout was Arizona, which created a Medicaid program only in 1982 (Gruber, 2003).

There are large differences across states in per-capita Medicaid expenditures. Expenditures per Medicaid beneficiary in fiscal year 2007 were $8450 in New York and $3168 in California, compared with an overall average of $5163 (Gilmer and Kronick, 2011). These differences partly arise from the considerable discretion states have to set reimbursement levels to health care providers and to set eligibility rules. They also arise from differences in patterns of procedure use, outcomes and the underlying characteristics of populations, such as the percentages of elderly and disabled (e.g., Fisher et al., 2003a, 2003b). The partisan make-up of

*   We thank Lara Shore-Sheppard for helpful discussions.
[1]   The 138 percent includes an income disregard of 5 percent of the federal poverty level; eligibility is based on adjusted income up to 133 percent of the poverty level.

the state legislature appears to affect state eligibility rules for children, with states with more Democrats in the legislature having more generous eligibility rules; the political party of the governor and partisan control of the legislature are not significantly related to program generosity, however (Baughman and Milyo, 2008).

This chapter provides an overview of the economics of Medicaid. After explaining how the program is structured, we briefly discuss the economics of health insurance and then delve into two key issues: take-up and crowd-out. The chapter then turns to the evidence on the effects of Medicaid on health and other behaviors. We conclude with some thoughts on the future of Medicaid and important areas for future research.

PROGRAM STRUCTURE

To be eligible for Medicaid, a person must meet resource and categorical restrictions. The resource restrictions include having income below a specified low threshold that varies with family size and composition. States determine the income thresholds, subject to minimums and maximums set by the federal government. Some states also impose a limit on assets, although few states consider assets when determining children's eligibility (Department of Health and Human Services, 2010). Prior to the implementation of the ACA, the categorical restrictions in most states limited eligibility to people who belong to one of several demographic groups: children, parents of dependent children, pregnant women, the blind and disabled and the elderly. There is also a "medically needy" program for people who would otherwise be eligible but whose incomes are too high to qualify for Medicaid unless their medical expenses are subtracted from their income. During the 2000s, a few states extended coverage to low-income, non-disabled, non-elderly childless adults and/or parents.

The ACA encourages states to expand eligibility for Medicaid. Federal funding has been made available to states that expand eligibility to people with incomes below 138 percent of the federal poverty level. This extends coverage to non-disabled, childless adults of working age with relatively low incomes, a group that previously had a very low rate of Medicaid eligibility. If all states choose to participate in the ACA-related Medicaid expansions, up to 16 million additional people will become eligible for Medicaid by 2014. However, as of December 2013, 14 states were planning to participate in 2014, two at a later date and 23 had no plans to participate in the expansions, thus continuing the federalist nature of the current system (Kaiser Family Foundation, 2013).

Historically, Medicaid eligibility was limited to people receiving cash welfare benefits through the Aid to Families with Dependent Children (AFDC) or Supplemental Security Income (SSI) programs.[2] Welfare reform and other legislative changes during the 1980s and 1990s eroded the link between Medicaid and cash welfare programs. As Figure 6.1 shows, these changes led to a doubling in the percentage of the population covered by Medicaid at some point in a given year.

Medicaid eligibility was expanded dramatically for children and pregnant women beginning in the mid-1980s. The early phase of the expansions required states to cover several groups of poor pregnant women that did not meet the family structure requirements of the AFDC program. In the later phases of the expansion, states were first allowed to cover additional groups of low- and middle-income pregnant women and young children and then required to do so. For example, states were required to cover pregnant women and children under age six in families with incomes up to 133 percent of the federal poverty line by April 1990, and by July 1991 they were required to begin phasing in coverage for all children under age 19 in families with incomes up to 100 percent of the poverty line.[3] States also were given the option to extend coverage to pregnant women and children under age six in families with incomes up to 185 percent of the poverty line. States can extend coverage even further at their own expense.

As a result of the expansions, the fraction of all children aged 0–15 eligible for Medicaid increased from around 13 percent in 1983 to almost 31 percent in 1996. However, the fraction actually enrolled in Medicaid only increased from 13 percent to about 23 percent (Gruber, 2003). There are several potential reasons for such low take-up, as explored below. Another result of the expansions is that over one-third—and in some recent years over two-fifths—of births in the U.S. are covered by Medicaid each year.

There was considerable variation in the timing and extent of the expansions across states. For example, in July 1991, 29 states exceeded the required threshold of 133 percent of the poverty line for pregnant women and young children; six of those had expanded coverage just in the previous six months. Eligibility increases tended to be larger in the South, where states traditionally had very low income limits for AFDC eligibility, than in the Northeast and West, where AFDC programs tended to be relatively generous even before the expansions. In the mid-1990s, a number of states

---

[2] AFDC (reconfigured as Temporary Assistance for Needy Families (TANF) as part of the 1996 welfare reform law) provided monthly benefits to low-income families with minor children. SSI is a program administered by the Social Security Administration that pays monthly benefits to disabled, blind and elderly (65 and older) individuals with low incomes and assets.

[3] See Gruber (2003) for details on the expansions.

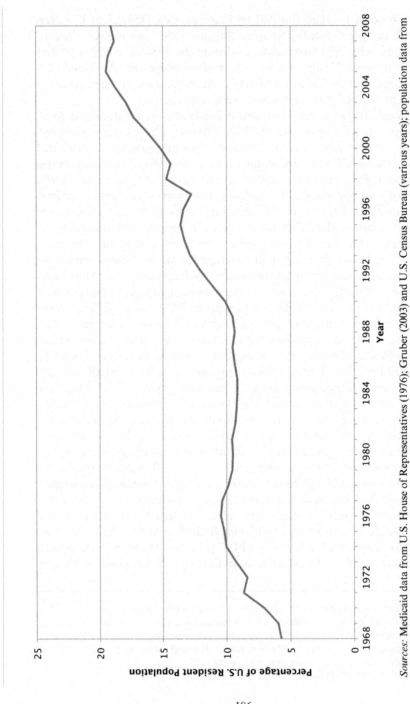

Sources: Medicaid data from U.S. House of Representatives (1976); Gruber (2003) and U.S. Census Bureau (various years); population data from www.census.gov.

Figure 6.1   Medicaid recipients as a percentage of the U.S. population, 1968–2008

received waivers from the traditional AFDC program that gave them even more latitude to expand Medicaid eligibility. Finally, the formal delinking of cash welfare for families with children from Medicaid eligibility that came with federal welfare reform devolved even more flexibility to the states in determining eligibility.

The State Children's Health Insurance Program (SCHIP, later shortened to CHIP) was created in 1997 to provide public health insurance to children in families with incomes too high to be eligible for Medicaid but typically too low to afford private health insurance. States were allowed to provide coverage to uninsured children in families with incomes up to 200 percent of the poverty line or 50 percentage points above their threshold for traditional Medicaid. This led to considerable cross-state variation in program generosity. States also differ in the degree of cost-sharing and the types of services covered and in whether expansions were implemented through the state's traditional Medicaid program or not. When the program was reauthorized in 2009, the minimum eligibility threshold was set at 200 percent of the poverty line. Together, Medicaid and CHIP covered one-third of all children in the U.S. in 2009 (Kaiser Family Foundation, 2010a). As discussed below, crowd-out from private insurance is a major concern with regard to Medicaid and CHIP.

Partly as a result of the expansions, women of child-bearing age and children comprised about 70 percent of Medicaid recipients in 2009. However, the elderly and the disabled accounted for the majority of program expenditures, largely because of the high cost of long-term care. Medicaid covers a large share of the low-income elderly and disabled. Nearly 8.8 million Medicare beneficiaries have incomes low enough to qualify for Medicaid. These people are called "dual eligibles." Medicaid covers these participants' Medicare premiums and cost-sharing and services not covered by Medicare, such as long-term care. In 32 states and D.C., SSI beneficiaries are automatically eligible for Medicaid. In another seven states, SSI beneficiaries are eligible for Medicaid but must file a separate application. The remaining states have rules for Medicaid eligibility that differ from the eligibility rules for SSI.

Another important component of Medicaid eligibility involves citizenship or legal residency.[4] Before welfare reform, most documented legal residents were eligible for safety net programs like Medicaid on the same terms as U.S. citizens. Unauthorized immigrants were typically ineligible for all benefits except emergency Medicaid. Emergency Medicaid

---

[4] Bitler and Hoynes (2013) survey immigrant eligibility for Medicaid and SCHIP as well as other safety net programs.

includes coverage for emergency medical conditions that can last for a limited period and can include pregnancy and limited post-partum care. The passage of the Personal Responsibility and Work Opportunity Reconciliation Act (PRWORA) and the Illegal Immigration Reform and Immigrant Responsibility Act in 1996 rescinded many benefits for documented (legal) immigrants. At the same time, responsibility for deciding eligibility for various immigrant groups shifted considerably to the states. Many states have chosen to cover both permanent residents and qualified alien immigrants as well as those permanently residing under color of law (e.g., New York). Federal law has since changed, allowing more groups of non-citizens to be covered. Medicaid participation declined among immigrants relative to U.S. natives after welfare reform (Watson, 2014).

A number of states have obtained what are termed section 1115 research and demonstration waivers that allow them to explore other ways of broadening coverage as well as to explore effects of other changes to Medicaid rules. For example, in addition to expanding eligibility, states can explore using different rules in different parts of the state, giving different benefits to different groups, restricting access to different providers or mandating use of managed care and changing reimbursements. However, states cannot alter some aspects of the program, such as services for pregnant women and children. States also can get family planning waivers to expand provision of family planning services to populations not otherwise eligible for Medicaid or SCHIP (e.g., Kearney and Levine, 2009). These experiments or pilots must not reduce access or quality of care, and they must be budget neutral. This is the authority under which Arizona first implemented a Medicaid program, which was in place from 1982 to 2006. This is also the same demonstration program through which the state of Massachusetts implemented parts of its health care reform.

Costs, Reimbursement and Managed Care

Medicaid accounts for about one-sixth of all health care spending, making it a large item in federal and state budgets. Indeed, Medicaid represents the largest transfer of funds from the federal government to the states. The federal government shares from a minimum of 50 percent to a maximum of 83 percent of Medicaid costs with states. The matching rates—called the "Federal Medical Assistance Percentage," or FMAP—were temporarily increased during 2008–11 because of the economic downturn.

States have engaged in a variety of creative tactics to increase federal funding and reduce their own financial contribution to their Medicaid program. These tactics involve taxes on health care providers; intergovernmental transfers (IGTs) from publicly owned providers to state or local governments; upper payment limits (UPLs), in which providers receive payments in excess of costs and then make IGTs back to the state; and disproportionate-share hospital (DSH) payments, which are federal funds given to states to allocate to hospitals that serve disproportionate numbers of low-income patients (the ACA reduces DSH payments, under the rationale that places that expand Medicaid to adults under 138 percent of the poverty level will need less reimbursement for uncompensated care for the uninsured).[5] A study offers this example: a state receives $10 million revenue from a hospital via a tax (or via an IGT if it is a public hospital). The state then makes a $12 million DSH payment to the hospital. If the state has a 50 percent FMAP, the state gets $6 million in federal matching funds. In the end, the hospital has netted $2 million, the state has netted $4 million and the federal government has paid $6 million, only one-third of which actually went to the hospital (Coughlin, Ku and Kim, 2000). The fact that states have considerable discretion over their Medicaid program creates room for such shenanigans to occur. In response, the federal government has imposed restrictions aimed at ending such tactics and has cut the size of the DSH program (and will do so more as ACA is implemented). This is important since research indicates that DSH funding is associated with reduced mortality if states are not able to expropriate it (Baicker and Staiger, 2005).

In an effort to control Medicaid program costs, states impose caps on how much they will reimburse health care providers. These caps vary greatly across states. Medicaid reimbursement levels fell in inflation-adjusted terms over 2003–08, and Medicaid reimbursement levels were only 72 percent of Medicare reimbursement levels in 2008 (Zuckerman, Williams and Stockley, 2009). Low reimbursement levels have made some health care providers unwilling to treat patients covered by Medicaid. Twenty-eight percent of physicians surveyed in 2008 reported their practices were not accepting any new Medicaid patients (Boukus, Cassil and O'Malley, 2009). Medicaid reimbursement levels appear to affect participants' access to doctors (Shen and Zuckerman, 2005) and to dentists (Buchmueller, Orzol and Shore-Sheppard, 2015).

Many states also have turned to managed care programs as a way to control costs.[6] Medicaid managed care programs either pay a fixed monthly

---

[5]   Practically, this provides additional financial incentive for states to adopt the Medicaid expansion. States that do not adopt the expansion not only forgo almost 100 percent federal funding, but do so in the context of reduced DSH payments.

[6]   Another reason cited for implementing managed care is that it enables enrollees to improve their health outcomes by being part of a health care system that encourages preventive care and improves access to primary care.

fee to a managed care provider (called "capitated" plans because costs are made on a per patient basis) or combine a fixed fee to a primary care provider with fee-for-service payments to other providers (called "primary care case management"). About 70 percent of Medicaid recipients receive some or all of their Medicaid-covered services through managed care (Kaiser Family Foundation, 2010a). There is considerable variation across states. In some states, the vast majority of Medicaid recipients are enrolled in managed care while two states (Alaska and Wyoming) do not have a Medicaid managed care program at all. Mandatory managed care requires one of two kinds of waivers, either the 1115 research and demonstration waivers described above or a section 1915(b) freedom of choice waiver.[7] As early as September 1995, 42 states and the District of Columbia had implemented section 1915(b) waivers (Rowland and Hanson, 1996).

Findings are mixed about the extent to which mandates to move Medicaid recipients to managed care plans reduce expenditures (Duggan, 2004; Duggan and Hayford, 2013; Herring and Adams, 2011) and about the extent to which the move to managed care has affected utilization (Howell et al., 2004; Baker and Afendulis, 2005; Bindman et al., 2005; Currie and Fahr, 2005; Kaestner et al., 2005). Until recently, most Medicaid managed care was provided to women and children. Some studies project big cost savings from shifting the aged and disabled Medicaid populations to managed care, although research on the cost savings regarding the disabled is mixed (e.g., Lo Sasso and Freund, 2000; Coughlin, Long and Graves, 2008/2009; Burns, 2009). We discuss impacts on health below.

Long-term care accounts for over one-third of total Medicaid spending. Medicaid covers institutional services in residential facilities, including room and board, at Medicaid-certified nursing homes, which provide skilled nursing care, rehabilitation and long-term care and predominately serve the aged and younger individuals with physical disabilities, and at other institutions that serve individuals with mental retardation and developmental disabilities. Since 1983, Medicaid has provided some long-term care via home and community-based services in some states through what are termed home and community-based service waivers.

Finally, Medicaid subsidizes hospitals that serve a large share of low-income patients (e.g., the uninsured or those with Medicaid) under the DSH program. Funds are allocated to states, which then distribute them

---

[7] Introduced in the Omnibus Budget Reconciliation Act of 1981, s. 1915(b) waivers allow states to implement mandatory managed care for a subset of the state or a subset of the state's Medicaid beneficiaries.

to qualifying hospitals. The 2010 health insurance reform law will reduce DSH payments during 2014–20.

OVERVIEW OF THE ECONOMICS OF HEALTH INSURANCE

Like markets for other forms of insurance, the market for health insurance involves two classic asymmetric information problems: adverse selection and moral hazard. Adverse selection arises when people who expect to have higher-than-average health care costs are more likely to seek health insurance. This is a problem if insurers cannot charge higher prices to policyholders who are likely to have higher claims. Moral hazard arises when having health insurance changes people's choices in ways that increase health care costs. For example, people with insurance might visit the doctor for minor ailments because they know the insurer bears part of the cost of the visits.

Because Medicaid must cover all individuals and families that meet the eligibility requirements, the program experiences adverse selection. The population eligible for Medicaid is also likely to be adversely selected—in worse health than others—given the positive relationship between health and income in the U.S. This is part of why Medicaid is publicly funded: the people it covers would not be able to pay the premiums of actuarially-fair private insurance plans, insurance that charged them fees that covered their expected claims. Medicaid therefore subsidizes—typically at a 100 percent rate—their health insurance. The subsidy is designed to ensure that certain groups have health care coverage and therefore access to health care. This may be socially optimal since some health care involves positive externalities, benefits to people besides the recipients themselves. These positive externalities are thought to be particularly large for children and pregnant women, the groups that were the focus of the Medicaid expansions during the 1980s and 1990s. Research on Wisconsin's Medicaid program that included premiums and copays for relatively high-income participants suggests that participation and health care visits are very responsive to such costs (Dague, 2014).

In theory, the fact that Medicaid makes health care essentially free for participants should create moral hazard as well. However, not all providers accept Medicaid patients, and seeking health care requires spending time and effort in addition to (usually) money. These factors may limit the extent to which Medicaid patients consume "too much" health care. It is also not clear that Medicaid patients receive the same quality of care as privately-insured patients. This is another asymmetric information problem—health care providers are better informed than patients in general, and perhaps even more so than Medicaid patients. Medicaid patients then will receive the optimal quantity and quality of care only if providers are concerned about providing it, either because of professional ethics or because of regulations or other forces.

It is difficult to assess whether Medicaid participants receive the same quality of health care as other patients. Medical care is a credence good—its quality often cannot be measured either before or after it is received. Even if research shows differences in medical care or health outcomes between Medicaid participants and other people, the source of those differences may be unclear. There are likely to be differences between Medicaid participants and other people that researchers cannot observe that would result in differences in medical care and health outcomes regardless of the quality of care. Studies on the effects of Medicaid therefore tend to focus on relatively simple outcomes that would respond quickly to the availability of health insurance, such as the likelihood that a young child made a well-child visit in the last year or that a pregnant woman received prenatal care during the first trimester, rather than on more complex health outcomes.[8]

How Medicaid structures its payments to providers may affect participants' medical care and health outcomes. Providers who are paid a flat fee per Medicaid patient—the capitated managed care model—may not be willing to take on relatively unhealthy patients, or perhaps any Medicaid patients at all if payments are too low. However, capitated models should create incentives for cost-effective preventative care, conditional on a provider being willing to take on a patient. Medicaid managed care programs based on a fee-for-service model, in contrast, may create incentives for providers to supply services that are relatively profitable even if they are not cost-effective. Research shows that financial incentives tend to affect providers in the ways predicted by economic theory (e.g., Adams, Bronstein and Florence, 2003; Quast, Sappington and Shenkman, 2008). Interestingly, Garthwaite (2012) shows that the introduction of SCHIP led to both a decrease in hours spend by pediatricians on patient care and an increase in the share of physicians participating in the program.

An additional consideration is that states have flexibility to set provider reimbursement levels. Levels are almost always set lower than Medicare or private reimbursement levels, and this is often cited as a reason for providers to stop accepting Medicaid patients. Yet the evidence is not as damning as one might expect. Cunningham and May (2006) report that 85 percent

---

[8]   A further challenge we discuss below is that health itself likely does not respond right away to the availability of health insurance.

of physicians were serving Medicaid patients in 2004–05. Zuckerman et al. (2004) report that in 2001, 54 percent of all physicians and 67 percent of specialists were accepting most or all new Medicaid patients.

Medicaid also has the power to affect prices for prescriptions. Since a large number of people obtain pharmaceutical coverage from Medicaid, this suggests the program can influence prices. Medicaid uses the average private-sector price to decide what it will pay, which gives drug makers an incentive to increase private prices if Medicaid will be a large purchaser (Duggan and Scott-Morton, 2006). The federal structure of the Medicaid program may reduce its power to influence prices for other aspects of health care, however, since states differ in their reimbursement rates to providers and coverage of some services.

Economic theory also predicts that targeted programs like Medicaid affect participants' behavior along other dimensions. People may change their behavior in order to qualify for the program. For example, families may work less in order to keep their income below the program threshold, women may opt not to marry and the elderly may spend down their assets in order to be eligible for Medicaid. The empirical evidence on these theories is discussed below.

Government transfer programs like Medicaid affect the general population, not just participants and providers. Transfer programs are funded via taxes, which distort people's behavior. However, targeted programs like Medicaid cost less than universal programs that cover the entire population. There is an efficiency tradeoff—targeted programs may create more behavioral distortions since people change their behavior to be eligible, but they require less tax revenue than a universal program would and hence create fewer tax-related distortions. An additional inefficiency with regard to Medicaid involves crowd-out, displacement from private insurance to public insurance.

CROWD-OUT

Individuals and families may opt not to have private health insurance if they are eligible for Medicaid or may drop existing private insurance if they become eligible for public insurance. This is termed "crowd-out" in the economics literature.[9] People covered by Medicaid typically have

---

[9] Crowd-out also can occur if employers do not provide employer-sponsored health insurance because a large proportion of their employees have other options, such as Medicaid.

far lower out-of-pocket health care costs than people with private health insurance since Medicaid is highly subsidized. From a broader perspective, however, crowd-out does not necessarily confer any savings; it transfers costs from certain individuals and families (and possibly their employers) to taxpayers without necessarily improving health. Indeed, if Medicaid recipients receive worse medical care, crowd-out may be a public health concern as well as a fiscal problem. On the other hand, to the extent that the transfers are welfare enhancing for low-income families by freeing up funds otherwise used for health insurance and societal preferences put more weight on income to the bottom of the distribution than on income accruing higher up, crowd-out could be welfare enhancing.

Findings on the extent of crowd-out are mixed. In the first and seminal paper in this literature, Cutler and Gruber (1996) estimate that the crowd-out rate was almost 50 percent during 1987–92: For every two people who took up Medicaid as a result of the expansions, one person dropped or did not take up private coverage. In a now-standard approach, this paper used survey data on income and demographics for a national sample of children and state rules concerning eligibility to simulate state eligibility rates. This approach avoids endogeneity problems associated with modeling take-up of private or public insurance as a function of family's own Medicaid eligibility. If a researcher simply regressed outcomes on own eligibility (as imputed by the researcher), a host of issues could arise. First, there could be measurement error because none of the survey data sets typically used to assess these questions contains all of the information needed to determine eligibility and there is reporting error in existing survey measures.[10] Secondly, there is the concern than even though a researcher controls for observable factors that determine eligibility, there might still be unobserved factors that are associated with both take-up and health. Finally, there are concerns with reverse causality: families with sick children may have lower income and qualify for Medicaid because of the illness.

Subsequent research reports a wide range of estimates of the extent of crowd-out. Studies report crowd-out rates ranging from 0 to 60 percent (e.g., Dubay and Kenney, 1996; Blumberg, Dubay and Norton, 2000; Shore-Sheppard, 2000; Lo Sasso and Buchmueller, 2004; Ham and Shore-Sheppard, 2005a; Gruber and Simon, 2008; Shore-Sheppard, 2008). Estimates differ because of different data sets, different control variables and different time periods. Research that examines the sensitivity of crowd-

---

[10]   The instrumental variable strategy Cutler and Gruber (1996) and subsequent research uses cannot solve the measurement error problem if instrumenting for a binary variable.

out estimates to data, specifications and time periods seems warranted. Recent work by Shore-Sheppard (2008) is an important step towards understanding the role of specification and time-period differences.[11]

Crowd-out can occur among employers, who subsidize most of the private health insurance in the U.S., as well as among families. Research looking at firm- as well as family-level decisions finds that expanded Medicaid did not affect whether employers offer insurance to workers but may have changed the probability that firms offer family coverage (Shore-Sheppard, Buchmueller and Jensen, 2000).

The issue of crowd-out extends beyond Medicaid and CHIP. The 2010 Affordable Care Act was scheduled to expand Medicaid coverage to all non-elderly people with incomes up to 133 percent of the poverty line along with a 5 percent earnings disregard; require people to have health insurance or pay a fine; and set up state-run health exchanges. The Supreme Court ruled that this expansion of Medicaid is optional, and as of July 2016, only 31 states and DC have expanded Medicaid in this fashion. It will be interesting to see how many newly eligible people drop private coverage for Medicaid in expansion states and how many employers stop making health insurance available to their employees and their families as more options open up via the Medicaid expansion and the exchanges.

TAKE-UP

Take-up is the extent to which people who are eligible for a program actually enroll in the program and receive program benefits. As with many other public assistance programs, take-up of Medicaid is incomplete. Using an updated version of the method in Currie and Gruber (1996a, 1996b) and Gruber and Yelowitz (2000), Gruber (2003) reports that take-up was quite high for children aged 0–15 during the early 1980s but fell as the program expanded. This is not surprising since the expansions extended eligibility to those with higher incomes and better access to private insurance.

There are several potential reasons for incomplete take-up of Medicaid.

---

[11] Recent work using administrative data from Wisconsin by Dague et al. (2014) suggests crowd-out between 4 and 18 percent for children and parents. Shore-Sheppard's preferred estimates suggest little crowd-out and indicate that the lack of inclusion of age-specific trends drives this difference from Cutler and Gruber's findings.

First, not all eligible people may be aware that they are eligible.[12] In fact, Sonier, Boudreaux and Blewett (2013) project that a large share of the increase in participation in Medicaid under the ACA will come from this already eligible population (a so-called "welcome-mat" effect), based on findings that the Massachusetts Health Reform led to a large increase in Medicaid enrollment among those previously eligible. Those who are aware of their potential eligibility for Medicaid may face barriers to enrolling in the program. Beyond paperwork hurdles, participating in a means-tested program may involve stigma (Moffitt, 1983). Immigrant families may also be concerned about whether applying for Medicaid will trigger removal of any unauthorized family members or harm their ability to naturalize or sponsor relatives to immigrate. Heightened federal immigration enforcement appears to have "chilled" Medicaid participation among children in immigrant families, even when the children are U.S. citizens (Watson, 2014).

Another possible reason for low take-up is perceived low quality of Medicaid. The fact that some health care providers do not accept Medicaid because of low reimbursement rates further reduces people's incentive to enroll in the program. In addition, eligible individuals and families have relatively little incentive to apply for Medicaid until they need medical care.

However, medical care providers, especially hospitals, have an incentive to enroll eligible patients who do not have private health insurance to ensure that they get paid. Some eligible people therefore get enrolled in Medicaid at the time care is rendered. As noted by Aizer (2003), this means that the population enrolled in Medicaid tends to be less healthy than the population eligible for Medicaid. This can lead to biased estimates of the effect of Medicaid on health unless studies correct for the fact that individuals are more likely to be enrolled in Medicaid if they have needed medical care.

Researchers have taken advantage of the expansions to inform estimates of take-up. For example, Ham, Ozbeklik and Shore Sheppard (2014) find average effects of the expansions on take-up that differ somewhat across demographic groups. Estimates range from 0.41 for whites to 0.62 for non-whites and also vary in other predictable ways, with higher rates for more disadvantaged groups.

Take-up appears to affect estimates of the effect of the Medicaid expan-

---

12 For example, Aizer and Currie (2004) find that among immigrant women, greater use of public prenatal care by women of the same background (ethnicity and race) is associated with more own use but that much of this association goes away once they control for the hospital of delivery, casting some doubt on whether it is driven by information sharing.

sions. Card and Shore-Sheppard (2004) take advantage of law changes that required states to make low-income children born after a particular date or of a particular age eligible for Medicaid. Using a regression discontinuity approach that compared children on either side of these age cutoffs, they find evidence of smaller effects of the Medicaid expansions on children's coverage than Currie and Gruber (1996a) and Cutler and Gruber (1996). They attribute the difference to very low take-up rates among the newly eligible.

EFFECTS ON HEALTH

Lack of health insurance is likely to increase mortality and morbidity since the uninsured are less able to afford medical care, on average. However, it is difficult to determine the true effect of health insurance on people's health because of adverse selection. Most economics studies use quasi-experimental techniques to reduce the bias created by adverse selection in estimates of program effects. These studies rely on cross-state variation in policies or changes in policies within states—so-called "natural experiments" or quasi-experiments—to identify the effects of health insurance. Only a few studies use true experiments in which some individuals were randomly assigned health insurance coverage while others were not. Research on the effects of Medicaid on health relies on cross-state or within-state variation since to date only the Oregon Health Insurance Experiment randomized control trial has been run to evaluate the effects of Medicaid.

Studies on the effects of Medicaid on health face several challenges. One challenge is creating the correct counterfactual and comparison group: would Medicaid participants have no insurance or private insurance if they were not covered by Medicaid? The true answer is likely some of each, which implies that Medicaid may benefit some groups—people who would otherwise have no insurance—more than others—people who are crowded out of private coverage. Studies that report null effects of Medicaid therefore may be capturing offsetting effects on different groups.

Data limitations are another challenge. Studies often use data sets that lack information on individuals' insurance coverage, which makes it impossible to estimate the structural effect of Medicaid coverage on health outcomes. Alternatively, data sets with good measures of health outcomes, health care coverage and health care utilization often lack good measures of income, which are necessary to impute eligibility for Medicaid. Research that uses instruments for simulated eligibility—the approach pioneered by Cutler and Gruber (1996) for studying the effect of the Medicaid expansions on health insurance coverage—identifies only the local average treatment effect, or the effect of Medicaid among individuals made eligible by the expansions, not the effect of extending Medicaid eligibility to a random person or even the average effect of eligibility. Studies frequently report reduced-form effects that give the relationship between a measure of Medicaid eligibility—not actual Medicaid participation—and health. Although their results are indirect evidence on Medicaid's effects, reduced-form studies avoid the selection bias that can plague some structural studies. Controlling for selection into Medicaid requires being able to identify at least one exogenous factor that affects individuals' decision whether to take up Medicaid coverage. Few data sets or research strategies meet that challenge. Thus, both reduced-form and the more structural studies have limitations. In practice, there are few structural papers in this literature.

Finally, studies that rely on cross-state differences or within-state changes in Medicaid policy implicitly assume that these differences or changes are exogenous. This may not be the case (e.g., Baughman and Milyo, 2008). Although states may be unlikely to change Medicaid eligibility based on health outcomes, they can and do change Medicaid eligibility rules as economic conditions change, and those changes in economic conditions do affect health outcomes. Studies therefore face difficulty isolating the impact of changes in Medicaid on health outcomes.

Health Outcomes among Children

Research indicates that being eligible for Medicaid increases children's access to medical care. For example, the eligibility expansions that occurred between 1984 and 1992 decreased the probability that a child went without a doctor's visit during the last year by one-half and increased the probability that a child visited a doctor's office in the last two weeks by two-thirds (Currie and Gruber, 1996a). Increases in Medicaid eligibility resulted in more hospitalizations of children as well, particularly for conditions for which hospitalization could not be avoided by obtaining appropriate primary care (Currie and Gruber, 1996a; Dafny and Gruber, 2005). However, Medicaid may reduce child hospitalizations for ambulatory-care-sensitive conditions, which tend to be avoidable with appropriate primary care (Kaestner, Joyce and Racine, 2001; Aizer, 2003, 2007; Dafny and Gruber, 2005). This suggests that Medicaid may increase use of preventative care.

Medicaid eligibility may improve children's health as well. The Medicaid expansions are associated with reductions in child mortality (Currie and Gruber, 1996a; Bacon-Goodman, 2016; Wherry and Meyer, 2016). However, there is less evidence of a positive impact on morbidity. One study concludes that Medicaid's impact on health outcomes may occur only over time by putting children on a better health trajectory as they age (Currie, Decker and Lin, 2008).

Looking at the rollout of Medicaid during the late 1960s and early 1970s, Almond, Decker and Simon (2010) find that Medicaid availability is associated with a decrease in the likelihood of giving birth at a public hospital and an increase in hospital length-of-stay among non-white women. Medicaid availability is positively associated with hospitalizations among children whose household head had relatively little education. Medicaid availability does not appear to have affected maternal mortality or early childhood mortality, however.

Studies have reached mixed conclusions about the effect of Medicaid managed care versus traditional fee-for-service care on infant and children's health. It is important for research that examines voluntary managed care plans to control for potential selection of healthier people into such plans, which would bias results towards finding pro-health effects. Research therefore tends to focus on mandatory managed care plans. Managed care is associated with less emergency room usage and more outpatient and specialist visits (Baker and Afendulis, 2005; Garrett, Davidoff and Yemane, 2003), which suggests increased preventative care. Troublingly, managed care is associated with higher incidence of low birth weight, prematurity and neonatal death in a California study, perhaps because it lowered the likelihood a mother received prenatal care during the first trimester of the pregnancy (Aizer, Currie and Moretti, 2007). Other research, however, finds that managed care did not adversely affect infant health outcomes in some other states (e.g., Conover, Rankin and Sloan, 2010; Levinson and Ullman, 1998).

Health Outcomes among Infants and Pregnant Women

There is a sizable literature on the effect of Medicaid on health outcomes related to pregnancy and birth since pregnant women and infants were a target of the eligibility expansions of the late 1980s and early 1990s. Findings are mixed. Several national-level studies find that Medicaid eligibility improved prenatal care and some birth outcomes (e.g., Currie and Gruber, 1996b; Dubay et al., 2001) while others find little effect (e.g., Dave et al., 2010/2011). Studies of specific states also find little effect of Medicaid on prenatal care and birth outcomes (e.g., Epstein and Newhouse, 1998; Piper, Ray and Griffin, 1990). The results may be mixed because of differences in study methodology and study populations. For example, it appears to matter whether studies examine potential eligibility for Medicaid versus actual Medicaid enrollment. Whether Medicaid is compared to no insurance or to private insurance also seems to affect results. Medicaid eligibility appears to reduce the quantity and intensity of care during childbirth compared to private insurance but improve it relative to no insurance (Currie and Gruber, 2001). More recent variation driven by welfare reform-induced declines in cash welfare participation may have reduced use of prenatal care, offsetting some of the expansion effects (Currie and Grogger, 2002).

The literature is more conclusive that Medicaid managed care does not improve prenatal care. On balance, studies suggest that managed care delays the start of prenatal care (e.g., Aizer, Currie and Moretti, 2007; Kaestner, Dubay and Kenney, 2005). However, managed care may reduce smoking rates among pregnant women and repeat C-section rates (Howell et al., 2004).

Medicaid's effect, if any, on birth outcomes has the potential to matter well beyond infancy. Increases in Medicaid and CHIP eligibility are associated with increases in test scores later in childhood, probably by improving health status at birth (Levine and Schanzenbach, 2009).

Health Outcomes among Non-elderly Adults

Other than pregnant women, there is little research on the effects of Medicaid on non-elderly adults' health outcomes.[13] This is not surprising since non-elderly adults are eligible for Medicaid only if they meet the resource and categorical restrictions, which has largely limited the eligible population to very low-income parents (often mothers) of dependent children and the blind or disabled. The late 1980s and early 1990s expansions increased cancer-screening rates among mothers and reduced the fraction of parents who reported they needed to see a doctor but did not because of cost (e.g., Busch and Duchovny, 2005). Research also indicates that Medicaid increases access to care for mothers relative to not having any insurance but not relative to private insurance (e.g., Long, Coughlin and King, 2005). One early study that examined effects of cutbacks in Medicaid (known as MediCal in California) in the early 1980s, when a number of medically indigent adults lost their benefits, found evidence of worse health outcomes (Lurie et al., 1984). States that extended eligibility to low-income, non-disabled childless adults during the 2000s saw a decrease in mortality and an improvement in self-reported health relative to neighboring states that did not expand eligibility (Sommers, Baicker and Epstein, 2012).

---

[13]   Dague et al. (2014) study the expansion of a state public insurance program to childless adults who had high rates of chronic illness but were otherwise much like the population to be covered by the ACA-related Medicaid expansions. They find that expanded eligibility led to increases in outpatient care and emergency room use but a decrease in preventable hospitalizations.

There is a larger literature on the effects of Medicaid managed care on adults' health outcomes. This literature has focused on the likelihood of using an emergency room or of seeing a health care provider in the last year. Some of this research does not distinguish between Medicaid recipients who voluntarily enrolled in managed care versus those who had no choice as part of their Medicaid coverage. That makes it difficult to evaluate the results given the possibility of selection bias, as discussed earlier. On balance, research suggests that managed care may reduce the likelihood of visiting an emergency room and may increase the likelihood of having seen a health care provider in the last year (Hurley, Freund and Paul, 1993; Rowland et al., 1995; Garrett and Zuckerman, 2005). There are few rigorous studies of the effect of Medicaid managed care on adult health outcomes other than those related to provider access.

An exciting recent study examines the effects of becoming eligible to participate in Medicaid via a lottery (Finkelstein and Baicker, 2011; Finkelstein et al., 2012; Baicker, Taubman et al., 2013; Taubman et al., 2014). In 2008, Oregon used a lottery to randomly offer Medicaid to a subset of a population of childless adults aged 19–64. The lottery was implemented in a way that allowed researchers to examine the health effects of Medicaid participation among a more randomly selected group of adults who had access to Medicaid (won the lottery) and did not have access (lost the lottery) than usual studies of program participants and non-participants. Data was collected from other sources to add to the administrative data. The findings are striking: Winning the "Medicaid lottery" is associated with a large increase in health care utilization (including emergency rooms) and to some extent with an improvement in self-rated health and mental health and increased rates of diabetes detection and management but not with an improvement in measured physical health outcomes.

Health Outcomes among Elderly Adults

Research consistently indicates that "dual eligible" elderly have worse health status and greater health service usage than elderly people who participate only in Medicare (Pezzin and Kasper, 2002). However, Medicaid eligibility and enrollment is likely endogenous with respect to health outcomes since the poor tend to have worse health. The fact that Medicaid has far more extensive coverage of long-term care than Medicare likely makes endogeneity bias worse for studies of the elderly than for studies of children and non-elderly, non-disabled adults. Because there have been relatively few changes in Medicaid eligibility for the elderly, researchers have had little opportunity to take advantage of natural experiments that would help identify the health effects of Medicaid among the elderly. However, there have been changes in Medicaid rules regarding long-term care that researchers have exploited. Results suggest that Medicaid policies have little effect on whether the elderly enter a nursing home instead of receiving care at home (e.g., Norton and Kumar, 2000; Grabowski and Gruber, 2007).

EFFECTS ON OTHER BEHAVIORS

Welfare Participation and Labor Supply

Before the welfare reforms of the late 1990s, participation in the main cash welfare program—Aid to Families with Dependent Children—conferred automatic eligibility for Medicaid. For families with young children, the health care coverage associated with Medicaid might quite realistically have created a substantial incentive to participate in welfare. It is a challenge to separate the effects of Medicaid from those of AFDC since most individuals participated in both. Early studies in this literature, such as Blank (1989) and Winkler (1991), found little effect of Medicaid on welfare participation.[14] Moffitt and Wolfe (1992) use longitudinal data from the Survey of Income and Program Participation and model the value associated with Medicaid with a family-specific proxy for health care expenditures. They find large and significant effects of Medicaid on welfare participation, with the effects concentrated among those with high-expected health care expenditures.

As with the question of insurance coverage and crowd-out, the more recent literature uses variation in Medicaid eligibility parameters associated with the expansions of the late 1980s and early 1990s to examine effects on welfare participation. Yelowitz (1995) takes advantage of the fact that these expansions decoupled eligibility for Medicaid from eligibility for AFDC for families with children, creating a notch in families' budget constraints for families with no other access to health insurance coverage. Using data from the Current Population Survey, Yelowitz finds that the expansions, as parameterized by the difference in the percent of the poverty level at which eligibility for AFDC and Medicaid differed, led to a large and significant increase in AFDC participation. Ham and Shore-Sheppard (2005b) look at the same question, with a more flexible specification that allows the thresholds for Medicaid and AFDC to

---

[14]   See Currie and Madrian (1999) for a more general discussion of the difficulties of looking at effects of health insurance on labor market outcomes. For a more thorough discussion of the older literature on Medicaid, see Moffitt (1992).

have their own effects and that incorporates more institutional features to calculate AFDC eligibility calculation. They find no impact of the expansions on AFDC receipt and are able to reject the specification used by Yelowitz (1995). Results from the Oregon "Medicaid lottery" indicate that Medicaid participation increases receipt of food stamps but had little impact on receipt of other government benefits (Baicker et al., 2014).

Studies have also used the expansions to examine effects on labor supply. Yelowitz (1995) finds that the expansions of the late 1980s and early 1990s led to an increase in labor supply, while Ham and Shore-Sheppard (2005b) find no effect on labor supply. Dave et al. (2015) find a negative effect of the expansions on employment among women who recently gave birth. After Tennessee disenrolled a large number of childless adults from its public health insurance program in 2005, employment and job search increased among childless adults in the state relative to other Southern states (Garthwaite, Gross and Notowidigdo, 2015). Results from the Oregon "Medicaid lottery," in contrast, do not indicate a significant effect of Medicaid participation on employment or earnings (Baicker et al., 2014; Finkelstein et al., 2013). Meyer and Rosenbaum (2001) look at the combined effects of a host of social programs (such as AFDC, Medicaid and welfare reform waivers) and the tax system (the Earned Income Tax Credit) on the labor supply of single mothers, incorporating various incentive effects. They find that Medicaid had little impact on labor supply while the tax system had the largest impact.

Several studies use the staggered introduction of Medicaid across states over time in the late 1960s and early 1970s to look at the effect of Medicaid on AFDC participation and labor supply. Decker and Selck (2012) find that the introduction of Medicaid explained about 10 percent of the increase in AFDC caseloads. Using individual data, they find the increase occurred because of an increase in take-up, not because of an increase in eligibility or a decline in labor force participation. Strumpf (2011) also finds no effects on labor supply.

Another mechanism through which Medicaid can affect labor supply is job lock. Job lock posits that access to employer-provided health insurance induces employees to stay at employers they otherwise would have left. Hamersma and Kim (2009) look at the effect of Medicaid expansions of parental coverage and find that expanded eligibility reduces job lock among unmarried women, with few other effects.

Marriage and Fertility

Medicaid also may affect marriage and fertility behavior. Until the expansions, Medicaid was tightly linked to participation in cash welfare programs, the largest of which—AFDC—was largely restricted to single mothers. Economic theory therefore predicts that AFDC and Medicaid reduce the incentive to marry and increase the incentive to have children. Research on the introduction of Medicaid during the late 1960s and early 1970s finds evidence of the predicted positive effect on single motherhood (Decker, 2000). The 1980s and 1990s Medicaid expansions, in contrast, decoupled Medicaid from AFDC and therefore increased Medicaid eligibility for two-parent families. This had a positive effect on marriage rates (Yelowitz, 1998). The expansions also may have increased birth rates because they reduced the cost of health care for pregnant women and children, but recent research finds there was little effect on fertility (DeLeire, Lopoo and Simon, 2011; Zavodny and Bitler, 2010), while some older work finds some impacts (e.g., Joyce and Kaestner, 1996).

Medicaid also can affect fertility through its coverage of family planning services, including contraceptives and abortion. Expanding women's eligibility for family planning services reduces births by increasing contraceptive use (Kearney and Levine, 2009). States can opt to cover abortion via Medicaid at their own expense. Such coverage is positively associated with abortion rates and negatively associated with birth rates (Zavodny and Bitler, 2010).

Savings

Medicaid may affect people's savings behavior. There are several reasons to expect Medicaid to reduce how much money people save. First, like any insurance program, Medicaid reduces the need for precautionary savings to cover uncertain health care expenses. Second, Medicaid imposes asset tests for eligibility. Until the mid-1980s, there was an asset cap of $1000 for AFDC eligibility, which also conferred Medicaid eligibility. While that cap has been dropped, Medicaid continues to impose asset limits for dual eligibles. This gives elderly and disabled people with low incomes an incentive to not exceed those limits. However, Medicaid may boost savings among some recipients by freeing up money that they otherwise would spend on health insurance and health care.

One difficulty with estimating the effect of Medicaid on savings is that Medicaid eligibility is endogenous with respect to savings, particularly when asset limits are in effect. Gruber and Yelowitz (1999) therefore use an identification strategy similar to Currie and Gruber (1996a, 1996b) to simulate Medicaid eligibility in order to examine its relationship with savings during the late 1980s and early 1990s. They conclude that Medicaid eligibility substantially reduced families' level of assets and the likelihood that a family had any assets at all. Gittleman (2011) reports that some of Gruber and Yelowitz's results are sensitive to the choice of cohort and empirical model. Gross and Notowidigdo (2011) find that the Medicaid expansions were associated with a decrease in personal bankruptcies but had no effect on business bankruptcies. Using data from the Oregon Health Insurance Experiment, Finkelstein et al. (2012) find that one year of access to Medicaid for low-income adults without children led to a statistically significant decline in the presence of medical debt and both medical and overall collections, but no significant effect on overall bankruptcy or a summary measure of overall access to credit.

The adverse effect on savings is likely to be concentrated in the middle of the income and wealth distributions. People with very low incomes and wealth typically do not have enough assets to be concerned about Medicaid's asset limit. If faced with an adverse health event, their assets are likely to quickly fall below Medicaid's limit. People with very high incomes or wealth are unlikely to ever qualify for Medicaid coverage and are likely to have private health insurance. Consistent with this, Maynard and Qiu (2009) find evidence that Medicaid has a strong negative effect on savings for households in the middle of the wealth or income distributions.

Medicaid may have particularly large effects on savings among the elderly because it has considerably more extensive coverage of long-term care than Medicare. However, research suggests that these effects are fairly small. For example, Gardner and Gilleskie (2012) report that doubling the asset limit for nursing home coverage would increase the percentage of elderly with positive assets by about 1 percentage point and would increase average assets by less than 10 percent.

Medicaid's coverage of long-term care may affect the market for long-term care insurance as well. Long-term care insurance is implicitly a form of savings. Very few people buy long-term care insurance, partly because such insurance tends to be expensive and not actuarially-fairly priced. The existence of Medicaid and the implicit tax it levies on private long-term care insurance further reduces the incentive to purchase such insurance. Brown and Finkelstein (2011) provide an overview of research in this area. They conclude that Medicaid does reduce the market for long-term care insurance. As with savings, however, the effect appears to be relatively small.

CONCLUSION

What the future holds for Medicaid depends heavily on politics and the macroeconomy. In the wake of the 2007–09 recession, high unemployment boosted the number of people eligible for Medicaid at the same time as tax revenues shrank. Fiscal woes motivated a number of Republican governors and members of Congress to press for changes to the 2010 ACA that would allow states to drop Medicaid enrollees without forfeiting federal funds. Several states have moved toward making cuts that do not put federal funds at risk. A few governors have even threatened that their states might stop participating in the program altogether.

The joint federal-state structure of Medicaid gives rise to striking differences across states. The federal government provides more generous matching funds to poorer states, but states still must bear a share of Medicaid costs. Poorer states therefore tend to have less generous Medicaid programs: lower provider reimbursement rates, coverage of fewer health care services and lower eligibility thresholds. This results in considerable disparities in access to care across states. A national system with uniform rules across states would help eliminate such disparities and would be more equitable. It also would smooth across regional business cycles and give the federal government more power to influence health care prices and achieve economies of scale.

The federal-state structure of Medicaid does have some advantages. It allows for experimentation across states. Such experimentation can reveal cost-effective programs that other states then adopt. In addition, researchers have long relied on variation across states to examine the effects of Medicaid and other public policies.

We conclude by highlighting some important avenues for future research. Assessing the effects of ACA-related expansions on health, labor market outcomes and other behaviors among previously underserved groups (non-disabled, childless adults of working age with relatively low incomes) is clearly a critical research area. Here, variation will come from several sources. First, there will be cross-state variation in Medicaid eligibility generosity for childless adults (and some for parents as well) since not all states are participating in the expansions (and even among the expanders, the timing is not uniform). Secondly, regardless of whether they have expanded Medicaid or not, states are now required to use a new version of countable income for determining eligibility— modified adjusted gross income—and to use a consistent income disregard (5 percent). This movement to a considerably more uniform system creates cross-state variation that researchers can couple with over-time variation in how and when states implement the expansions and make other changes to their Medicaid systems.

Another critical need is for more randomized control trials that examine the effects of Medicaid on health and other outcomes. The Oregon Health Insurance Experiment offers an excellent model of how to design such studies. More such experiments in other areas are needed and their results are likely to be of great interest to researchers and policymakers alike.

Another hole in the literature is systematic reviews of existing studies of Medicaid, particularly those that evaluate managed care. A large literature examines the consequences of the shift to managed care from fee-for-service on providers' decision-making and Medicaid participants' health outcomes. This literature indicates that reimbursement structure affects providers' decision-making but is mixed on whether the shift to managed care has improved health outcomes. In addition, more research on the cost effectiveness of managed care is needed. One study concludes that managed care actually increases government spending, not lowers it, and does so without improving health outcomes (Duggan, 2004). This is an important and disturbing possibility given that states continue to look to managed care to reduce Medicaid costs.

REFERENCES

Adams, E. Kathleen, Janet M. Bronstein and Curtis S. Florence. 2003. "The Impact of Medicaid Primary Care Case Management on Office-Based Physician Supply in Alabama and Georgia," 40 *Inquiry* 269–82.

Aizer, Anna. 2003. "Low Take-Up in Medicaid: Does Outreach Matter and for Whom?" 93 *American Economic Review Papers & Proceedings* 238–41.

Aizer, Anna. 2007. "Public Health Insurance, Program Take-Up and Child Health," 89 *Review of Economics and Statistics* 400–15.

Aizer, Anna, and Janet Currie. 2004. "Networks or Neighborhoods? Correlations in the Use of Publicly-Funded Maternity Care in California," 88 *Journal of Public Economics* 2573–85.

Aizer, Anna, Janet Currie and Enrico Moretti. 2007. "Does Managed Care Hurt Health? Evidence from Medicaid Mothers," 89 *Review of Economics and Statistics* 385–99.

Almond, Douglas, Sandra Decker and Kosali Simon. 2010. "The Impact of Medicaid's Introduction on the Use of Health Care Services, Health Outcomes, and Birth Rates," Mimeo.

Bacon-Goodman, Andrew. 2016. "Public Insurance and Mortality: Evidence from Medicaid Implementation," forthcoming. *Journal of Political Economy*.

Baker, Laurence, and Christopher Afendulis. 2005. "Medicaid Managed Care and Health Care for Children," 40 *Heath Services Research* 1466–88.

Baicker, Katherine, Amy Finkelstein, Jae Song and Sarah Taubman. 2014. "The Impact of Medicaid on Labor Force Activity and Program Participation: Evidence from the Oregon Health Insurance Experiment," 104 *American Economic Review* 322–8.

Baicker, Katherine, and Douglas Staiger. 2005. "Fiscal Shenanigans, Targeted Federal Health Care Funds, and Patient Mortality," 120 *Quarterly Journal of Economics* 345–86.

Baicker, Katherine, Sarah Taubman, Heidi Allen, Mira Bernstein, Jonathan

Gruber, Joseph Newhouse, Eric Schneider, Bill Wright, Alan Zaslavsky and Amy Finkelstein. 2013. "The Oregon Experiment—Effects of Medicaid on Clinical Outcomes," 368 *New England Journal of Medicine* 1713–22.

Baughman, Reagan, and Jeffrey Milyo. 2008. "How Do States Formulate Medicaid and SCHIP Policy? Economic and Political Determinants of State Eligibility Levels," Mimeo.

Bindman, Andrew, Arpita Chattopadhyay, Dennis Osmond, William Huen and Peter Bacchetti. 2005. "The Impact of Medicaid Managed Care on Hospitalizations for Ambulatory Care Sensitive Conditions," 40 *Health Services Research* 19–38.

Bitler, Marianne, and Hilary Hoynes. 2013. "Immigrants, Welfare and the U.S. Safety Net," in David Card and Steven Raphael, eds., *Immigration, Poverty and Socioeconomic Inequality*. New York: Russell Sage Foundation.

Blank, Rebecca. 1989. 'The Effect of Medical Need and Medicaid on AFDC Participation," 24 *Journal of Human Resources* 54–87.

Blumberg, Linda, Lisa Dubay and Stephen Norton. 2000. "Did the Medicaid Expansions for Children Displace Private Insurance? An Analysis Using the SIPP," 19 *Journal of Health Economics* 33–60.

Boukus, Ellyn, Alwyn Cassil and Ann S. O'Malley. 2009. "A Snapshot of U.S. Physicians: Key Findings from the 2008 Health Tracking Physician Survey," Data Bulletin Results from HSC Research No. 35. www.rwjf.org/files/research/hscbulletin35sept2009.pdf.

Brown, Jeffrey R., and Amy Finkelstein. 2011. "Insuring Long-Term Care in the United States," 25 *Journal of Economic Perspectives* 119–42.

Buchmueller, Thomas C., Sean Orzol and Lara D. Shore-Sheppard. 2015. "The Effect of Medicaid Payment Rates on Access to Dental Care among Children," 1 *American Journal of Health Economics* 194–223.

Burns, Marguerite. 2009. "Medicaid Managed Care and Cost Containment in the Adult Disabled Population," 47 *Medical Care* 1069–76.

Busch, Susan H., and Noellia Duchovny. 2005. "Family Coverage Expansions: Impact on Insurance Coverage and Health Care Utilization of Parents," 25 *Journal of Health Economics* 876–90.

Card, David, and Lara Shore-Sheppard. 2004. "Using Discontinuous Eligibility Rules to Identify the Effects of the Federal Medicaid Expansions on Low-Income Children," 86 *Review of Economics and Statistics* 752–66.

Conover, Christopher, Peter Rankin and Frank Sloan. 2001. "Effects of Tennessee Medicaid Managed Care on Obstetrical Care and Birth Outcomes," 26 *Journal of Health Politics, Policy, and Law* 1291–324.

Coughlin, Teresa, Sharon Long and John Graves. 2008/2009. "Does Managed Care Improve Access to Care for Medicaid Beneficiaries with Disabilities? A National Study," 45 *Inquiry* 395–407.

Coughlin, Teresa, Leighton Ku and Johnny Kim. 2000. "Reforming the Medicaid Disproportionate Share Hospital Program," 22 *Health Care Financing Review* 137–57.

Cunningham, Peter, and Jessica May. 2006. "Medicaid Patients Increasingly Concentrated among Physicians," Tracking Report No. 16, Center for Studying Health System Change.

Currie, Janet, Sandra Decker and Wanchuan Lin. 2008. "Has Public Health Insurance for Older Children Reduced Disparities in Access to Care and Health Outcomes?" 27 *Journal of Health Economics* 1407–652.

Currie, Janet, and John Fahr. 2005. "Medicaid Managed Care: Effects on

Children's Medicaid Coverage and Utilization of Care," 89 *Journal of Public Economics* 85–108.

Currie, Janet, and Jeffrey Grogger. 2002. "Medicaid Expansions and Welfare Contractions: Offsetting Effects on Prenatal Care and Infant Health," 21 *Journal of Health Economics* 313–35.

Currie, Janet, and Jonathan Gruber. 1996a. "Health Insurance Eligibility, Utilization of Medical Care, and Child Health," 111 *Quarterly Journal of Economics* 431–66.

Currie, Janet, and Jonathan Gruber. 1996b. "Saving Babies: The Efficacy and Cost of Recent Changes in the Medicaid Eligibility of Pregnant Women," 104 *Journal of Political Economy* 1263–96.

Currie, Janet, and Jonathan Gruber. 2001. "Public Health Insurance and Medical Treatment: The Equalizing Impact of the Medicaid Expansions," 82 *Journal of Public Economics* 63–90.

Currie, Janet, and Brigitte Madrian. 1999. "Health, Health Insurance, and the Labor Market," in Orley Ashenfelter and David Card, eds., *Handbook of Labor Economics Volume 3*. Amsterdam: Elsevier.

Cutler, David, and Jonathan Gruber. 1996. "Does Public Insurance Crowd Out Private Insurance?" 111 *Quarterly Journal of Economics* 391–430.

Dafny, Leemore, and Jonathan Gruber. 2005. "Public Insurance and Child Hospitalizations: Access and Efficiency Effects," 89 *Journal of Public Economics* 109–29.

Dague Laura. 2014. "The Effect of Medicaid Premiums on Enrollment: A Regression Discontinuity Approach," 47 *Journal of Health Economics* 1–12.

Dague, Laura, Thomas DeLeire, Donna Friedsam, Lindsey Leininger, Sarah Meier and Kristen Voskuil. 2014. "What Fraction of Medicaid Enrollees Have Access to Private Insurance? Estimates from Administrative Data," 51 *Inquiry* 1–14.

Dave, Dhaval, Sandra Decker, Robert Kaestner and Kosali Simon. 2010/2011. "The Effect of Medicaid Expansions on Health Insurance Coverage of Pregnant Women: An Analysis Using Deliveries," 47 *Inquiry* 315–30.

Dave, Dhaval, Sandra Decker, Robert Kaestner and Kosali Simon. 2015. "The Effect of Medicaid Expansions in the Late 1980s and Early 1990s on the Labor Supply of Pregnant Women," 1 *American Journal of Health Economics* 165–93.

Decker, Sandra. 2000. "Medicaid, AFDC and Family Formation," 32 *Applied Economics* 1947–56.

Decker, Sandra, and Frederic Selck. 2012. "The Effect of the Original Introduction of Medicaid on Welfare Participation and Labor Supply," 10 *Review of Economics of the Household* 541–56.

DeLeire, Thomas, Lenard Lopoo and Kosali Simon. 2011. "Medicaid Expansions and Fertility in the United States," 48 *Demography* 725–47.

Department of Health and Human Services. 2010. "Connecting Kids to Coverage: Continuing the Progress," 2010 CHIPRA Annual Report. www.insurekids.gov/professionals/reports/chipra/2010_annual.pdf, accessed 4/12/2012.

Dubay, Lisa, Theodore Joyce, Robert Kaestner and Genevieve Kenney. 2001. "Changes in Prenatal Care Timing and Low Birth Weight by Race and Socioeconomic Status: Implications for the Medicaid Expansions for Pregnant Women," 36 *Health Services Research* 373–98.

Dubay, Lisa, and Genevieve Kenney. 1996. "Revisiting the Issues: The Effects of Medicaid Expansions on Insurance Coverage of Children," 6 *The Future of Children* 152–61.

Duggan, Mark. 2004. "Does Contracting Out Increase the Efficiency of Government Programs? Evidence from Medicaid HMOs," 88 *Journal of Public Economics* 2549–72.

Duggan, Mark, and Tamara Hayford. 2013. "Has the Shift to Managed Care Reduced Medicaid Expenditures? Evidence from State and Local-Level Mandates," 32 *Journal of Policy Analysis and Management* 505–35.

Duggan, Mark, and Fiona Scott-Morton. 2006. "The Distortionary Effects of Government Procurement: Evidence from Medicaid Prescription Drug Purchasing," 121 *Quarterly Journal of Economics* 1–30.

Epstein, Arnold, and Joseph Newhouse. 1998. "Impact of Medicaid Expansions on Early Prenatal Care and Health Outcomes," 19 *Health Care Financing Review* 85–99.

Finkelstein, Amy, and Katherine Baicker. 2011. "The Effects of Medicaid Coverage," 365 *New England Journal of Medicine* 683–5.

Finkelstein, Amy, Sarah Taubman, Bill Wright, Mira Bernstein, Jonathan Gruber, Joseph Newhouse, Heidi Allen, Katherine Baker and the Oregon Health Study Group. 2012. "The Oregon Health Insurance Experiment: Evidence from the First Year," 127 *Quarterly Journal of Economics* 1057–106.

Fisher, Elliott, David Wennberg, Therese Stukel, Daniel Gottlieb, F.L. Lucas and Etiole Pinder. 2003a. "The Implications of Regional Variations in Medicare Spending. Part 1: The Content, Quality and Accessibility of Care," 138 *Annals of Internal Medicine* 273–87.

Fisher, Elliott, David Wennberg, Therese Stukel, Daniel Gottlieb, F.L. Lucas and Etiole Pinder. 2003b. "The Implications of Regional Variations in Medicare Spending. Part 2: Health Outcomes and Satisfaction with Care," 138 *Annals of Internal Medicine* 288–98.

Gardner, Lara, and Donna Gilleskie. 2012. "The Effects of State Medicaid Policies on the Dynamic Savings Patterns and Medicaid Enrollment of the Elderly," 47 *Journal of Human Resources* 1082–127.

Garthwaite, Craig. 2012. "The Doctor Might See You Now: The Supply Side of Public Health Insurance Expansions," 4 *American Economic Journal: Economic Policy* 190–215.

Garthwaite, Craig, Tal Gross and Matthew Notowidigo. 2014. "Public Health Insurance, Labor Supply, and Employment Lock," 129 *Quarterly Journal of Economics* 653–96.

Garrett, Bowen, Amy J. Davidoff and Alshadye Yemane. 2003. "Effects of Medicaid Managed Care Programs on Health Services Access and Use," 32 *Health Services Research* 575–94.

Garrett, Bowen, and Stephen Zuckerman. 2005. "National Estimates of the Effects of Mandatory Medicaid Managed Care Programs on Health Care Access and Use, 1997–1999," 43 *Medical Care* 649–57.

Gilmer, Todd, and Richard Kronick. 2011. "Differences in the Volume of Services and in Prices Drive Big Variations in Medicaid Spending among US States and Regions," 30 *Health Affairs* 1316–24.

Gittleman, Maury. 2011. "Medicaid and Wealth: A Re-Examination," 11 *B.E. Journal of Economic Analysis and Policy*.

Grabowski, David, and Jonathan Gruber. 2007. "Moral Hazard in Nursing Home Use," 26 *Journal of Health Economics* 560–77.

Gross, Tal, and Matthew Notowidigdo. 2011. "Health Insurance and the

Consumer Bankruptcy Decision: Evidence from the Expansion of Medicaid," 95 *Journal of Public Economics* 767–78.

Gruber, Jonathan. 2003. "Medicaid," in Robert A. Moffitt, ed., *Means-Tested Transfer Programs in the United States*. Cambridge, MA: National Bureau of Economic Research.

Gruber, Jonathan, and Kosali Simon. 2008. "Crowd-Out 10 Years Later: Have Recent Public Insurance Expansions Crowded Out Private Health Insurance?" 27 *Journal of Health Economics* 201–17.

Gruber, Jonathan, and Aaron Yelowitz. 1999. "Public Health Insurance and Private Savings," 107 *Journal of Political Economy* 1249–74.

Ham, John, and Lara Shore-Sheppard. 2005a. "The Effect of Medicaid Expansions for Low-Income Children on Medicaid Participation and Private Insurance Coverage: Evidence from the SIPP," 89 *Journal of Public Economics* 57–83.

Ham, John, and Lara Shore-Sheppard. 2005b. "Did Expanding Medicaid Affect Welfare Participation?" 59 *Industrial and Labor Relations Review* 452–70.

Ham, John, Serkan Ozbeklik and Lara Shore-Sheppard. 2014. "Estimating Heterogeneous Take-Up and Crowd-Out Responses to Existing Medicaid Income Limits and their Nonmarginal Expansions," 49 *Journal of Human Resources* 872–905.

Hamersma, Sarah, and Matthew Kim. 2009. "The Effect of Parental Medicaid Expansions on Job Mobility," 28 *Journal of Health Economics* 761–70.

Herring, Brad, and E. Kathleen Adams. 2011. "Using HMOs to Serve the Medicaid Population: What Are the Effects on Utilization and Does the Type of HMO Matter?" 20 *Health Economics* 446–60.

Howell, Embry, Lisa Dubay, Genevieve Kenney and Anna Sommers. 2004. "The Impact of Medicaid Managed Care on Pregnant Women in Ohio: A Cohort Analysis," 39 *Health Services Research* 825–46.

Hurley, Robert E., Deborah A. Freund and John E. Paul. 1993. *Managed Care in Medicare: Lessons for Policy Design*. Ann Arbor, MI: Health Administration Press.

Joyce, Theodore, and Robert Kaestner. 1996. "The Effect of Expansions in Medicaid Income Eligibility on Abortion," 33 *Demography* 181–92.

Kaestner, Robert, Lisa Dubay and Genevieve Kenney. 2005. "Managed Care and Infant Health: An Evaluation of Medicaid in the US," 60 *Social Science and Medicine* 1815–33.

Kaestner, Robert, Theodore Joyce and Andrew Racine. 2001. "Medicaid Eligibility and the Incidence of Ambulatory Care Sensitive Hospitalizations for Children," 52 *Social Science and Medicine* 305–13.

Kaiser Family Foundation. 2010a. *Medicaid and Managed Care: Key Data, Trends and Issues*. Washington, D.C.: Kaiser Family Foundation. www.kff.org/medicaid/upload/8046.pdf.

Kaiser Family Foundation. 2013. *Status of State Action on the Medicaid Expansion Decision, as of December 11, 2013*. Washington, D.C.: Kaiser Family Foundation. http://kff.org/health-reform/state-indicator/state-activity-around-expanding-medicaid-under-the-affordable-care-act/.

Kearney, Melissa S., and Phillip B. Levine. 2009. "Subsidized Contraception, Fertility, and Sexual Behavior," 91 *Review of Economics and Statistics* 137–51.

Levine, Phillip B., and Diane Schanzenbach. 2009. "The Impact of Children's Public Health Insurance Expansions on Educational Outcomes," in David

Cutler, Alan Garber, and Dana Goldman, eds., *Frontiers in Health Policy Research, Vol. 12*. Berkeley, CA: Berkeley Electronic Press.

Levinson, Arik, and Frank Ullman. 1998. "Medicaid Managed Care and Infant Health," 17 *Journal of Health Economics* 351–68.

Long, Sharon, Teresa Coughlin and Jennifer King. 2005. "How Well Does Medicaid Work in Improving Access to Care?" 40 *Health Services Research* 39–58.

Lo Sasso, Anthony, and Thomas Buchmueller. 2004. "The Effect of the State Children's Health Insurance Program on Health Insurance Coverage," 23 *Journal of Health Economics* 1059–82.

Lo Sasso, Anthony, and Deborah Freund. 2000. "A Longitudinal Evaluation of the Effect of Medi-Cal Managed Care on Supplemental Security Income and Aid to Families with Dependent Children Enrollees in Two California Counties," 38 *Medical Care* 937–47.

Lurie, Nicole, Nancy B. Ward, Martin F. Shapiro and Robert H. Brook. 1984. "Termination from Medi-Cal—Does It Affect Health?" 311 *New England Journal of Medicine* 480–84.

Maynard, Alex, and Jiaping Qiu. 2009. "Public Insurance and Private Savings," 24 *Journal of Applied Econometrics* 282–308.

Meyer, Bruce D., and Dan T. Rosenbaum. 2001. "Welfare, the Earned Income Tax Credit, and the Labor Supply of Single Mothers," 116 *Quarterly Journal of Economics* 1063–114.

Moffitt, Robert A. 1983. "An Economic Model of Welfare Stigma," 73 *American Economic Review* 1023–35.

Moffitt, Robert. 1992. "Incentive Effects of the U.S. Welfare System: A Review," 30 *Journal of Economic Literature* 1–61.

Moffitt, Robert, and Barbara Wolfe. 1992. "The Effect of the Medicaid Program on Welfare Participation and Labor Supply," 74 *Review of Economics and Statistics* 615–26.

Norton, Edward, and V. Kumar. 2000. "The Long-Run Effect of the Medicare Catastrophic Coverage Act," 37 *Inquiry* 174–87.

Pezzin, Liliana E., and Judith D. Kasper. 2002. "Medicaid Enrollment and Elderly Medicare Beneficiaries: Individual Determinants, Effects of State Policy, and Impact on Service Use," 37 *Health Services Research* 827–47.

Piper, Joyce M., Wayne A. Ray and Marie R. Griffin. 1990. "Effects of Medicaid Eligibility Expansion on Prenatal Care and Pregnancy Outcome in Tennessee," 264 *Journal of the American Medical Association* 2219–23.

Quast, Troy, David E. Sappington and Elizabeth Shenkman. 2008. "Does the Quality of Care in Medicaid MCOs vary with the form of Physician Compensation?" 17 *Health Economics* 545–50.

Rowland, Diane, and Kristina Hanson. 1996. "Medicaid: Moving to Managed Care," 15 *Health Affairs* 150–2.

Rowland, Diane, Sara Rosenbaum, Lois Simon and Elizabeth Chait. 1995. *Medicaid and Managed Care: Lessons from the Literature*. Washington, D.C.: Kaiser Commission on the Future of Medicaid.

Shen, Yu-Chu, and Stephen Zuckerman. 2005. "The Effect of Medicaid Payment Generosity on Access and Use among Beneficiaries," 40 *Health Services Research* 723–44.

Shore-Sheppard, Lara. 2000. "The Effect of Expanding Medicaid Eligibility on the Distribution of Children's Health Insurance Coverage," 54 *Industrial and Labor Relations Review* 59–77.

Shore-Sheppard, Lara. 2008. "Stemming the Tide: The Effect of Expanding Medicaid Eligibility on Health Insurance Coverage," 8 *B.E. Journal of Economic Analysis & Policy*.

Shore-Sheppard, Lara, Thomas Buchmueller and Gail Jensen. 2000. "Medicaid and Crowding Out of Private Insurance: A Re-Examination Using Firm-Level Data," 19 *Journal of Health Economics* 61–91.

Sommers, Benjamin D., Katherine Baicker and Arnold M. Epstein. 2012. "Mortality and Access to Care among Adults after State Medicaid Expansions," 367 *New England Journal of Medicine* 1025–34.

Sonier, Julie, Michel Boudreaux and Lynn Blewett. 2013. "Medicaid 'Welcome-Mat' Effect of Affordable Care Act Implementation Could Be Substantial," 32 *Health Affairs* 1319–25.

Strumpf, Erin. 2011. "Medicaid's Effect on Single Women's Labor Supply: Evidence from the Introduction of Medicaid," 30 *Journal of Health Economics* 531–48.

Taubman, Sarah, Heidi Allen, Bill Wright, Katherine Baicker, Amy Finkelstein and the Oregon Health Study Group. 2014. "Medicaid Increase Emergency Department Use: Evidence from Oregon's Health Insurance Experiment," 343 *Science* 263–8.

U.S. Census Bureau. Various years. *Statistical Abstract of the United States*. Washington, D.C.: U.S. Department of Commerce.

U.S. House of Representatives, Committee on Interstate and Foreign Commerce, Subcommittee on Health and the Environment. 1976. *Data on the Medicaid Program: Eligibility, Services, Expenditures Fiscal Years 1966–76*. Washington, D.C.: U.S. Government Printing Office.

Watson, Tara. 2014. "Inside the Refrigerator: Immigration Enforcement and Chilling Effects in Medicaid Participation," 6 *American Economic Journal: Economic Policy* 313–18.

Wherry, Laura R., and Bruce D. Meyer. 2016. "Saving Teens: Using a Policy Discontinuity to Estimate the Effects of Medicaid Eligibility," 51 *Journal of Human Resources* 556–88.

Winkler, Anne. 1991. "The Incentive Effects of Medicaid on Women's Labor Supply," 26 *Journal of Human Resources* 308–37.

Yelowitz, Aaron S. 1995. "The Medicaid Notch, Labor Supply, and Welfare Participation: Evidence from Eligibility Expansions," 110 *Quarterly Journal of Economics* 909–39.

Yelowitz, Aaron S. 1998. "Will Extending Medicaid to Two-Parent Families Encourage Marriage?" 33 *Journal of Human Resources* 833–65.

Zavodny, Madeline, and Marianne P. Bitler. 2010. "The Effect of Medicaid Eligibility Expansions on Fertility," 71 *Social Science and Medicine* 918–24.

Zuckerman, Stephen, Joshua McFeeters, Peter Cunningham and Len Nichols. 2004. "Changes in Medicaid Physician Fees, 1998–2003: Implications for Physician Participation," *Health Affairs* Supplementary Web Exclusives W-3-398-84.

Zuckerman, Stephen, Aimee Williams and Karen Stockley. 2009. "Trends in Medicaid Physician Fees, 2003–2008," 28 *Health Affairs* 510–19.

7. Entrepreneurial creative destruction and legal federalism

John A. Dove and Russell S. Sobel

I. INTRODUCTION

Federalism has been at the heart of the American political tradition since the country's founding. Within that tradition federalism has come to mean a system of governance whereby specific and distinct powers and responsibilities are delegated to different levels of government. Thus, the system is one in which both the states and federal government have separate and autonomous roles from one another.

A large literature has evolved to examine how government spending and taxes are determined within a federal system (the literature on "fiscal federalism"), much of it founded in the seminal work of Charles Tiebout (1956). This analysis centered on the overall consequences that would result from competition between various governmental units and jurisdictions in tax and expenditure policies. Specifically, if citizens have perfect information, are perfectly mobile, and if there are a large number of jurisdictions with no spillover effects occurring between jurisdictions due to the provision of public goods, then each citizen will self-select into a jurisdiction based on his or her preference for public goods and willingness to pay for those goods through taxation. This competition over mobile resources, much as market competition does, can lead to greater efficiency within the public sector's fiscal policies.

When the assumption of no spillover or externality effects is relaxed, however, there may be an incentive for localities to "overproduce" those public goods that create a negative externality and "under-produce" those goods which create a positive externality, potentially leading to a "race-to-the-bottom" in policy (Konisky 2007; Oates 2001; Revesz 1996, 1997). This has led to a general consensus in the literature that the powers of government should be decentralized to the lowest level that fully internalizes all costs and benefits associated with the policy decision (Inman and Rubinfeld 1997).

A more recent body of literature following in the vein of Tiebout has also developed within legal scholarship. This "legal federalism" attempts to apply the lessons of economic theory to provide insight into the devolution of both legal and regulatory rule making (Bratton and McCahery 1997). Most notably this work has focused on the impact of environmental policy and regulation (Stewart 1977a, 1977b; Konisky and Woods 2009; Konisky 2010), corporate law and corporate chartering (Bebchuk 2002; Bebchuk and Cohen 2003; Bebchuk, Cohen and Ferrell 2002; Cary 1974; Romano 1985), banking and financial regulation (Scott 1977; Butler and Macey 1988; Garten 1996) and antitrust enforcement (Easterbrook 1983; Lynch 2001; Posner 2004; Greve 2005). Ultimately, the application of economic analysis within the legal framework of federalism has led to an important assertion: that competition is instrumental in shaping numerous outcomes at state and local levels of government due to the fact that regulatory policy has a significant impact upon locational choice of firms and individuals. Overall, this literature – like its counterpart in fiscal federalism – has resulted in a long-standing debate as to whether decentralization and devolution of regulatory responsibility leads to a "race-to-the-top" and is thus welfare enhancing or a "race-to-the-bottom" and would therefore decrease welfare.

This chapter expands on the concept of horizontal legal federalism, or competition between states, by focusing on its impact on innovation and entrepreneurship. In addition, we consider this question from an entirely new direction by considering how entrepreneurial innovation itself helps to drive the process of dynamic legal evolution (the application of law into new areas), under a system of legal federalism. Specifically, our work is an attempt to lay a slightly new framework within which to consider legal federalism using concepts from Schumpeter's theory of entrepreneurial "creative destruction" (Schumpeter 1982) within the marketplace.

We first argue that businesses and entrepreneurs must constantly manage a portfolio of legal risks just as they must manage financial and other market risks. For any given business, some of these legal risks depend on the principal place of business or incorporation, while others do not. Given this, the impact of legal variation on the locational choice of entrepreneurs will vary greatly depending on the nature of the specific business and the product or service sold. Jurisdictions that increase the expected legal risk businesses face will ultimately hamper some types of business activity more than others. For example, an entrepreneurial LASIK eye surgeon's legal risk for medical malpractice will mainly depend on home state laws while a large national manufacturer, even with only one manufacturing facility, will face product liability risk across all 50 states. Malani and Reif (2010), for example, find that doctors' expectations of legal changes within a specific state generate significantly different results in their location decisions after controlling for the current laws.

Next, we argue that the Schumpeterian notion of entrepreneurial "creative destruction", which creates new and revolutionary products within the marketplace while simultaneously rendering others obsolete (Schumpeter 1942), sets in motion a process of creative destruction within the existing body of law, as law must be applied or created in response to new innovations and technological advances.

Innovations like the internet create a need for applications of law into the digital arena, while innovations like the automobile require new applications of precedent from existing laws. Similarly, medical innovations in cloning and stem cells create a need for entirely new areas of law to be developed. Therefore, what matters most to an entrepreneur is the *predictability* with which a jurisdiction's laws will be applied into these new areas. For entrepreneurs to be willing to make large up-front investments in research, development, and manufacturing facilities, they need to be fairly certain how the existing laws in the state in which they locate will be applied and interpreted into the new areas related to the innovative good or service produced by the entrepreneur. From this, we suggest that a system of decentralized federalism with horizontal competition automatically sets up the evolutionary process necessary for specific locations to spontaneously create new bodies of law and legal precedent most conducive to these new entrepreneurial innovations, allowing for certain jurisdictions to specialize in and capitalize on legal comparative advantages.

Lastly, we consider how the variation in law present under horizontal legal federalism is a key determinant of the overall productivity of an area's existing entrepreneurial resources. Following the logic of Baumol (1990), the differences in economic incentives created by differences in legal structures impact whether an economy's entrepreneurs spend their time and talents engaging in productive (versus unproductive) activities. Areas with laws that make it easy for entrepreneurial individuals to profit in the private marketplace will create incentives for innovation and growth, while those areas with laws that make it profitable to engage in attempts to transfer wealth through the legal and political systems will incentivize these same individuals to spend their time and talents engaging in lawsuit abuse and lobbying activities, destroying wealth in the process.

Most important in this context is the role that horizontal competition plays in minimizing unproductive entrepreneurship. Just as we argue for productive entrepreneurship, unproductive entrepreneurs also prefer those locations offering a predictable comparative advantage within the specific legal context most conducive to them. However, following Weingast (1995) we suggest that horizontal competition over legal regimes creates an automatic check against the expansion of unproductive entrepreneurship and is thus superior to greater centralization.

Therefore, our work suggests a new means by which to approach the decision to either decentralize or centralize certain aspects of the rule making and regulatory authority based around this portfolio of legal risk as well as our notion of legal creative destruction. Just as experimentation within the marketplace and the entrepreneurship this fosters is crucial to economic progress, so too might a system of greater decentralization within the legal sphere help to foster this by capitalizing on local and dispersed knowledge (Hayek 1945), and thus better avoid the potential for suboptimal path dependence, a risk associated with greater centralization (North 1990).

We support these conclusions empirically with data from the Institute for Legal Reform's *State Liability Systems Ranking* for each of the 50 states as well as state-level data on the locational choices of Fortune 500 companies, patent activity, and establishment birth rates. Our findings lend evidence to the conjecture that firms will locate in jurisdictions that not only minimize their bundle of legal risk, but also where entrepreneurial creative destruction is most welcomed by predictable application of law in new areas.

II. ENTREPRENEURSHIP, RISK, RETURN AND THE LAW

There exists a very strong and definite relationship between entrepreneurial activity and the law. In order to better understand this it is important to dissect two important aspects associated with any entrepreneurial or business decision: risk and return. All economic activity involves some varying degree of risk attached to it. Therefore, those activities must simultaneously provide a return on investment suitable enough to cover not only the opportunity cost associated with undertaking such activity, but also the associated risk. Naturally, entrepreneurs prefer a larger return and smaller risk.

Within this framework there are ultimately two potential forms of risk that can develop: market risk and legal risk. Market risk is simply the financial risk associated with the failure of an entrepreneurial venture in the marketplace. This market risk arises due to the imperfect knowledge and information about market participants by entrepreneurs trying to capitalize on dispersed and unique knowledge in order to seek out arbitrage opportunities and meet consumer demand (Hayek 1945; Kirzner 1978, 1997). These opportunities are known to be successes or failures only once discovered through the resulting signal of profit and loss attached to an activity. Entrepreneurs unable to properly forecast consumer preferences therefore incur the loss associated with those incorrect decisions. It is this loss that can be thought of as the risk associated with the marketplace. The unique feature of market risk that distinguishes it from legal risk is that an entrepreneur is able to control his or her maximum exposure to market risk through the ability to control the initial financial investment.

The second type of risk that entrepreneurs may face is legal risk. There are two important characteristics attached to legal risk. First, unlike market risk, entrepreneurs cannot limit or control their maximum exposure. An entrepreneur running a restaurant chain who opens a location in a new state may draw a lawsuit in this new jurisdiction. However, a case heard in this new venue may result in a legal liability that far exceeds the investment made in that establishment, forcing the firm to drain resources away from operations in other locations. This type of legal risk can best be illustrated through punitive damages awards, or other civil and criminal penalties.

As the legal system currently stands choice of venue is generally tilted in favor of the plaintiff, which may lead to suboptimal outcomes as the plaintiff does not necessarily fully internalize all of the externalities associated with a given legal remedy. For example, suppose a relatively more stringent antitrust statute exists within West Virginia, and a suit is brought forth within a West Virginia court under West Virginia law against an out-of-state firm. With a successful suit under a stricter law, the benefits now accrue to individuals within West Virginia, while the cost spills over onto individuals and firms in other states. Further, this increases the risk exposure for both potential and actual entrepreneurs operating within other states without adversely affecting litigious behavior in West Virginia.

Tabarrok and Helland (1999) and Helland and Tabarrok (2002) provide evidence of this effect in regard to the incentive effects that elected and unelected state level judges face when deciding upon both compensatory and punitive awards. Specifically, they find strong evidence to support the hypothesis that an elected judiciary within a state is more likely to provide a larger award to an in-state plaintiff, especially if the defendant is an out-of-state business or corporation. Further, their work suggests that average tort awards were largest when out-of-state defendants went before judges who are elected in partisan elections (versus judges elected in non-partisan elections or those who are appointed).

Secondly, predictability of the application of law will have a large influence on decision making, and as such is a major component of entrepreneurial activity. Ultimately, predictability within the law creates an automatic incentive for individuals to commit to and undertake long-term plans and business decisions, while also clearly defining a known and delimited sphere within which each entrepreneur may operate without fear of adverse consequence (Hayek 1960). Within this context, consistency in the law and its enforcement are welfare enhancing in that they reduce the inherent uncertainty attached to the unknown future of the marketplace. These multiple layers of legal risk that arise constantly require entrepreneurial and business decision makers to manage a bundle of legal risks within their given portfolio. While firms and entrepreneurs are able to control the home state risk they face given the freedom to choose where to locate or incorporate, the risk associated with economic activity across multiple states is far less controllable or predictable.

Given the current context as laid forth, what becomes most relevant for business and entrepreneurial decision making is the ability to manage this portfolio of legal risk. Thus, when making decisions firms and entrepreneurs must be able to assess and weigh the probability of the type of risk they may be faced with. This implies that it will be the overall probability of the *type of risk* which will affect the *type* of business and entrepreneurial activities that will take place within a given state or location. This we will address in Section IV.

III. ENTREPRENEURIAL INNOVATION AND THE EVOLUTION OF THE LAW

It is essential to understand entrepreneurship as a process of creative destruction (Schumpeter 1942). In other words, entrepreneurship leads to new innovative goods and services that make previous inventions and discoveries obsolete. This creates a constant disequilibrating process within the marketplace as these new discoveries emerge. The significance of this process can be seen when viewing its impact on legal and legislative institutions. By definition this process creates a need or demand for making new areas of law, or applying existing law to new areas not previously discovered or considered before. The net result from this process of both legal and market creative destruction will be one in which Schumpeterian entrepreneurship will migrate to those locations which create a legal environment that adapts the most predictably to these new innovations. Easterbrook (1996) suggests a similar justification for the law, by arguing that what needs to be developed is a sound *general* law that is easily applicable to new issues as they emerge. He applies his analysis to cyberspace law, arguing that what must come first is a sound intellectual property law, of which the principles developed from that can be applied to particular issues regarding cyberspace and the internet.

This occurs due to the very nature of creative destruction. With the advent of a new innovation or technological breakthrough a simultaneous need for legislative or judicial entrepreneurship emerges. In other words, new bodies of law or precedent will eventually emerge as new and unforeseen legal issues surrounding entrepreneurial discoveries arise. However, the trajectories along which these legal changes may take, like technological changes, are inherently unpredictable.

In this context, greater horizontal competition between jurisdictions sets in motion a process that allows jurisdictions to discover how to best reduce the variance associated with legal unpredictability and simultaneously draw in those entrepreneurs most in need of minimizing their particular legal risk exposure associated with their own activities, and who simultaneously require predictability within the body of law most significantly related to their activities. Therefore, a decentralized legal system offers the potential for multiple new applications or areas of law to emerge and compete, while a centralized legal system would alternatively create a set of uniform legal standards in order to deal with issues arising from new Schumpeterian discoveries. This greater centralization increases the probability that the chosen legal regime will be inferior, yet may also be extremely costly to change, with the overall result being path dependence along a suboptimal trajectory (North 1990). When legal discovery is left to 50 different governing bodies, this competitive process will result in an evolutionary process of legal trial and error (Hayek 1960). Over time, the dominant legal regime would become the one most sought after by entrepreneurs, with the ensuing benefits accruing to the jurisdiction or jurisdictions adopting that regime.

Within this framework each state initially competes over new applications or bodies of law. Through legal evolution some states are able to develop comparative advantages over a given subset of the law, occurring as this body of law influences firm and entrepreneurial locational choice. Over time states that have legislatively created the most conducive law to a given entrepreneurial activity will enjoy an inflow of that activity. This leads to increased precedent being set within the courts of that state and an increased knowledge at the judicial level over only a small subsection of the law. Delaware provides a ready example of this behavior in regard to corporate law.

The first modern body of corporate law was passed in 1896 in the state of New Jersey (Cary 1974). For a time the state saw an inflow of corporate chartering. However, shortly thereafter Delaware passed its own legislation governing corporate behavior. This led to a period in which the two states competed with one another, with Delaware clearly emerging ahead. As such, Delaware has now enjoyed the creation and discovery of legal precedents for nearly a century within a highly technical and specialized area of the law. Further, many of the legal changes that do occur across the states regarding corporate law emerge from Delaware (Romano 1985). Thus,

Delaware has been able to capitalize on its comparative advantage within corporate law and has increased the predictability associated with the evolutionary and competitive process of the law. The result has been an inflow of entrepreneurial activity, notably corporate governance. Not only has the state legislature adhered to a binding set of rules governing corporate law, so too has the judiciary through a long history of consistent legal precedent.

Overall, these predictions suggest an alternative or at least supplementary view in regard to the clustering of entrepreneurial industries. Often the clustering of innovative industries is attributed to specific resources in a given area. However, it would seem that industrial clusters may also (or primarily) develop in response to legal comparative advantages and legal predictability.

IV. DATA

Differences in state legal systems with respect to the treatment of businesses and entrepreneurs are admittedly difficult to measure. Probably the most comprehensive and consistent index available is from the Institute for Legal Reform's biannual report *State Liability Systems Ranking*. Overall, the study includes a nationally representative sample of 1482 senior legal representatives of business firms with annual revenues of at least $100 million. The survey measures perceptions over a set of ten different components of the legal liability system of each state.[1] Each respondent was required to give a letter grade to each of the subcategories and then to the overall legal environment of each state. From this the Harris Poll created both an overall score from a 100-point scale (0 being the worst and 100 the best) as well as a 5-point grade (again 0 being the worst and 5 being the best). Our goal is to use this ranking of legal quality as a proxy for legal predictability.

As an initial inspection of how this legal index correlates with a state's overall economic performance, Figure 7.1 plots a state's income growth against the legal index score.

On the x-axis is the average legal system quality score from 2002–2007, compared against each state's average annual economic growth rate from 1995–2005 on the y-axis. The figure shows a positive correlation between a state's legal quality and its economic growth rate. Specifically, the higher the score a state receives on the legal index the higher has been a state's

---

[1]   Appendix 7.1 provides a list of each of the ten subcategories along with the top five and bottom five performing state in each category and each state's overall score.

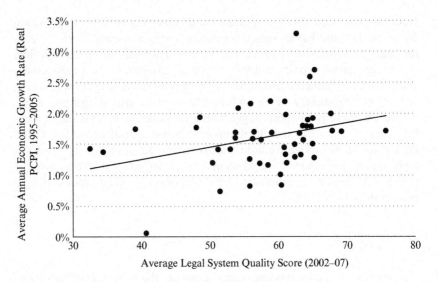

Figure 7.1   State legal system scores and state income growth

average rate of economic growth. Figure 7.2 shows how the average legal system quality score correlates with state per capita income for 2005. Again, there is a definite positive correlation between a state's overall legal index score and per capita income. Thus, states with higher legal index scores are also wealthier. This may be a direct result associated with the increased predictability in these legal regimes.

In order to test our conjecture about the impact that legal regimes may have on entrepreneurial and business decisions we ran a set of negative binomial regressions, using the number of Fortune 500 companies incorporated in each state as our dependent variable. The model takes the following form:

$$y_i = \alpha + \sum_{i=1}^{5} \beta_{1i} X_i + \sum_{k=1}^{7} \beta_{ki} Z_i + \varepsilon_i \tag{7.1}$$

where y_i is the number of Fortune 500 companies incorporated within state i, X_i is a set of five of the subcomponents that we believe most convey dynamic legal predictability, and Z_i is a set of socioeconomic control variables.

We perform regressions using the overall liability system grade and the grades for each of the subcategories we believe best capture what could constitute legal predictability for entrepreneurial activities, along with our control variables for other economic and demographic factors that would influence the underlying rate of entrepreneurial and business activity. We

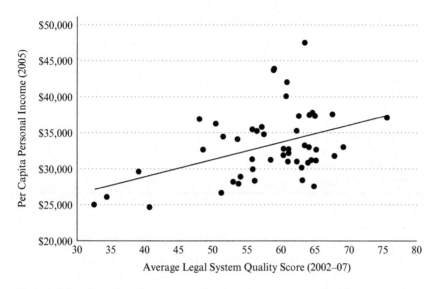

Figure 7.2   State legal system ranking and state income level

focus on six specific categories that we believe to be the most influential in regard to predictability. Along with the overall grade, these include "Discovery," "Scientific and Technical Evidence," "Judges' Impartiality," "Judges' Competence," and "Juries' Predictability."

We believe these to be the most significant determinants as more stringent rules of discovery minimize the risk of previously unknown evidence from entering the trial as it progresses. Further, the judge as agenda setter plays a vital role as to how a case actually progresses. Given that, knowing how and why a judge will proceed increases the ability to predict how this dynamic legal creative destruction may play out. Lastly, the jury as the ultimate fact finder will be the body to determine the outcome. Thus, knowing how this may play out also increases the ability for an entrepreneur to predict the direction that any newly derived legal precedent may go. Our estimates are reported in Table 7.1.[2]

For both the overall grade (column 1) and each of the subsequent subcategories the results are all positive and statistically significant. The marginal effects for the overall grade suggest that a one-point increase in a state's score leads to an increase of more than seven incorporations within that state. The two subcategories that have the largest impact on

---

[2]   Appendix 7.4 provides our full estimates results for each of the subcategories in our analysis.

Table 7.1   Number of Fortune 500 companies incorporated in state

Harris Score Area	Effect of a one unit increase in Harris Score on Fortune 500 Companies Incorporated
Overall Grade	7.28**
Discover	9.82***
Scientific and Technical Evidence	10.24***
Judges' Impartiality	7.37**
Judges' Competence	7.81**
Juries' Predictability	9.16**

Notes:
Negative Binomial Results.
Table presents estimated marginal effects of only the legal variable coefficients. Full results in Appendix 7.4.
Statistical significance indicated as follows: *** = 1%; ** = 5%; * = 10%.

incorporations appear to be "discovery" (column 2) and "scientific and technical evidence" (column 3). Both of these suggest that with a one-point increase in a state's grade for each of these subcategories, the number of incorporations increases by 9.82 and 10.24 respectively. Further, columns 4 and 5 both refer to the importance of a judge's predictability. Specifically, column 4, judges' impartiality suggests that a one-point increase in that category's grade increases the number of incorporations by 7.37 while column 5, judges' competence, increases the number of incorporations by 7.81. Lastly, column 6, juries' predictability suggests that a one-point increase in the category's grade increases the number of incorporations by 9.16.

Overall, our results give rise to some very important implications. The location of a firm seems to ultimately be driven by the importance of being able to fairly present and use scientific and technical evidence and discovery procedures within the courtroom of a given state. This would seem to comport with our conjecture about the ultimate importance of Schumpeterian entrepreneurial and legal creative destruction. In other words, as we suggested, a firm has any number of legal risks that may be unavoidable. However, the most important for a firm to avoid are those most damaging to a new and never before known technology or technological discovery. Thus, when faced with a legal challenge concerning such an innovation a firm will look to the location which will be most willing to accept the necessary and highly technical evidence derived from these entrepreneurial discoveries. Therefore, it will be those jurisdictions most willing to push the process of Schumpeterian legal creative destruction that will be the ones to see a rise in the number of firms located within that jurisdiction.

V. LEGAL SYSTEMS AND THE ALLOCATION OF ENTREPRENEURIAL EFFORTS – BAUMOL'S PRODUCTIVE AND UNPRODUCTIVE ENTREPRENEURSHIP

Based on the work of Baumol (1990), modern economic literature acknowledges that not all entrepreneurial activities are wealth-enhancing for a society. Creative individuals may spend their time and talents earning wealth for themselves either by producing goods and services for others voluntarily (productive entrepreneurship), or by attempting to secure wealth transfers through the political and legal process (unproductive entrepreneurship). The allocation of entrepreneurship across these two alternatives is driven by the relative payoff or personal reward, which in turn is a function of the incentives created by legal systems. Put simply, an entrepreneurial individual located in one state may have started a cutting edge engineering company, while had she located in another state may have instead started a new personal injury law firm or lobbying firm, depending on the relative profitability of these industries in each state.

From this it is possible to understand that it is the quality of the legal institutions found within a state that will have the greatest impact on the type of entrepreneurship that will develop. When legal systems create a system of economic predation, the prevalence of unproductive entrepreneurship will increase (Buchanan 1975; Frye and Shleifer 1997). Thus, it is the quality of the legal institutions and the ability of those institutions to constrain the ability for individuals to undertake such unproductive behavior that plays a crucial role in economic growth, development and well-being.

To this point our analysis has applied to all types of entrepreneurship, whether productive or unproductive. In other words, unproductive entrepreneurs also face a bundle of legal risks that must constantly be managed. Further, the same process of creative destruction also occurs within these areas, requiring changes in both the law and legal precedent. Therefore, just as productive entrepreneurs seek out those locations that provide legal predictably, so too do unproductive entrepreneurs. However, this also brings out the importance of horizontal legal federalism, in that through competition the results of unproductive entrepreneurship may over time be minimized.

In this context, areas that provide legal predictability that rewards or encourages unproductive entrepreneurship and economic predation will see declines in overall economic well-being and outmigration, or exit, in accordance with Tiebout (1956). If one jurisdiction has legal rules that are detrimental to prosperity, it simultaneously has the unintended consequence of increasing the competitiveness and well-being of entrepreneurs in neighboring states (Weingast 1995). Therefore, under legal federalism there is an automatic check on the extent to which unproductive entrepreneurship might emerge (becoming increasingly strong as the ability to exit occurs), in contrast to a centralized legal system.

In the context of our current work we attempt to understand how exactly changes in a state's liability index score may impact not only economic outcomes, but also the type of entrepreneurship that individuals pursue. As we discussed earlier, some of a business's legal risks depend on the principal place of business or incorporation, while others do not. However, clearly the home state legal environment matters significantly, and we will be able to see the extent of this in our empirical results. In order to do this we consider how a state's liability score (the overall score for each state), impacts three key economic indicators for each state. As a first approximation of each, we plot the individual liability rankings against: (1) Sobel (2008)'s measure of the ratio of productive to unproductive entrepreneurship in each state (we term this the "Baumol ratio"); (2) the establishment birth rate for large firms in each state; and (3) the number of patents produced in each state. Figures 7.3, 7.4, and 7.5 show each respectively.

In the figures, there appears to be a strong, positive correlation between a state's legal climate as measured by its liability system rank and the three variables measuring innovation and productive entrepreneurship. Overall, these indicators suggest that states with sounder legal institutions have a

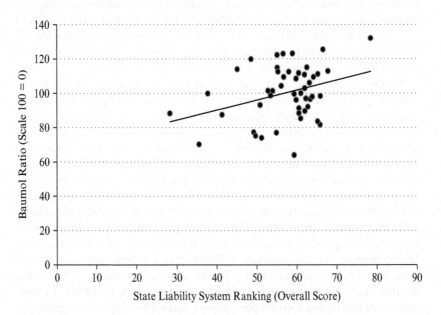

Figure 7.3　Comparison of Baumol ratio against state liability index

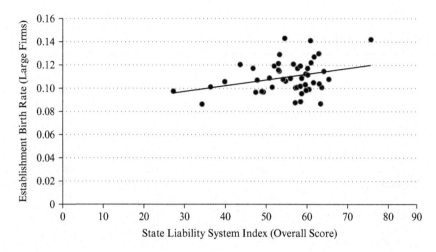

Figure 7.4   Comparison of large establishment birth rate and state liability index

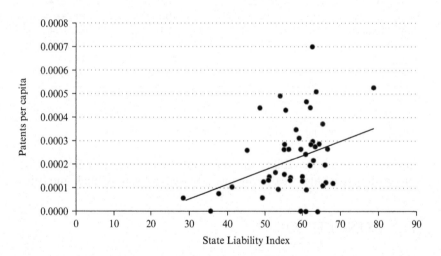

Figure 7.5   Comparison of patents per capita and state liability index

larger establishment birth rate for large firms, a larger number of patents produced, and a significantly larger number of productive relative to unproductive entrepreneurs. Regression lines fit to these relationships all show positive and significant correlations as is shown in Table 7.2 below.

These results strongly suggest that a sounder legal system in each state

Table 7.2　Productive entrepreneurship measures by state regression results

	Dependent Variables		
	Baumol Ratio	Patents per 100,000	Large Firm Birth Rate (per 100)
Constant	30.51	5.96	44.62**
	(0.15)	(0.02)	(2.34)
State Liability Index	0.4672**	4.22*	0.9153**
	(2.04)	(1.59)	(2.04)
Median Age	−5.77***	1.52	−0.3560**
	(3.81)	(0.92)	(2.52)
Median Household Income	−0.0035**	0.0001	0.0001*
	(2.53)	(0.05)	(1.53)
Per Capita Income	0.0118***	0.0018	0.0005*
	(3.98)	(0.57)	(1.88)
Population Density	−0.0165	0.001	0.0027**
	(1.36)	(0.94)	(2.45)
Percent College Degree	−0.8623	0.0266	−0.0654
	(1.22)	(0.30)	(0.94)
Percent Male	1.4249	0.0177	−0.4894*
	(0.37)	(0.01)	(1.38)
Observations	48	48	48
R-Squared	0.4987	0.3522	0.4000

Notes:
Absolute value of t-statistics in parenthesis.
Statistical significance indicated as follows: *** = 1%; ** = 5%; * = 10%.

appears to reduce the ability for unproductive entrepreneurship to arise, thus leading to greater wealth enhancing activities by individuals and firms.

VI.　CONCLUSION

This chapter has attempted to add to the literature on legal federalism by examining the impact that it has on innovation and entrepreneurship. Business firms face different bundles of legal risks that they must manage, some heavily depending on their location, some not. This proportion will vary widely across different types of businesses, and thus variations in state legal systems will have disproportionate impacts on some types of firms relative to others.

Most importantly, this chapter has tried to bring attention to the idea that the predictability of the evolution and application of law into new areas in a state is a very important determinant of the environment created for entrepreneurial endeavors. Because the Schumpeterian process of creative destruction creates new goods and services to which existing law must be extended, it is a driver of legal evolution. A substantial upfront investment by an entrepreneur in a location will critically depend on how well he or she can forecast the future application of local law onto the new good or service being produced.

Through entrepreneurial creative destruction entirely new bodies of laws must be developed in order to deal with what are entirely new and previously unknown innovations and discoveries. Therefore, we contend that each state competes over these new bodies of law and eventually through the evolutionary process of trial-and-error comes to discover certain areas of comparative advantages in which they specialize. This in turn drives entrepreneurs to naturally select into those states that are most conducive to not only Schumpeterian entrepreneurial discovery, but also are those best able to cope with potentially uncertain legal contingencies that may emerge due to this process. The returns to entrepreneurial discovery in that field will also be higher in those areas, causing the state's existing resources to naturally flow into those activities in the spirit of Baumol (1990).

As entrepreneurs drive change, legal systems must evolve. A system of decentralized legal federalism is the system best able to cope with this process of the discovery of how to apply existing law into new areas. With multiple jurisdictions attempting to apply law into new areas, those with existing comparative advantages and the best and most efficient systems for dynamic legal evolution will succeed and prosper. In turn, this helps to create (or explain) the geographic clustering of entrepreneurial enterprises in certain legal jurisdictions.

REFERENCES

Baumol, William J. 1990. "Entrepreneurship: Productive, Unproductive, and Destructive." 98 *The Journal of Political Economy* 893–921.
Bebchuk, Lucian. 1992. "Federalism and the Corporation: The Desirable Limits on State Competition in Corporate Law." 105 *Harvard Law Review* 1435–510.
Bebchuk, Lucian and Alma Cohen. 2003. "Firm's Decisions When to Incorporate." 46 *Journal of Law and Economics* 383–425.
Bebchuk, Lucian, Alma Cohen, and Allen Ferrell. 2002. "Does the Evidence Favor State Competition in Corporate Law?" 90 *California Law Review* 1775–821.
Bratton, William A. and Joseph A. McCahery. 1997. "The New Economics of Jurisdictional Competition: Devolutionary Federalism in a Second-Best World." 86 *Georgetown Law Journal* 201–78.

Buchanan, James M. 1975. *The Limits of Liberty: Between Anarchy and Leviathan*. Chicago, IL: University of Chicago Press.

Butler, Henry and Jonathan Macey. 1988. "The Myth of Competition in the Dual Banking System." 73 *Cornell Law Review* 677–713.

Cary, William L. 1974. "Federalism and Corporate Law: Reflections upon Delaware." 83 *Yale Law Journal* 663–705.

Easterbrook, Frank H. 1983. "Antitrust and the Economics of Federalism." 26 *Journal of Law and Economics* 23–50.

Easterbrook, Frank H. 1996. "Cyberspace and the Law of the Horse." *University of Chicago Legal Forum* 207–16.

Frye, Timothy and Shleifer, Timothy. 1997. "The Invisible Hand and the Grabbing Hand." 87 *The American Economic Review* 354–8.

Garten, Helen A. 1996. "Devolution and Deregulation: The Paradox of Financial Reform." 14 *Yale Law and Policy Review* 65–97.

Greve, Michael S. 2005. "Cartel Federalism? Antitrust Enforcement by State Attorneys General." 72 *The University of Chicago Law Review* 99–122.

Hayek, Friedrich. 1945. "The Use of Knowledge in Society." 35 *The American Economic Review* 519–30.

Hayek, Friedrich. 1960. *The Constitution of Liberty*. Chicago, IL: University of Chicago Press.

Helland, Eric and Alexander Tabarrok. 2002. "The Effect of Electoral Institutions on Tort Awards." 4 *American Law and Economics Review* 341–70.

Inman, Robert P. and Daniel L. Rubinfeld. 1997. "Rethinking Federalism." 11 *Journal of Economic Perspectives* 43–64.

Kirzner, Israel M. 1978. *Competition and Entrepreneurship*. Chicago, IL: University of Chicago Press.

Kirzner, Israel M. 1997. "Entrepreneurial Discovery and the Competitive Market Process: An Austrian Approach." 35 *Journal of Economic Literature* 60–85.

Konisky, David M. 2007. "Regulatory Competition and Environmental Enforcement: Is there a Race to the Bottom?" 51(4) *American Journal of Political Science* 853–72.

Konisky, David M. 2010. "Public Preferences for Environmental Policy Responsibility." 41 *Publius: The Journal of Federalism* 76–100.

Konisky, David M. and Neil D. Woods. 2009. "Exporting Air Pollution? Regulatory Enforcement and Environmental Free Riding in the United States." 63 *Political Research Quarterly* 771–82.

Lynch, Jason. 2001. "Federalism, Separation of Powers, and the Role of State Attorneys General in Multi-state Litigation." 101 *Columbia Law Review* 1998–2032.

Malani, Anup and Julian Reif. 2010. "Accounting for Anticipation Effects: An Application to Medical Malpractice Tort Reform." NBER Working Paper No. 16593.

North, Douglass C. 1990. *Institutions, Institutional Change and Economic Performance*. Cambridge: Cambridge University Press.

Oates, Wallace E. 2001. "A Reconsideration of Environmental Federalism." Resources for the Future Discussion Paper 01-54.

Posner, Richard. 2004. "Federalism and the Enforcement of Antitrust Laws by State Attorneys General." 2 *The Georgetown Journal of Law and Public Policy* 5–16.

Revesz, Richard L. 1996. "Federalism and Interstate Environmental Externalities." 144 *University of Pennsylvania Law Review* 2341–416.

Revesz, Richard L. 1997. "Federalism and Environmental Regulation. A Normative Critique." in John Ferejohn and Barry R. Weingast, eds., *The New Federalism: Can the States Be Trusted?* Stanford: Hoover Institution Press.

Romano, Roberta. 1985. "Law as Product: Some Pieces of the Incorporation Puzzle." 1 *Journal of Law, Economics and Organization* 225–83.

Scott, Kenneth E. 1977. "The Dual Banking System: A Model of Competition in Regulation." 30 *Stanford Law Review* 1–50.

Schumpeter, Joseph A. 1942 [2003]. *Capitalism, Socialism and Democracy.* London and New York: George Allen and Unwin Ltd.

Sobel, Russell S. 2008. "Testing Baumol: Institutional Quality and the Productivity of Entrepreneurship." 23 *Journal of Business Venturing* 641–55.

Stuart, Richard B. 1977a. "The Development of Administrative and Quasi-Constitutional Law in Judicial Review of Environmental Decisionmaking: Lessons from the Clean Air Act." 62 *Iowa Law Review* 713–69.

Stuart, Richard B. 1977b. "Pyramids of Sacrifice? Problems of Federalism in Mandating State Implementation of National Environmental Policy." 86 *Yale Law Journal* 1196–272.

Tabarrok, Alexander and Eric Helland. 1999. "Court Politics: The Political Economy of Tort Awards." 42 *Journal of Law and Economics* 157–88.

Tiebout, Charles M. 1956. "A Pure Theory of Local Expenditures." 64 *The Journal of Political Economy* 416–24.

Weingast, Berry R. 1995. "The Economic Role of Political Institutions: Market Preserving Federalism and Economic Development." 11 *Journal of Law, Economics and Organization* 1–31.

APPENDIX 7A.1

The Ten Sub-categories Ranked within the Institute for Legal Reform's "State Liability Systems Ranking"

(1) Overall treatment of tort and contract litigation
(2) Having and enforcing meaningful venue requirements
(3) Treatment of class action suits and mass consolidation suits
(4) Damages
(5) Timeliness of summary judgment or dismissal
(6) Discovery
(7) Scientific and technical evidence
(8) Judges' impartiality
(9) Judges' competence
(10) Juries' fairness

APPENDIX 7A.2

Overall Score and Overall Grade of Each State's Tort Liability System as Ranked by the Institute for Legal Reform's "State Liability Systems Ranking"

State	Rank	Overall Score	Overall Grade	State	Rank	Overall Score	Overall Grade
Delaware	1	77.2	4.1	Vermont	26	61.6	3.5
North Dakota	2	71.1	4	Ohio	27	59.7	3.4
Nebraska	3	69.7	3.9	Michigan	28	59.5	3.4
Indiana	4	69.6	3.8	Washington	29	61.6	3.4
Iowa	5	69.4	3.8	Nevada	30	59.8	3.4
Virginia	6	68.1	3.8	Oklahoma	31	59	3.4
Utah	7	67.8	3.7	Missouri	32	56.1	3.3
Massachusetts	8	65.6	3.7	Texas	33	56.3	3.2
Minnesota	9	65.3	3.7	New Jersey	34	57.8	3.2
South Dakota	10	65.6	3.7	Pennsylvania	35	56.6	3.2
Maine	11	65.2	3.6	Hawaii	36	56.4	3.2
Arizona	12	65	3.6	Kentucky	37	54.4	3.2
Colorado	13	65.8	3.6	Alaska	38	56.6	3.2
North Carolina	14	64	3.6	South Carolina	39	55.1	3.1
New York	15	62.5	3.6	Rhode Island	40	55.2	3.1
Idaho	16	63.9	3.6	Florida	41	53.9	3.1
Kansas	17	64.6	3.6	New Mexico	42	53.9	3.1
New Hampshire	18	64.2	3.6	Montana	43	52.4	3
Tennessee	19	63.7	3.5	Arkansas	44	48.7	2.9
Wyoming	20	64.5	3.5	Alabama	45	45.5	2.8
Georgia	21	60.9	3.5	Illinois	46	47.9	2.8
Wisconsin	22	62.8	3.5	California	47	47.2	2.7
Maryland	23	63.2	3.5	Mississippi	48	40	2.5
Oregon	24	63	3.5	Louisiana	59	39.6	2.4
Connecticut	25	62.1	3.5	West Virginia	50	35.1	2.2

APPENDIX 7A.3

Overall Grade of Each State's Tort Liability System Based on Each Sub-category as Ranked by the Institute for Legal Reform's "State Liability Systems Ranking"

Subcategory	Top 5 States	Grade	Bottom 5 States	Grade
Having and Enforcing	Delaware	4.2	Illinois	3.1
Meaningful Venue	Iowa	4	Alabama	3.1
Requirements	Indiana	3.9	Mississippi	2.9
	Virginia	3.9	Louisiana	2.9
	Arizona	3.9	West Virginia	2.6
Overall Treatment of Tort	Delaware	4.1	Alabama	2.8
and Contract Litigation	North Dakota	3.8	California	2.7
	Nebraska	3.8	Mississippi	2.5
	Utah	3.8	Louisiana	2.5
	Iowa	3.7	West Virginia	2.3
Treatment of Class	Delaware	3.9	Illinois	2.6
Action Suits and Mass	Nebraska	3.8	Mississippi	2.5
Consolidation Suits	Utah	3.7	California	2.4
	Indiana	3.7	Louisiana	2.4
	North Dakota	3.6	West Virginia	2
Damages	Delaware	3.9	Illinois	2.6
	Nebraska	3.9	California	2.5
	Indiana	3.9	Louisiana	2.4
	North Dakota	3.8	Mississippi	2.3
	Iowa	3.8	West Virginia	2.1
Timeliness of Summary	Delaware	3.9	California	2.8
Judgment or Dismissal	North Dakota	3.8	Illinois	2.7
	Nebraska	3.6	Mississippi	2.6
	Indiana	3.6	Louisiana	2.5
	Idaho	3.6	West Virginia	2.4
Discovery	Delaware	3.9	Illinois	3
	Iowa	3.8	California	2.9
	Nebraska	3.7	Louisiana	2.8
	Indiana	3.7	Mississippi	2.7
	Utah	3.7	West Virginia	2.6
Scientific and Technical	Delaware	4.1	Alabama	2.9
Evidence	Colorado	3.8	Arkansas	2.7
	Utah	3.7	Mississippi	2.6
	Massachusetts	3.7	Louisiana	2.6
	Nebraska	3.6	West Virginia	2.6

Subcategory	Top 5 States	Grade	Bottom 5 States	Grade
Judges' Impartiality	Delaware	4.4	Arkansas	3.1
	North Dakota	4.1	Alabama	2.8
	South Dakota	4	Mississippi	2.6
	Nebraska	3.9	Louisiana	2.4
	Indiana	3.9	West Virginia	2.4
Judges' Competence	Delaware	4.4	Arkansas	3
	North Dakota	4	Alabama	3
	Nebraska	3.9	Mississippi	2.8
	Maine	3.9	Louisiana	2.7
	Massachusetts	3.9	West Virginia	2.6
Juries' Fairness	Nebraska	4.1	California	2.8
	North Dakota	4	Alabama	2.7
	Iowa	4	Mississippi	2.5
	Delaware	3.9	Louisiana	2.5
	South Dakota	3.9	West Virginia	2.3

APPENDIX 7A.4

Negative Binomial Regression Results; Dependent Variable: State of Incorporation for Each of the Fortune 500 Companies

Independent Variables	1	2	3	4	5	6	7	8	9	10	11
Constant	13.51 (27.37)	20.29 (30.41)	9.41 (21.04)	35.25 (36.78)	15.23 (28.25)	11.20 (20.30)	17.59 (20.19)	10.41 (28.45)	10.41 (28.45)	25.59 (29.45)	25.41 (35.23)
Overall Score	2.38** (0.57) [7.28]										
Overall Treatment of Tort and Contract Litigation		2.26** (0.60) [7.26]									
Overall Treatment of Class Actions			2.19** (0.46) [6.85]								
Punitive Damages				1.41 (0.49) [4.79]							
Timeliness of Summary Judgment					2.08* (0.63) [7.34]						
Discovery						3.26*** (0.67) [9.82]					

235

Independent Variables	1	2	3	4	5	6	7	8	9	10	11
Scientific and Technical Evidence							3.98*** (0.67) [10.24]				
Judges' Impartiality								2.34** (0.60) [7.37]			
Judges' Competence									2.47** (0.58) [7.37]		
Juries' Predictability										2.63** (0.82) [9.16]	
Juries' Fairness											1.69* (0.59) [6.12]
Median Age	-0.44*** (0.18) [-1.26]	-0.42*** (0.18) [-1.22]	-0.34*** (0.17) [-1.14]	-0.31*** (0.17) [-1.06]	-0.41** (0.18) [-1.44]	-0.42*** (0.17) [-1.27]	-0.30*** (0.17) [-0.78]	-0.38*** (0.17) [-1.21]	-0.39*** (0.17) [-1.21]	-0.36*** (0.18) [-1.26]	-0.31** (0.17) [-1.14]
Median Household Income (in Thousands)	-0.32** (0.08) [-0.91]	-0.31** (0.08) [-0.90]	-0.31*** (0.07) [-0.90]	-0.31*** (0.07) [-0.92]	-0.33*** (0.07) [-1.02]	-0.32*** (0.08) [-0.91]	-0.24*** (0.09) [-0.58]	-0.30*** (0.08) [-0.88]	-0.30*** (0.08) [-0.88]	-0.34*** (0.08) [-1.02]	-0.32*** (0.07) [-0.97]
Per Capita Personal Income (in Thousands)	1.16*** (0.29) [3.28]	1.12*** (0.30) [3.25]	1.12*** (0.28) [3.19]	1.12** (0.31) [3.27]	1.23*** (0.30) [3.72]	1.17*** (0.28) [3.29]	0.31*** (0.86) [2.09]	1.13*** (0.29) [3.24]	1.13*** (0.30) [3.26]	1.23*** (0.30) [3.68]	1.17*** (0.29) [3.55]
and Area (per 100,000 miles)	-0.23 (0.48) -0.27 [-0.64]	-0.17 (0.50) [-0.62]	-0.17 (0.45) [-0.48]	-0.31 (0.42) [-0.91]	-0.46 (0.38) [-1.40]	-0.21 (0.41) [-0.60]	0.03 (0.48) [0.09]	-0.25 (0.51) [0.73]	-0.25 (0.51) [0.74]	-0.40 (0.38) [-1.21]	-0.40 (0.41) [-1.21]

	(1)	(2)	(3)	(4)	(5)	(6)	(7)	(8)	(9)	(10)	(11)
Population Density	1.14	1.28	1.03	2.23	0.75	1.50	2.17	1.11	1.19	0.93	0.91
(in Thousands)	(1.10)	(1.12)	(0.98)	(3.40)	(1.00)	(1.12)	(1.11)	(1.04)	(1.11)	(1.15)	(1.10)
	[3.20]	[3.69]	[2.93]	[6.49]	[2.28]	[4.21]	[5.28]	[3.20]	[3.45]	[2.78]	[2.74]
Percent College	-0.19	-0.18	-0.16*	-0.19	-0.18	-0.18*	-0.19*	-0.23	-0.23	-0.22	-0.22
Degree	(0.06)	(0.06)	(0.05)	(0.08)	(0.06)	(0.05)	(0.05)	(0.07)	(0.07)	(0.09)	(0.10)
	[-0.54]	[-0.52]	[-0.51]	[-0.66]	[-0.82]	[-0.56]	[-0.50]	[-0.74]	[-0.74]	[-0.77]	[-0.82]
Percent Male	-0.05	-0.12	-0.13**	-0.62	-0.22*	-0.19*	-0.36*	-0.13*	-0.13*	-0.48	-0.45
	(0.37)	(0.39)	(0.38)	(0.71)	(0.53)	(0.37)	(0.37)	(0.52)	(0.52)	(0.56)	(0.66)
	[-0.16]	[-0.36]	[-0.43]	[-2.13]	[-0.79]	[-0.58]	[-0.93]	[-0.41]	[-0.41]	[-1.68]	[-1.65]
Overdispersion Results	255.58	278.07	208.43	306.55	333.39	281.77	175.46	274.27	274.27	381.31	391.29
Log-Pseudolikelihood	-118.81	-119.72	-113.30	-107.77	-121.06	-118.14	-115.17	-119.13	-119.13	-121.05	-121.85
Pseudo R-Squared	0.12	0.12	0.13	0.11	0.11	0.13	0.15	0.12	0.12	0.11	0.10
Observations	50	50	50	50	50	50	50	50	50	50	50

Notes:
Statistical significance indicated as follows: *** = 1%; ** = 5%; * = 10%.
Robust Standard Errors in Parentheses.
Marginal Effects in Brackets.

8. Federalism and the rise of state consumer protection law in the United States

Joshua D. Wright[a]

INTRODUCTION

Consumer protection legislation has proliferated within the United States over the last several decades. The early 1960s heralded the dawn of this proliferation, as a general discontent with the ability of market forces, the Federal Trade Commission ("FTC"), and state common law to protect consumers fueled important legislative reactions (Butler and Wright, 2011, p. 167). Indeed, state legislatures responded to these criticisms by formulating and enacting a diverse collection of legislation often referred to as state Consumer Protection Acts ("CPAs") (Schwartz and Silverman, 2005, p. 15). The original purpose of these state CPAs was to supplement the FTC's objective of shielding consumers from "unfair or deceptive acts or practices,"[1] and by 1981, every state had its own version of a CPA— some even had enacted more comprehensive consumer protection schemes (Sovern, 1991, p. 446).

This expansive trend has continued in recent years, exacerbated by the potent combination of the onset of the financial crisis, the rise of behavioral law and economics, and the increasingly broad interpretation of state CPAs (which themselves had already given greater latitude to consumer protection regimes). Yet despite the meteoric rise of consumer protection laws, its effect upon overall consumer welfare remains unclear; conflicting

[a] Elyse Dorsey provided superb research assistance. This chapter draws upon previous work on state Consumer Protection Acts with, separately, Henry Butler and Eric Helland. (Butler and Wright, 2011; Wright and Helland 2011). I am grateful to the Searle Civil Justice Institute for financial support, and to Henry Butler, David Evans, Eric Helland, Jonathan Klick, Bruce Kobayashi, and Todd Zywicki for helpful comments and discussions on these issues. All errors are my own.
[1] 15 U.S.C. § 45(a)(1) (2006).

economic theories of consumer protection yield divergent predictions for consumer welfare. Consumer protection legislation may serve important economic functions, potentially correcting market failures and informational asymmetries; however, such legislation may also generate over-deterrence as expanded liability increases firms' marginal costs, resulting in higher market prices and otherwise deterring procompetitive conduct. Empirical evidence indicates legislators often fail to take into account the serious costs—both intended and unintended—passed on (at least in part) to consumers as the result of the expansion of consumer protection legislation.

State CPAs provide a valuable opportunity to observe competitive federalism in action as they implicate important challenges associated with concurrent regulation. The potential for competitive federalism to enhance consumer outcomes by improving state law arises because each state has its own CPA. Competitive federalism reflects the notion that market principles can be translated to, and lead to efficiency within, legislative decision-making. It suggests that competition between state governments will compel jurisdictions to compete for the optimal provision of laws and public services (Buchanan, 1995; See also Stearns and Zywicki, 2009, ch. 6; Musonda and Bulliard, 2004, p. 9).[2] Indeed, jurisdictional competition may play a significant role in disciplining regulatory institutions, thereby mitigating potentially adverse consumer welfare effects arising from over-reaching regulation (Kobayashi and Ribstein, 2007).

However, the benefits of competitive federalism do not obtain under all circumstances,[3] and may be critically limited when comprehensive federal regimes exist or when jurisdictional competition is restricted. Whether or not the welfare enhancing effects of jurisdictional competition are realized depends primarily upon the firm's costs of exiting the jurisdiction (Buchanan, 1995; Kobayashi and Ribstein, 1997, p. 10). Exit is the most direct manner by which firms can discipline costly legislative decisions, preventing (or forcing the repeal of) suboptimal imposition of taxes and regulations (Epstein, 1992). By allowing firms to avoid the consequences of legislative decisions, exit imposes constraints upon legislators, forcing them to internalize the costs of their decisions and leading to more efficient

---

[2] "[B]y differentiating public goods consumption by location it improves the incentives for individuals to reveal their true preferences in public goods" (Musonda and Bulliard, 2004, p. 9).

[3] Tiebout describes the necessary conditions for the benefits of competitive federalism to be realized: "(1) people and resources are mobile, (2) the number of jurisdictions is large, (3) jurisdictions are free to select any set of laws they desire, and (4) there are no spillovers" (Kobayashi and Ribstein, 2007).

results. When exit is too costly to adequately restrain the governing entity, legislative decisions may impose deadweight losses.

Whether exit is feasible, in turn, depends primarily upon the ability of firms to contract for the law of an alternative jurisdiction, without physically relocating to that jurisdiction (Kobayashi and Ribstein, 1997, p. 10). Indeed, the economics literature recognizes the role choice of law provisions serve in enhancing jurisdictional competition (See, e.g., Buchanan, 1995; Epstein, 1992; O'Hara and Ribstein, 2000, p. 631). Choice of law provisions permit firms to select the regulatory regime best tailored to their particular endeavors, thereby augmenting competition between jurisdictions to supply desirable regulatory frameworks (O'Hara and Ribstein, 2000, p. 633). Empirical evidence demonstrates choice of law provisions facilitate jurisdictional competition and have important economic effects (Klick et al., 2006; Klick et al., 2009). For instance, while studies have found that franchise regulations restricting the ability of franchisors to terminate franchises tend to diminish franchising in favor of less efficient owner-operated outlets, choice of law provisions mitigate this inefficiency by allowing firms to avoid cumbersome or harmful restrictions (Klick et al., 2009, pp. 378–9). In the state CPA context, however, it is unlikely such negative effects will be tempered. Firms cannot contract out of state CPA liability, as most state statutes do not allow for choice of law provisions.[4] Thus, the beneficial effects of jurisdictional competition as a constraint upon state CPA development are severely weakened.

The impediments to jurisdictional competition between states with respect to CPAs do not alone imply that the regulation of consumer protection should be hastily surrendered to the FTC and other federal regulators, such as the new Consumer Financial Protection Bureau (CFPB).[5] However, the CFPB would in fact assume many of the powers previously delegated to the FTC—plus significant additions—thereby supplanting the FTC's consumer protection efforts (Kovacic, 2009, p. 20).[6] Further

---

[4] See, e.g., California's Unfair Competition Law, Ca. Bus. & Prof. Code §§ 17200–17210 (previously, Ca. Civil Code § 3369); New York's Deceptive Business Acts and Practices Statute, N.Y. Gen. Bus. §§ 349–350-f-1.

[5] Dodd-Frank Wall Street Protection and Reform Act, 12 U.S.C. § 5301 (2010). The CFPB is created in a mammoth piece of legislation that regulates nearly every aspect of the financial services industry. The CFPB consolidates federal consumer protection authority—leading some to question whether the FTC's consumer protection programs will persist—but does not preempt state authority. Rather, the CFPB encourages state CPA action in the same manner the FTC has.

[6] "Yet the CFPA Act will have the effect of divesting the FTC of all of its financial consumer protection functions in a manner that provides no assurances

responsibilities for enforcing consumer protection law would be shifted away from the FTC and to the states. Former FTC Chairman William E. Kovacic expressed concern that the CFPB "will not improve consumer financial protection, but [rather] degrade it," by thrusting a novel agency with incredibly broad-sweeping authority, which lacks the FTC's institutional knowledge and constraints, into a place of prominence (Kovacic, 2009, p. 20). Despite these concerns, the FTC's troubled history in this area suggests that more rigorous analyses of the actual effects of state CPA and federal consumer protection enforcement are required to inform a sensible division of responsibilities.

We examine the available evidence on state and federal consumer protection enforcement to discern their likely effects upon consumer welfare. Our primary focus is to understand the role of state CPAs in the consumer protection landscape with an eye toward drawing lessons concerning whether state CPAs manifest the benefits of competitive federalism, embody a failure of this principle, or neither. Part I documents the dramatic rise of consumer protection legislation within the United States. Part II details recent expansions and amendments to state CPA statutes. Part III discusses the empirical evidence available on the consumer welfare effects of these statutes, focusing upon two recent studies: (1) comparing enforcement under state CPAs to FTC enforcement; and (2) measuring the effects of state CPAs upon automobile insurance premiums. These studies cast significant doubt upon the ability of jurisdictional competition to constrain state CPAs. Part IV concludes.

I.   THE DRAMATIC RISE OF CONSUMER PROTECTION LEGISLATION

Three forces present in the 1960s combined to catalyze the rapid rise of state CPAs: (1) dismay over the FTC's perceived ineptitude at protecting consumers; (2) popular demand for greater consumer protection (and greater regulation of business as a whole); and (3) dissatisfaction with common law causes of action, which were perceived as insufficient and far too stringent (Butler and Wright, 2011, p. 167). These three forces implicate each of the current tools for consumer protection: federal regulation; market forces; and state common law (See Muris, 2004).

---

that the new regulatory body will attain the FTC's existing level of effectiveness or develop an institutional platform that yields future enhancements" (Kovacic, 2009, p. 20).

FTC critics vociferously decried its inadequacies along numerous dimensions, including that it: misallocated its limited resources (American Bar Association, 1969, pp. 26–8); had succumbed to political favoritism and to regulatory capture (Cox et al., 1969, pp. 130–40); and erroneously shielded producers in its consumer protection endeavors (Posner, 1969, p. 71).[7] These critics argued that market forces could no longer curtail adverse consumer outcomes or adequately deter producers from bad acts as the marketplace was too impersonal (Lovett, 1972, p. 725; Withrow, 1967, p. 64)[8] and favored producers (Norstrand, 1969, p. 175).[9] Indeed, critics asserted that this new market paradigm rendered common law causes of action ineffective as consumer protection institutions. Common law actions allegedly suffered from myriad shortcomings: most were far too expensive to efficiently enforce, while others doctrinally did not fit a regime of prospective consumer protection.[10] For example, common law requirements did not allow for prospective injunctions.

State legislatures quickly reacted to this maelstrom of criticism by enacting CPAs. In 1962, eight states had CPAs; within 20 years, these statutes had been incorporated as important components of each state's consumer protection initiative (Pridgen and Alderman, 2009, § 210, app. at 3A). These state CPAs were originally intended to fill perceived gaps in FTC enforcement and to enhance consumer outcomes on the market. Early state CPAs almost universally granted the state Attorney General authority to seek (and courts to grant) injunctions proscribing certain behaviors or practices—some even permitted the state Attorney General to seek restitution on behalf of harmed consumers.[11] Many contemporary state

---

[7] "A perusal of FTC rules and decisions reveals hundreds of cases in which prohibitory orders have been entered against practices, not involving serious deception, by which sellers have attempted to market a new, often cheaper, substitute for an existing product" (Posner, 1969, p. 71).

[8] "The difficulties being faced by the consumer today are best understood in terms of the new 'impersonality' of the market place" (Withrow, 1967, p. 64). See also National Association of Attorneys General Committee on the Office of Attorney General, 1971, pp. 395–6 (hereinafter Attorney General Report).

[9] "[The] consumer has lost the leverage he once had in the marketplace. The disgruntled buyer can no longer hash out differences with his shopkeeper-neighbor; he is now confronted by impersonal bigness where responsibility and liability forever lie just one department away" (Norstrand, 1969, p. 175).

[10] Common law causes of action—including deceit, misrepresentation, and breach of warranty—had relatively high burdens of proof and limited remedies (See Schwartz and Silverman, 2005, pp. 6–7).

[11] See, e.g., 1960 *New Jersey Laws*, ch. 39, at § 5.

CPA attributes derive from uniform and model statutes established in the late 1960s (National Association of Attorneys General Committee on the Office of Attorney General, 1971, p. 400). The Uniform Deceptive Trade Practices Act, for instance, created a private right of action for consumers and permitted injunctive relief absent a demonstration of actual damages or of intent to deceive (Commissioners on Uniform State Laws, 1964, pp. 253, 262).

The Model Unfair Trade Practices and Consumer Protection Law ("UTPCPL") was another influential model statute arising at this time. The FTC itself crafted the UTPCPL, intending it to be a comprehensive and enticing consolidation of traditional and contemporary aspects of consumer protection regimes. In its 1970 rendering, the UTPCPL described three possible bases for finding practices unlawful (Council of State Governments, 1969, p. 142): (1) Section 5 of the FTC Act could be used to define and proscribe the limits of unlawful practices (Council of State Governments, 1970); (2) prohibited conduct could be defined as "false, misleading, or deceptive acts or practices in the conduct of any trade or commerce"—notably, this definition omitted a broad "unlawful practices" component (Pridgen and Alderman, 2009, § 210); and (3) a "laundry list" approach proscribed 12 competition-focused behaviors alongside one provision addressing consumers (See Council of State Governments, 1969; see also Pridgen and Alderman, 2009, § 210). Additionally, and comparable to many modern state CPA statutes, the UTPCPL intentionally strived to retain standards and requirements analogous to the relevant FTC provisions. Indeed, the UTPCPL noted that "due consideration and great weight" should be given to the FTC's own interpretations (Council of State Governments, 1969). Similarly, 28 states' CPAs currently reference the FTC (Pridgen and Alderman, 2009, § 210, app. at 3B).

These references reflect the fact that most state CPAs were first enacted to supplement perceived shortcomings in consumer protection by deliberately mimicking FTC enforcement actions. Yet most contemporary state CPAs encompass a far greater range of conduct than their original counterparts. For instance, many state CPAs do not include a public interest requirement, although this remains a crucial limitation upon FTC enforcement. Several others broadly or vaguely define "injury" to a party and establish liberal—if any—standing requirements (Searle Civil Justice Institute, 2009; Butler and Johnston, 2010, p. 9).

Moreover, state CPAs have become increasingly favorable and generous to consumer litigants. The relaxation of traditional FTC and common law requirements has helped to fuel an increase of 119 percent in the number of CPA decisions reported in federal district and state appellate courts between 2000 and 2007 (Searle Civil Justice Institute, 2009, p. 20). This dramatic spike is especially pronounced within states whose CPAs are most friendly to consumer plaintiffs (Searle Civil Justice Institute, 2009, p. 20).

The emerging and widespread popularity of behavioral law and economics has further accelerated the creation and adoption of consumer protection legislation. Recently, behavioral law and economics has gained considerable traction within the literature—indeed, hundreds of law review articles referencing "behavioral economics" have been written just within the last decade,[12] and behaviorist arguments underlie recent consumer protection legislation as influential as the Dodd-Frank Act.[13] Behaviorist consumer protection proposals include disclosure requirements, limiting consumer choice, and establishing default rules that favor agency-approved products, all of which would allegedly improve consumer decision-making and outcomes.[14] Several of these proposals manifest themselves within the Dodd-Frank Act, which drastically alters the current framework of consumer protection. Dodd-Frank establishes a "floor," a minimal level of protection enforced at the federal level, and further encourages states to supplement this basic protection with their own regulations. The likely effect of this encouragement is likely to further expand state consumer protection legislation.

II.   EXPANSIONS OF AND AMENDMENTS TO STATE CPAS

Today each state has its own CPA—all of which allow for private actions. Yet most states have amended their CPAs several times over the years, yielding wide variation between contemporary state CPA regimes (Pridgen and Alderman, 2009, § 210, app. at 3A). These recent amendments, coupled with expansive judicial interpretations, have generally broadened consumer rights and seem on net to have increased consumer incentives to file suit in a myriad of ways. For example,

---

[12]   As of August 24, 2010, a search of the Westlaw JLR database reveals 1789 articles in legal periodicals referencing "behavioral economics." A search on Google Scholar results in 2150 legal opinions and articles referencing the same term.

[13]   Dodd-Frank Wall Street Reform and Consumer Protection Act, 12 U.S.C. § 5301 (2010); Bar-Gill and Warren, 2008 (arguing that a stronger federal consumer protection agency utilizing behaviorist knowledge and tools would enhance consumer outcomes).

[14]   See Evans and Wright, 2010 (documenting the behaviorist literature).

some statutes allow for class actions and private claims, while others repeal the "public interest" requirements to sue under the state CPA statute. Moreover, some state CPAs have abbreviated or eliminated rigorous common law requirements for establishing a prima facie case, along with traditional burdens of proof, thereby tipping adjudications toward consumers (Rice, 1969, p. 307). Proponents of these amendments invoke 1960s arguments contending that consumers must have adequate incentives to file suit in order for state CPAs to have any supplemental deterrent effect. Yet critics contend that these amendments increase the prospect of harassment of legitimate business conduct (Lovett, 1972, p. 744) and that ambiguous consumer protection laws are ripe for abuse of discretion through judicial interpretation (See, e.g., Rice, 1969, p. 340).

Despite the potential for serious negative consumer welfare affects, the trajectory of state consumer protection law is clear: it has changed in favor of consumer plaintiffs. One recent study conducted by the Searle Center ("Searle Study") sought to measure just how pronounced this change is (Searle Civil Justice Institute, 2009). Economic theory postulates that the expected value of a claim to a potential, generic consumer plaintiff should influence the level of litigation arising under a given state CPA.[15] Accordingly, the Searle Study generated an index (the "State CPA Index") to assess the overall "plaintiff friendliness" of state CPAs, to compare against the level of CPA litigation within states. The Study coded 27 variables present within 2008 state CPA statutes as either "benefits" to or "restrictions" upon consumer suits.[16] The following two figures illustrate the Study's findings. Figure 8.1 depicts the State CPA Index for the states with the most state CPA litigation, as measured by the number of judicial decisions. Figure 8.2 focuses upon the State CPA Index within the ten states exhibiting the greatest number of state

---

[15]   Specifically, theory predicts that the higher the expected value of a claim, the higher the level of litigation will be, and vice versa.

[16]   For details on the creation of the State CPA Index, see Searle Civil Justice Institute, 2009. The Study demonstrated that the State CPA Index is positively correlated with the log of reported state CPA decisions (Searle Civil Justice Institute, 2009). The figures' findings understate the changes in state CPAs over the time period because changes that supplement the definition of illegal conduct under the state CPA are excluded. The exclusion is to facilitate comparison between state CPAs which are vague (and thus do not list types of illegal conduct) and those that include such a list. For example, a state CPA which adds a significant number of acts to its definition of illegal conduct over time need not be more "plaintiff friendly" than a state CPA which includes only a vague description (i.e., "unfair and deceptive") of the prohibited conduct.

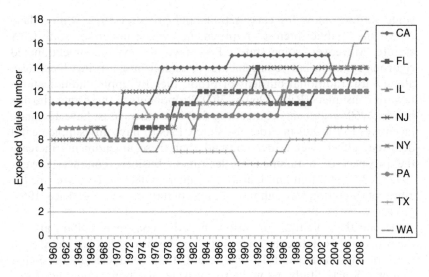

Figure 8.1   State CPA index for top states (states with > 80 decisions in either Federal, District or State Appellate Courts, 2007)

CPA changes between initial state CPA adoption and 2009. Each displays the incredible increase in the ease of filing state CPA claims over the last several decades.

Indeed, as the two figures demonstrate, the willingness and ability of consumers to file suit has risen dramatically within many states, reflecting the larger trend of increasingly pro-consumer state CPA statutes nationwide. This trend has important implications for analyzing the effects—both positive and negative—of consumer protection legislation.

III.   EMPIRICAL EVIDENCE OF STATE CPAS' EFFECTS UPON CONSUMER WELFARE

Theories underlying state CPA legislation yield ambiguous consumer welfare predictions; yet they portend, in many instances, the likelihood of serious harms to overall welfare (Butler and Johnston, 2010, pp. 44–53). Competition between jurisdictions may play an important role in mitigating these harmful effects, but before it can definitively be said to do so, several factors must be rigorously analyzed. Theories underlying likelihood of both positive and negative consumer welfare effects must be articulated; the overall environment must be analyzed to determine whether the conditions requisite to jurisdictional competition are present;

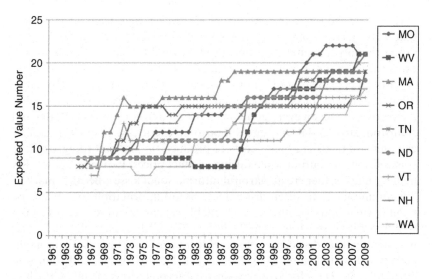

Figure 8.2 State CPA index for top movers (change = 8 or more units)

and the empirical evidence addressing which of these effects appear to prevail must be examined.

A. The Economics of Consumer Protection

State CPAs generally impose liability upon two broad categories of behavior: (1) selling practices; and (2) marketing communications, including advertising. This liability theoretically may compel sellers to internalize the social costs of deceptive selling or marketing practices, thereby enhancing both efficiency and consumer welfare. For instance, state CPAs may grant recourse to consumers who would otherwise bear the costs of a producer's misleading statements; this burden shifting increases economic efficiency and consumer welfare by forcing the party responsible for creating the cost to pay for it. Consistent with this argument, state CPA proponents claim that "gaps" in FTC enforcement, irrational consumer behavior, and inadequate incentives for plaintiffs to bring small but meritorious claims justify increased state CPA liability. These proponents further contend that state CPAs may alleviate informational asymmetries by compelling sellers to accurately disclose information uniquely within their possession regarding the quality of their products.[17]

---

[17]   For example, one common CPA claim involves "vanishing premiums": life insurance sales agents promise customers that premiums will "vanish" entirely

However, economic theory further recognizes significant social harms that may derive from expanded state CPA liability. State CPAs may raise prices to consumers by increasing, beyond the optimal amount, the expected liability for conduct associated with the production, marketing, and sale of consumer goods and services. In this respect, state CPA liability in the market for consumer goods and services may amount to "what is effectively a tax on every good or service sold to consumers" (Butler and Johnston, 2010, p. 44). By functioning as an excise tax, state CPA liability can increase firms' marginal costs of production, and accordingly reduce competition and output while raising product prices. Expanded state CPA liability may further create harmful informational losses. Because marketing communications often disseminate useful information to consumers, liability rules that discourage this valuable exchange can reduce consumer welfare (Butler and Johnston, 2010, pp. 47–8).[18] For example, such rules may deter partial disclosures of valuable information, because firms might perceive such disclosures as likely to trigger liability (Butler and Johnston, 2010, nn. 130–31). Moreover, expansive interpretations of state CPA language may create welfare losses by introducing additional uncertainty into firms' business decisions.[19]

Accordingly, the potential social benefits of expanded state CPA liability must be offset against the attendant potential social costs. Unfortunately, economic theory and empirical evidence do not dictate one uniquely optimal level of state CPA liability. The potentially adverse effects of continually increasing liability, however, indicate that this increase may have diminishing marginal returns. In the consumer protection context,

---

after a few years of payments, because the policy will pay for itself out of dividend or investment income. However, these claims rely upon highly implausible assumptions regarding investment performance; using more realistic assumptions, the premiums would never vanish. Yet consumers are unlikely to identify the deceptive nature of these claims. A CPA, then, could theoretically enhance outcomes in life insurance markets, as consumers would have a cause of action that would address not only their own harms, but further prevent future misleading claims. See *Broberg v. Guardian Life Ins. Co. of America*, 90 Cal. Rptr. 3d 225 (Ct. App. 2009).

[18]   On the economic value of information, and advertising in particular, see Bagwell, 2005; Dixit and Norman, 1978; Nelson, 1974; Klein and Leffler, 1981.

[19]   Indeed, the Searle Study finds that CPA statutory language strongly affects the total level of CPA litigation within a state (Searle Civil Justice Institute, 2009, p. 26). Businesses must expend resources in an effort to discern how vague CPA standards will be enforced; judges must expend further resources defining illegal conduct and differentiation between meritorious and frivolous claims. These added costs may be passed on to consumers in the form of higher prices or reduced innovation.

expanding liability may yield positive consumer welfare effects up to some threshold level, but expansion past this critical level portends over-deterring business conduct that is beneficial to consumers.

While the foregoing tradeoffs are well recognized even by state CPA advocates,[20] little data currently exists illuminating the actual effects of expanded liability upon consumers. Despite the murkiness of the empirics, the question guiding the analysis is clear: whether the rise in consumer protection legislation optimally deters consumer abuse. Preliminary empirical evidence indicates the answer to this question is no, and that the costs of expanded consumer protection legislation may overwhelm the purported benefits. Given these early indications, it is important to analyze the potential mitigating effects of competitive federalism and jurisdictional competition. Competitive federalism may enhance consumer welfare by compelling states to compete with one another to offer the optimal regulatory system. However, effective jurisdictional competition arises only under certain circumstances—namely, when the costs of contracting out of liability are low enough to make exit a viable constraint upon legislative behavior. Accordingly, its mitigating effects may not be realized if exit is too costly.

Indeed, exit is a crucial component of jurisdictional competition, and its absence in the state CPA context is notable. This absence casts doubt upon the ability of jurisdictional competition to alleviate state CPAs' adverse consumer welfare effects. In order to properly discipline legislative decisions, firms must be able to meaningfully exhibit their displeasure with the regulatory regime—thereby providing valuable feedback information (Kobayashi and Ribstein, 1997, p. 10). Firms typically create this feedback by contractually exiting the jurisdiction (Kobayashi and Ribstein, 1997, p. 10), but businesses are unable to contract out of state CPA liability. If a firm is operating within a given state, then it is subject to that state's CPA rules. Given the lack of a viable exit option, the ability of competitive federalism to restrain states' creation of CPAs appears minimal.

However, note that the available evidence necessarily presents a limited picture of the effects of changes to consumer protection regimes. Competition between jurisdictions may well play an important role in correcting suboptimal legislative decisions (Kobayashi and Ribstein, 1997, p. 1),[21] yet these benefits would only be realized in the long-run,

---

[20]   See, e.g., Sovern, 2006, pp. 1705–9 (recognizing that state CPAs can increase transaction costs and arguing for regulation that would prevent firms from passing these costs on to consumers).

[21]   "Our analysis ... emphasizes the importance of a dynamic rather than static perspective on state law. Theory and data indicating that state law is inefficient

after competition has had sufficient time to exert its pressure and to force welfare-enhancing changes. While jurisdictional competition may compel states to reconsider alternative and existing solutions that they initially overlooked, or to scale back broad liability provisions, these effects are not immediate.

Examining the existing empirical evidence for preliminary effects of consumer protection legislation, therefore, serves an important function— assisting in discerning whether the rise of state CPA legislation is likely to benefit consumers, or instead portends unwarranted harms to consumer welfare. The Searle Center recently examined the relationship between state CPAs and consumer welfare in both a "Shadow FTC" Study and a study of automobile insurance premiums, each of which provides useful data for this analysis.

B. Shadow FTC Study

The Searle Center's Shadow FTC study offers empirical evidence illuminating how enforcement of state consumer protection legislation compares to the FTC's consumer protection enforcement (Searle Civil Justice Institute, 2009). In this study, an expert panel analyzes the facts of actual, litigated state CPA cases. Overall, the panel finds that state CPAs seem to find unlawful conduct that would not be illegal under the relevant FTC standard—casting doubt upon the proposition that state CPA liability has marginally benefited consumers (Searle Civil Justice Institute, 2009, pp. 49–50).

In fact, the study reveals that *most* state CPA claims do not state cognizable consumer protection violations under FTC standards: the Searle Study finds that only 22 percent of state CPA claims would constitute illegal conduct under the FTC standards (Searle Civil Justice Institute, 2009, p. 39). Moreover, the FTC would likely pursue significantly fewer of these claims (just 12 percent) (Searle Civil Justice Institute, 2009, p. 39). While this latter finding appears consistent with state CPAs' objective of supplementing FTC enforcement, the Searle Study further finds that nearly 40 percent of state CPA claims in which the consumer plaintiff prevailed at trial would not amount to illegal conduct under the pertinent FTC standard (Searle Civil Justice Institute, 2009, p. 49). This indicates that state CPAs are imposing liability upon a very different type of

---

may be incomplete because they examine only states' initial attempts to externalize costs rather than the ultimate outcome of state competition" (Kobayashi and Ribstein, 1997, p. 1).

conduct than would the FTC. Additionally, this latter finding demonstrates the substantial overbreadth of state CPAs, in even the strongest of cases. The FTC necessarily faces significant and built-in enforcement restraints—including its public interest requirement (Braucher, 2006, n. 1)[22]—that are crafted to minimize harmful error costs. Such costs may have significant and negative repercussions, potentially chilling innovation and increasing prices to consumers. State CPAs, however, seem to evade these constraints, by condemning conduct of a different nature than that reached under FTC standards.

Indeed, serious questions arise as to whether state CPAs create net benefits for consumers, given that they allow such different and more expansive claims. Moreover, many state CPAs create costly uncertainty by utilizing vague statutory definitions of illegal conduct.[23] Firms must then expend valuable resources attempting, in the first instance, to predict how these ambiguous standards will be enforced; subsequently, judges must expend further resources defining illegal conduct, and distinguishing between meritorious and trivial claims. These expenditures increase costs that may, in turn, be passed on to consumers, both directly—in the form of higher prices—and indirectly.

Additionally, the Searle Study indicates that state CPA statutory language significantly affects the overall level of state CPA litigation within a state (Searle Civil Justice Institute, 2009, p. 50). Statutory language establishing more generous remedies and less rigorous claim requirements incentivizes more lawsuits—indicating that consumers are rationally responsive to state CPA incentives (Searle Civil Justice Institute, 2009, p. 50). Because consumer plaintiffs (or at least, their counsel) should be cognizant of the increased return on investment within states using vague state CPA language, further increases in state CPA litigation within these states is likely. This result is troubling, given the expense of litigation, the likely chilling effects, and the questionable consumer benefits deriving from expanded state CPA liability. However, the realization that statutory language matters suggests that legislators may increase or decrease state CPA litigation within their jurisdictions at relatively low cost. This realization in turn entails important implications for the federalism analysis: because the level of consumer protection within a given state is easily altered, competition along this dimension may be comparatively

---

[22]   5 U.S.C. § 53(b) (2000) (requiring that the FTC demonstrate claims are in the public interest before the court may grant a preliminary injunction).
[23]   These definitions are particularly pernicious as they deviate from the FTC's well-developed and well-understood standards.

easy, as states are not locked into regimes. Yet the ultimate effect of this realization is unclear, as the ease of alteration may increase uncertainty for firms that rely upon the current consumer protection laws in making business decisions and accordingly may suffer costly and unforeseen liability. Which of these effects predominates must be evaluated empirically.

C.   Automobile Insurance Premiums

The Searle Civil Justice Institute's Preliminary Report on Consumer Protection Acts and Costs to Consumers ("Report") provides evidence on how changes to state CPAs affect automobile insurance prices (Searle Civil Justice Institute, 2011). Automobile insurance provides a particularly appealing metric for analyzing the effects of state CPA amendments for numerous reasons, including that: it is the largest property casualty line of insurance; its prices are established independently on a state-by-state basis; its product lines are frequently subjected to state CPA litigation; and consumers purchase it without government subsidies (unlike health insurance) (Searle Civil Justice Institute, 2011, p. 3). Moreover, automobile insurance prices are arguably the closest approximation of a market price within the insurance industry, due to their being comparatively less regulated.[24]

The Report considers the impact of state CPAs from a myriad of perspectives. It uses the same State CPA Index discussed above to conduct three separate analyses: first, it examines the relationship between total state CPA changes and changes in average combined automobile insurance premiums; second, it analyzes the impacts of individual state CPA provisions upon average combined automobile insurance premiums; and finally, it evaluates the effect of individual state CPA provisions on the growth rate of average combined automobile insurance premiums (Searle Civil Justice Institute, 2011, p. 27). While the Report reveals useful information regarding the impact of state CPA changes upon automobile insurance premiums, it does have important limitations. Notably, without a comprehensive examination of the quality of

---

[24]   Automobile insurance companies retain considerable discretion over prices, as 28 states either have no filing laws or have file and use laws. According to the National Association of Insurance Commissioners, file and use (or use and file) laws require the rates to be submitted to the state insurance department but specific approval is not required (See National Association of Insurance Commissioners, 2009, p. 227). Although automobile insurance prices may not be the least regulated insurance product line, they are one of the least regulated that have all of the other benefits mentioned above.

automobile insurance offered, as well as the quantity demanded, the effects of these price increases are somewhat ambiguous (Searle Civil Justice Institute, 2011, pp. 7–12). Consumers may benefit despite price increases if they are accompanied by quality increases and increases in demand. To the contrary, if quality and demand remain the same (or decrease), then these price increases yield adverse consumer welfare effects.[25]

Overall, the Report finds that states with more plaintiff-friendly State CPA Index changes over the relevant time period are generally associated with higher automobile insurance premiums (Searle Civil Justice Institute, 2011, p. 27). For instance, an increase in one standard deviation from the average State CPA Index yields a 2.0 percent increase in combined average premiums. This increase translates to an additional \$17.81 paid by the average consumer annually, given an overall combined average annual premium of \$838.72 (Searle Civil Justice Institute, 2011, p. 28).

These price increases are observed only after states expand their CPAs beyond a certain threshold level, illustrating the concept of increasing marginal costs (Searle Civil Justice Institute, 2011, pp. 29–31). Consistent with the proposition that state CPAs can enhance consumer welfare by compelling firms to internalize the social costs of deceptive or misleading conduct, a nonlinear model shows that initial adoption of pro-plaintiff provisions reduces automobile insurance premiums (Searle Civil Justice Institute, 2011, p. 30). However, consumer prices increase after approximately 12 such amendments are incorporated into a state CPA (Searle Civil Justice Institute, 2011, p. 30). Figure 8.3 below illustrates these findings, comparing the linear to the nonlinear impact of the State CPA Index upon automobile insurance premiums.[26]

---

[25] Additionally, it is not entirely clear that the price effects for consumers capture the entire effect of CPA changes—other parties, such as automobile insurance company shareholders, may bear cost increases. However, demand for automobile insurance is likely relatively inelastic, given that all states require drivers to have automobile insurance. Consumers are unlikely to stop demanding automobile insurance merely because price increases. The price elasticity of demand for a particular product is calculated as the percent change in quantity demanded for the product over the percent change in the price of the product. Blackmon and Zeckhauser (1991) estimate a demand elasticity of −.57 for Massachusetts while Jaffee and Russell (1997) estimate a price elasticity of −.63 for California. Accordingly, economic theory predicts that consumers, and not shareholders, will bear the brunt of these cost increases, if the increases function analytically as a tax upon automobile insurance (Blackmon and Zeckhauser, 1991).

[26] The nonlinear coefficients are not independently statistically significant, but they are jointly significant, demonstrating that the relationship between State

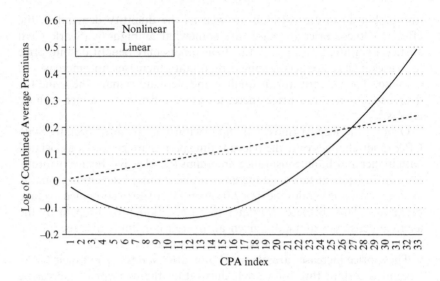

Figure 8.3   Linear versus nonlinear impact of the State CPA Index

Importantly, the Report further finds that certain state CPA provisions are more influential than others, confirming the Searle Study's finding that state CPA statutory language matters. Terms allowing for enhanced damages have the largest impact upon automobile insurance premiums—they are associated with increases ranging from 10–16 percent (Searle Civil Justice Institute, 2011, p. 31). Indeed, such terms alone may increase premiums by $80 annually (Searle Civil Justice Institute, 2011, p. 31). Provisions that allow for any recovery of restitution and for the recovery of attorney's fees for prevailing plaintiffs are likewise influential, raising premiums by approximately 14 percent and 8 percent respectively (Searle Civil Justice Institute, 2011, pp. 31–2).

IV.   CONCLUSION

The dramatic rise of consumer protection legislation has affected consumers in important respects, and thus warrants critical analysis. While such legislation can theoretically enhance consumer outcomes—by correcting market failures and informational asymmetries—it simultaneously

---

CPA Index and average automobile insurance premiums is nonlinear (Searle Civil Justice Institute, 2011, p. 29).

portends the realization of significant deadweight losses associated with diminished consumer choice, expanded liability for firms, and the chilling of procompetitive conduct. A proper analysis of the effects of state CPAs accordingly considers their costs and benefits in relation to other available solutions, including federal regulation, common law, and market forces. The empirical evidence available indicates that state CPAs impose significant costs upon consumers in certain circumstances. The Searle Study reveals that state CPAs have drastically increased liability for firms, and the Automobile Insurance Premiums Report finds that this increased liability translates into generally higher prices for consumers in the automobile insurance market. Accordingly, state CPAs appear to function as a costly tax upon firms, the negative effects of which likely overwhelm the purported benefits of increased regulation.

Yet state CPAs raise significant federalism challenges, given both their proliferation and the existence of concurrent federal regulation. Economic theory predicts that competition between jurisdictions may mitigate the harmful effects just identified, if firms are readily able to contract out of costly and non-optimal liability. However, this mitigation function is unlikely to arise with respect to state CPAs. While state CPAs could theoretically benefit from jurisdictional competition, the absence of a viable exit option significantly limits this potential by removing an important motivation for competing. Notably, despite the fact that CPA liability has observably raised various prices to consumers (e.g., automobile insurance premiums), virtually no state has meaningfully scaled back the plaintiff-friendliness of its CPA in recent years. Rather, as one scholar describes the situation, "[a]lthough there have been occasional legislative adjustments to these statutes, mostly broadening them further and occasionally cutting back their scope, repeal has *never* been attempted" (Braucher, 2006, pp. 829–30).[27] Quite the contrary, many states have retained—and more often increased—the ease of filing CPA claims. This continual expansion in the face of commensurate price increases indicates that competitive federalism has thus far not played a meaningful role in disciplining costly legislative decisions.

Given the FTC's documented trouble in this area, however, it is important to avoid dismissing potential state CPA benefits too readily. Importantly, consumers may realize long-run benefits deriving from

---

[27] Braucher further describes why courts are unlikely to play a meaningful role in curtailing the power of CPAs: "It is rather aggressive for judges—especially federal judges—to attempt to roll back the reach of popular state statutes" (2006, p. 832).

jurisdictional competition between state CPAs. It is possible that competition between jurisdictions is occurring, and simply has not had sufficient time to develop and to compel legislative action.

However, the lack of a viable exit option combined with the astounding popularity of consumer protection legislation (Braucher, 2006, p. 830) at both the state and federal level indicates that jurisdictional competition is unlikely to play an effective role in restraining state CPA development in the short to mid run, and perhaps even in the long-run. Accordingly, continued expansion of state CPAs may ultimately prove detrimental to consumer welfare, and legislators should consider incremental costs and benefits of legislation—and articulate tangible consumer benefits offsetting the costs of more legislation—before enacting further changes.

REFERENCES

American Bar Association. 1969. *Report of the ABA Commission to Study the Federal Trade Commission.*
Bagwell, Kyle. 2005. "The Economic Analysis of Advertising," Columbia University Department of Economics Discussion Paper Series, Paper No. 0506-01. Available at: www.stanford.edu/~kbagwell/Bagwell_Web/adchapterPost082605.pdf.
Bar-Gill, Oren, and Elizabeth Warren. 2008. "Making Credit Safer," 157 *University of Pennsylvania Law Review* 1–101.
Blackmon, Glenn, and Richard Zeckhauser. 1991. "Mispriced Equity: Regulated Rates for Auto Insurance in Massachusetts," 81 *The American Economic Review* 65–9.
Braucher, Jean. 2006. "Deception, Economic Loss and Mass-Market Customers: Consumer Protection Statutes as Persuasive Authority in the Common Law of Fraud," 48 *Arizona Law Review* 813–56.
Buchanan, James. 1995. "Federalism and Individual Sovereignty," 15 *CATO Journal.* Available at: www.cato.org/pubs/journal/cj15n2-3-8.html.
Butler, Henry, and Jason Johnston. 2010. "Reforming State Consumer Protection Liability: An Economic Approach," *Columbia Business Law Review* 1–103.
Butler, Henry, and Joshua Wright. 2011. "Are State Consumer Protection Acts Really Little-FTC Acts?" 63 *Florida Law Review* 163–92.
Commissioners on Uniform State Laws. 1964. *Handbook of the National Conference of Commissioners on Uniform State Laws and Proceedings of the Annual Conference Meeting in its Seventy-Third Year.*
Council of State Governments. 1969. *1970 Suggested State Legislation.*
Council of State Governments. 1970. *Unfair Trade Practices and Consumer Protection Law.*
Cox, Edward et al. 1969. *'The Nader Report' on the Federal Trade Commission.*
Dixit, Avinash, and Victor Norman. 1978. "Advertising and Welfare," 9 *The Bell Journal of Economics* 1–17.
Epstein, Richard. 1992. "Exit Rights under Federalism," 55 *Law and Contemporary Problems* 147–66.

Evans, David, and Joshua Wright. 2010. "The Effect of the Consumer Financial Protection Agency Act of 2009," 22 *Loyola Consumer Law Review* 277–335.

Jaffee, Dwight, and Thomas Russell. 1997. "The Causes and Consequences of Rate Regulation in the Auto Insurance Industry," in David Bradford ed., *The Economics of Property-Casualty Insurance*. University of Chicago Press.

Klein, Benjamin, and Keith Leffler. 1981. "The Role of Market Forces in Assuring Contractual Performance," 89 *The Journal of Political Econonomics* 615–41.

Klick, Jonathan, Bruce Kobayashi, and Larry E. Ribstein. 2006. "The Effect of Contract Regulation: The Case of Franchising," *George Mason University Law and Economics Research*, Paper No. 07-03. Available at: http://papers.ssrn.com/sol3/papers.cfm?abstract_id=951464.

Klick, Jonathan, Bruce Kobayashi, and Larry Ribstein. 2009. "Federalism, Variation, and State Regulation of Franchise Termination," 3 *Entrepreneurial Business Law Journal* 355–517.

Kobayashi, Bruce, and Larry Ribstein. 1997. "Federalism, Efficiency and Competition." Available at: http://papers.ssrn.com/sol3/papers.cfm?abstract_id=110071.

Kobayashi, Bruce, and Larry Ribstein. 2007. "Introduction," in Bruce Kobayashi and Larry Ribstein eds, *The Economics of Federalism*. Edward Elgar Publishing.

Kovacic, William. 2009. "The Consumer Financial Protection Agency and the Hazards of Regulatory Restructuring," 1 *Lombard Street* 19–28.

Lovett, William. 1972. "State Deceptive Trade Practice Legislation," 46 *Tulane Law Review* 724–1073.

Musonda, Flora, and Pascal Bulliard. 2004. "The Modern Market System and Federalism," Institute of Freedom, Working Paper No. 3.

Muris, Timothy. 2004. "The Federal Trade Commission and the Future Development of U.S. Consumer Protection Policy," George Mason University School of Law, Law and Economics Working Paper Series No. 04-19. Available at: http://ssrn.com/abstract_id=545182.

National Association of Attorneys General Committee on the Office of Attorney General. 1971. *Report on the Office of Attorney General.*

National Association of Insurance Commissioners. 2009. *2006/2007 Auto Insurance Database Report.* Available at: www.naic.org/documents/newsroom_2007_auto_report_summary.pdf.

Nelson, Philip. 1974. "Advertising as Information," 82 *The Journal of Political Economy* 729–54.

Norstrand, H. Peter. 1969. "Treble Damage Actions for Victims of Unfair and Deceptive Trade Practices: A New Approach," 4 *New England Law Review* 171–8.

O'Hara, Erin Ann, and Larry Ribstein. 2000. "9600: Conflict of Laws and Choice of Law," in Boudewijn Bouckaert and Gerrit De Gist eds., *Encyclopedia of Law and Economics, Volume V: The Economics of Crime and Litigation*. Edward Elgar Publishing.

Posner, Richard. 1969. "The Federal Trade Commission," 37 *The University of Chicago Law Review* 47–89.

Pridgen, Dee and Richard Alderman. 2009. 1 *Consumer Protection and the Law.* Clark Boardman Callaghan.

Rice, David. 1969. "Exemplary Damages in Private Consumer Actions," 55 *Iowa Law Review* 307–43.

Schwartz, Victor, and Cary Silverman. 2005. "Common-Sense Construction of Consumer Protection Acts," 54 *University of Kansas Law Review* 1–72.

Searle Civil Justice Institute. 2009. *State Consumer Protection Acts, An Empirical Investigation of Private Litigation.* Available at: http://papers.ssrn.com/sol3/papers.cfm?abstract_id=1708175.

Searle Civil Justice Institute. 2011. *Preliminary Report on Consumer Protection Acts and Costs to Consumers: The Impact of State Consumer Protection Acts on Automobile Insurance Premiums.*

Sovern, Jeff. 1991. "Private Actions under the Deceptive Trade Practices Acts: Reconsidering the FTC Act as Rule Model," 52 *Ohio State Law Journal* 437–67.

Sovern, Jeff. 2006. "Toward a New Model of Consumer Protection Statutes: The Problem of Increased Transaction Costs," 47 *William and Mary Law Review* 1635–710.

Stearns, Maxwell, and Todd Zywicki. 2009. *Public Choice Concepts and Applications in Law.* West.

Withrow, James. 1967. "The Inadequacies of Consumer Protection by Administrative Action," 1967 *N.Y. State Bar Association Antitrust Law Symposiums* 58.

Wright, Joshua, and Eric Helland. 2011. "The Dramatic Rise of Consumer Protection Law," in F.H. Buckley ed., *The American Illness: Essays on the Rule of Law.* Yale University Press.

Index

Introductory Note
References such as '178–9' indicate (not necessarily continuous) discussion of a topic across a range of pages. Because the whole of this work is about 'federalism', use of this term (and certain others which occur throughout) as an entry point has been restricted. Please look under the appropriate detailed entries. Wherever possible in the case of topics with many references, these have either been divided into sub-topics or only the most significant discussions of the topic are listed.